CLIPPED WINGS

Cpl Peter Walker's Illustrated Diary of his
RAF Service in India & Burma 1942 – 1946

Elizabeth Dent (nee Walker)

Clipped Wings

Cpl Peter Walker's Illustrated Diary of his RAF Service in India & Burma 1942 – 1946

by

Elizabeth Dent

www.lizdenthistorian.co.uk

Copyright Elizabeth Dent © 2017

ISBN: 978-0-9955810-0-5

This book is produced by Elizabeth Dent in conjunction with **WRITERSWORLD**, and is produced entirely in the UK. It is available to order from most bookshops in the United Kingdom, and is also globally available via UK based Internet book retailers.

WRITERSWORLD
2 Bear Close Flats, Bear Close, Woodstock
Oxfordshire, OX20 1JX, England
☎ 01993 812500
☎ +44 1993 812500

www.writersworld.co.uk

The text pages of this book are produced via an independent certification process that ensures the trees from which the paper is produced come from well managed sources that exclude the risk of using illegally logged timber while leaving options to use post-consumer recycled paper as well.

CPL PETER WESTLAKE WALKER 1916-1983.
A qualified pilot who served in the RAF as a Leading
Aircraftman from 1942-1946.

CONTENTS

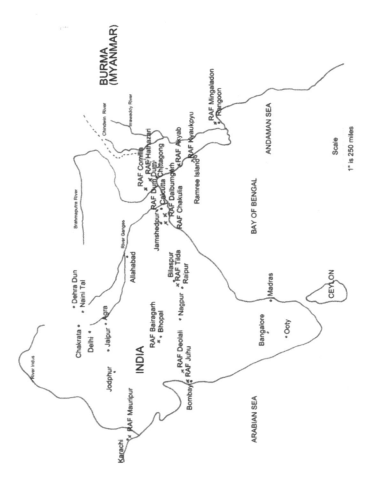

Map of India and Burma, showing sites of RAF stations in the 1940s.

PROLOGUE

Lest We Forget

This book is dedicated to all those young men and women who fought so bravely in World War II's 'Forgotten War of India and Burma', thousands never to return. We must never forget the sacrifices they made, giving 'baby boomers' like myself a life in post-war Britain.

Peter Westlake Walker, my father, was one of the lucky ones: surviving perhaps in part due to the fact that he was demoted from RAF pilot to mechanic when found to be colour-blind. Being a Leading Aircraftman (LAC) meant that Peter had time for letter writing, keeping diaries and taking photographs.

As his eldest child, growing up in the 1950s, my father would often regale me with stories of exotic places and creatures in a hot, faraway land. These tales enthralled me and thus began my own life-long fascination with India.

This book would never have been written save for several coincidences. Firstly, I managed to stop my mother from throwing out a tin trunk containing *"some stuff your father accumulated in India"*. It was not until some years later, whilst attending a family wedding in Australia, that one of the other guests, John Adams, prompted me to have a look for the old photos of planes I had inherited.

I recovered the trunk and imagine my surprise to find over 500 snapshots, a partially completed *Illustrated Diary of My Overseas Tour 1942-46*, three diaries, Pilot's Log Book and other original documents as well as over 30 letters written between 1942 and 1945, not to mention an RAF flying helmet and overalls: I quickly realised this was a real Pandora's Box!

Several years were spent researching and compiling the archive. In 2014, whilst lecturing/guiding an archaeological tour in Malta, one of the tour group turned out to be the mother of the 31 Squadron's Commanding Officer based in Norfolk. Through that contact, I was able to meet up with a former Commanding Officer, Ian Hall, who was about to publish *A Goldstar Century – 31 Squadron 1915-2015* and helped me greatly with my research, also leading to several of my father's photos being included in his book. In fact, in the earlier 31 Squadron's *First in the Indian Skies,* I found that the photo of my father in a Burmese *'basha'* had been incorrectly captioned as Bill Southworth!

Deciphering my father's tiny writing in his diaries and then cross-referencing his own activities with those events described in the letters written by his family, friends and RAF colleagues was quite a challenge.

By quoting from the letters and diaries verbatim, I realise that some of the words used by my father (such as Wogs and Ities) would now be politically incorrect so I do apologise for any offence this might cause, but these were the words used in the context of their time. My father was not a racist – quite the opposite in fact.

Chapter 1 describes Peter's family life, gaining his pilot's licence, joining the RAF and undertaking training courses throughout England and Wales. The remainder of the chapters form a narrative with diary entries, letters, original documents and relevant excerpts from RAF Operational Records, interspersed with accompanying photos (or 'snaps'). An *Editor's Note* at the beginning of each chapter gives a brief summary of events taking place.

Trying to sort out my father's 6cm x 8cm snaps into some sort of order was quite a feat as the majority were unmarked and just jumbled together in three small Kodak boxes. The numerous snapshots of old planes also posed somewhat of a problem since my aviation knowledge was negligible, but with help from family and friends I was soon able to tell a Lockheed from a Lysander! Many of the photos are of damaged Harts, Wapities and Lysanders; there are also a number of Dakotas as well as rarer ones such as Vengeance, Hudson, & Curtiss Mohawk.

A number of books concerning the Second World War, including a selection in the library of the RAF Museum at Colindale, were consulted so that events occurring elsewhere in the world would correspond with those in the Far East: a *'Chronology of War'* is provided at the end of each chapter.

My work was hampered by knowing shamefully little of Indian culture and geography, especially of the 1940s Indian sub-continent during the last years of the Raj. But having studied my father's RAF Record of Service & Medical Records, consulted photographs and films in the Special Collections Department of The Imperial War Museum, looked at maps at The British Library and at Operations Records of No. 37 Staging Post (India) and 31 Squadron (Burma) at The National Archives, slowly a picture began to emerge of a now long-vanished India: the India my father knew and loved.

This photo-journal paints a fascinating picture of what life was like for an RAF 'erk' (member of the invaluable ground crew) in the so-called 'Forgotten War of India and Burma'. How, at the age of 25, Peter's happy, family life was to be shattered when sent halfway around the world to serve his country as a Leading Aircraftman (LAC).

Firstly stationed for two and a half years at RAF Bairagarh near Bhopal in Central India where there was time for troop duties and tourism, before being sent to join No. 31 Squadron (Transport) and taking part in dangerous sorties flying into Burma. Then witnessing the Japanese surrender at Rangoon before finally hitching home by plane from Singapore in January 1946.

ACKNOWLEDGEMENTS

I would like to thank all those who have helped me over six years to complete this labour of love, especially:

My late mother, Dulcie, for safely storing the trunk in her attic.

My husband, Robert, for his encouragement and help with editing.

My children, Emily, Rebecca & Nicholas, for their patience and 'techie' advice.

My brother, Michael, for giving me our father's medals and filling in some missing links.

My brother-in-law, Hugh Dent MBE, for help with sorting out the chronology of World War II.

My cousin, Geraldine, and husband, Paul Sauvage, for their help with editing.

My Auntie Barbara and late Uncle Francis [Wall], for corroborating family events.

My Aunt Connie [Walker], for sharing her memories.

Ian Hall, former Commanding Officer of 31 Squadron, for his support and advice.

John Adams, of the Aviation Forum, for scanning photos and identifying the aeroplanes.

Pat Pelton, for her help with the book's format.

CHAPTER 1

PETER GETS HIS WINGS AND LOSES THEM
JULY 1939 – MARCH 1942

The Walker family's Hillman car (DYH 771) outside their
home in Hampstead Garden Suburb.

Peter was born in Talbot Road, Highgate on 9th December 1916 and
grew up with his parents, grand-parents and elder brother Eustace,
having a comfortable, happy childhood, with a wide circle of extended
family members and friends, many of whom attended Highgate's St
Augustine's Church. In fact, social life revolved around the church. Peter
played tennis with his good friend, Francis Wall, and cousin, Barbara
Caton (who were to get married after the war), together with his
girlfriend, Peggy Caswell.

Correspondence was very important to Peter although many letters
often took weeks to arrive and were subject to censorship; the only
other means of communication was by telegram, which he rarely used.
In all he wrote nearly 200 letters to his parents and over 200 to his

girlfriend, Peggy (Pegs): their long-distance romance provides an interesting backdrop to the correspondence between India, Burma and Blighty.

The letters depict what life was like in St Albans and London during the war. Virtually no mention of rationing is made, although food parcels were gratefully received: probably the 'stiff upper lip' prevailed. Interestingly, my father makes virtually no mention of VE or VJ Day, just 'Japanese peace rumours'.

The Walker family later moved to 25 Greenhalgh Walk, part of Hampstead Garden Suburb in Finchley; but this house was destroyed by bombs in 1940. Peter's parents moved house several times between London and St Albans, dodging the bombs but at the same time not living too far away from the family's business in Mayfair.

From 1928-34 Peter was privately educated at Highgate School, his housemaster being the Reverend Whitehead. It was at this school that Peter enjoyed his first taste of mechanical engineering: the headmaster had managed to procure two aeroplanes, which the boys could take to pieces and rebuild. So he became a member of the Aeronautical Class, learning about the rigging of a Snipe Aeroplane and the assembling of an Armstrong Siddeley Mark 3 engine. Peter was also a member of the Highgate Officers' Training Corps (OTC) from 1930 until July 1934 when he left school as a private.

He then joined his father and brother as 'Assistant Ironmonger' in the family business of W. R. Walker Ltd., Ironmongers & General Engineers (established in 1817) at 97 Mount Street, Mayfair, whilst also training as an electrician (Experience of Electrical Installations).

Peter was lucky enough to have his own car, an Austin Seven (OY 3906) and was able to drive to Hanworth Airfield to pursue his greatest passion – flying; he flew several of their fleet of Cirrus Swallows.

The London Air Park Flying Club was one of the earliest and most active of the Civil Air Guard (CAG) sections. This was a subsidised organisation set up to provide a pool of pilots in the event of war, as normal flying club rates were often beyond the means of 'the man in the street'. CAG units were usually attached to regular flying clubs such as the London Air Park at Hanworth.

Peter was appointed an Electrician at W.R. Walker Ltd. by
his Auntie Dorothy (Doll).

At the age of 23, Peter started flying lessons and, after dual instruction with Captain Stewart, gained his Pilot's Licence on 12th August 1939: he was now licensed to fly *"all types of landplanes"* but *"fit for daylight flying only"*.

The London Air Park Flying Club at Hanworth. The Cirrus
Swallow (G-AFHK) in the centre is one of the planes flown
by Peter.

RECORD OF FLIGHTS.

Date.	Aircraft.		Engine.		Journey.		Time of Departure	Time of Arrival	Time in Air.		Pilot. See Instructions (3) & (4) on flyleaf of this book.	Remarks.
	Type.	Markings	Type	H.P.	From	To	Hrs. Mins.	Hrs. Mins.	Hrs.	Mins.		
						Brought forward			6	45		
21-7-39	DA Swallow	G-AFHL	Cirrus	90	Hanworth	Local				20	Mr Brooks	Dual Instruction
"	"	"	"	"	"	"				20	Self	Solo
24-7-39	"	G-AFRM	"	"	"	"				15	Capt Stewart	Dual Instruction
"	"	"	"	"	"	"				25	Self	Solo
26-7-39	"	G-AFHL	"	"	"	"				30	Self	Solo
28-7-39	"	G-AFHL	"	"	"	"				15	Mr Brooks	Dual Instruction
"	"	"	"	"	"	"				25	Self	Solo (A Licence Test)
31-7-39	"	G-AFBD	"	"	"	"				10	Mr	Club Competition
						Carried forward			9	25		

Peter's Pilot's Log Book showing he went solo on 21st July
1939 in a Cirrus Swallow (G AFHL).

Not long after, on 30th August 1939, he received a letter saying that the
Civil Air Guard flying would now cease and in view of his qualifications
had been noted for probable war employment as a pilot after further
training, and was now part of the RAF Volunteer Reserve.

In October of that year, Peter attended an interview by the Royal Air
Force, but on 15th January 1940 was told he could not be enlisted as a
member of the Air Crew as he was colour blind. He replied to say he that

he would be willing to take up some training or trade for ground work as they suggested.

On 29th March, Peter enlisted under the usual wartime D.P.E. (Duration of the Present Emergency) terms and was sent to sign up at No. 2 Recruits Centre at Cardington in Bedfordshire (a site of acres of wooden huts) and then sent home until called forward for training in June. His official service number was 958707.

Peter and colleagues at No. 1 AACU, Farnborough.

Then he went first to 4 Wing of No. 4 School of Technical Training at St Athan in South Wales, followed in October to 4 Squadron, Clifton, York. In January 1941 he was sent to No. 7 School of Technical Training at Innsworth, Gloucestershire, to undertake conversion courses for Flight Mechanics and Flight Riggers. For a while he was based at the No. 1 AACU at Weston Zoyland, Somerset before finally, in April 1941, being sent to No. 1 Anti-Aircraft Co-operation Unit (AACU), Farnborough.

By the end of his training Peter had attained the rank of Leading Aircraftman (LAC) with superior proficiency both as a Flight Mechanic and as a Fitter, Grade 2, Engines.

Later on, his RAF Service Record shows that he had a Good Conduct Badge for Exemplary Conduct and that as a Fitter (Grade 2) Engines his proficiency was 'Superior' for 1942, 43 & 44.

In March 1942, just before being posted out to India, Peter received a letter from his good friend, Francis Wall, who had been posted with the Royal Artillery to El Alamein in 1941:

Dear Peter,

Many thanks for your airgraph of 11th December, which reached me some time ago, and all your news. I heard from Peggy recently, all about her 21st. I'm glad you managed to get leave and had a good time.

Since I last wrote to you from Base, I have rejoined the Unit thank goodness. When I got back, [brother] Martin and the lads were going on leave, so I was allowed to go too, and we had a very good time for five days. Saw some more good films 'Fantasia', 'Suspicion', 'Nice Girl' and others. Seen them? I wonder if you see the flicks often? Last week I saw 'Foreign Correspondent'.

We had several beanos during leave, and one night in particular painted one portion of Cairo a very moderate red! Prices in Cairo have doubled since last January (41) and leave proves a lot more expensive. In addition they have three meatless days a week and no pure white bread, though these don't worry us much! We stayed at one of the many Forces hostels where we were very comfortable till at least 9 a.m. each day. Martin and I played tennis one morning which was good fun. We have lately been on the move again, but details are taboo I'm afraid. Hoping you are OK and not too "brahmed".

Best luck, yours Francis

Luckily my father had the good sense to take his camera with him. He would be able to send photos home to family and friends as well as selling them to RAF colleagues, as part of his 'All India Series'. It is likely that the more relaxed conditions in the Indian sub-continent made it more conducive for servicemen to take photographs in the theatre.

Peter was fortunate to have sufficient funds to pursue his passion for photography and to buy the equipment needed for developing the photos in India. He made a note in his diary before leaving England to *"Get special tropical films in sealed tins; leave in camera no more than 24 hours; keep exposed film in airtight jar containing cork and tea leaves to absorb moisture."*

In April 1942, at the age of 26, Peter left England for the first time, sailing down the Clyde by troopship bound for India and wondering if he would ever see home again.

11 Sun—1st after Epiphany

GLASS MEASURE

603   1 - 0.

15 Thur Kodak amature

Printer — electric

62 - 0

12 Mon—Hilary Law Sittings begin

DEVELOPING DISH

8½ × 6½   hardalead   Pore

              1 - 4

5 × 4   9   2 - 3

16 Fri—● New Moon, 9.32 p.m.

ENLARGER — Kodak

home

78 - 0

13 Tues

PRINTING APPARATUS

3½ × 2½   1 - 6   FRAME

17 Sat

How to Make good Pictures

1 - 4

14 Wed

MAGNESIUM RIBBON

HOLDER   0 - 15

MAGNESIUM RIBBON

½ oz coil   0 - 15

Mems

HYPO 1lb 0 - 8

3 - 12

Details of the many items of photographic equipment that
Peter took with him.

Peter was fairly unusual in that, although privately educated and from a
middle class background, he did not serve in the upper echelons of the
RAF during the Second World War. Instead, found to be colour blind, he
was sent to the imperial outposts of India and Burma – not to fly the
planes but to maintain them. He later turned down the chance to apply
for commission as he was happy to remain an 'erk' and not an officer; in
recognition of his RAF service he received three medals, including the
Burma Star.

As my father missed his flying dreadfully, he volunteered to fly
whenever he could, flying as Second Pilot on occasions, and being
allowed to take the controls of a Dakota. But colour blindness was to
prevent him from flying officially and, when applying in 1944 to become
a Flight Engineer, he was again turned down, much to his dismay.

Chapter 1 – Chronology of War

Sept 1939: War was declared and the so-called 'Phoney War' followed. Prime Minister Neville Chamberlain made his famous speech. Germany invaded Belgium and The Netherlands.

May 1940: Winston Churchill took over as Prime Minister.

June 1940: Dunkirk evacuation of 224,328 British troops and 111,172 Allied troops.

July 1940: The Battle of Britain took place with dramatic dogfights all over southern Britain. The RAF was initially greatly outnumbered but was still able to inflict heavy losses on the Luftwaffe of which Herman Goering was the Commander-in-Chief. The role of RAF fighter planes (in particular Hurricanes and Spitfires) and anti-aircraft guns was vital in protecting Britain from more severe bombing and ultimately in preventing a German invasion.

Aug 1940: Goering switched his attacks from RAF airfields to London and other cities. The Luftwaffe launched 600 sorties a day with Britons dying in their hundreds.

Jan 1941: The 'Army of the Nile' attacked the Italians in the Western Desert with great success and Sir Archibald Wavell became a national hero; Italian prisoners of war were taken to India.

May 1941: The worst of the Blitz was over by now but air raids continued to bring destruction to many British cities: London, Sheffield, Manchester, Liverpool, Hull and many others suffered considerable damage throughout the Blitz despite the best efforts of RAF fighter pilots, anti-aircraft guns, barrage defences and blackouts.

June 1941: After military failures in North Africa (due to poor resources and bad luck), Churchill sacked General Wavell despite his success in securing oil reserves in Iraq, and exchanged him with Sir Claude Auchinleck, Commander-in-Chief in India. Wavell was a very intelligent, taciturn man who commanded respect from those who served under him, but Churchill allegedly never got on well with him.

Nov 1941: Auchinleck's long-delayed operation in the desert began with Operation Crusader.

Dec 1941: Japan's attack on Pearl Harbour when over 3,000 U.S. troops were killed and almost all planes and ships destroyed meant that America then entered the war. The conflict was now on a global scale with the Pacific Ocean being a vast area for major campaigns. Japan was in domination and the Allies struggled to cope.

Dec 1941: Burma was invaded by the Japanese army, commanded by General Tomoyaki Yamashita with air raids starting on Rangoon, killing over 7,000 in just two days. Amongst his troops he was known as 'The Tiger' and in capturing Singapore early in 1942 he was able to demonstrate his military prowess. Japanese forces cut off the 'Burma Road' into China, thus preventing the Americans from supplying resources to the Chinese by land.

British, Indian and Australian troops in Malaya were forced to retreat along the Malay Peninsula to the supposed safety of Singapore. However, approximately 9,000 Allied troops were killed and over 130,000 taken into captivity, many dying as a result of inhumane treatment by the Japanese as their prisoners-of-war.

Air Command Far East was starved of modern aircraft and crews in the first two years of war and there was a dearth of accurate military intelligence. People thought Singapore was impregnable and Japanese forces far inferior to the British ones but Japanese soldiers were masters of guerrilla fighting in the jungles and their soldiers were fanatical. Britain lost control of the seas with the loss of *HMS Prince of Wales* and *HMS Repulse*, so on 15th February 1942 Singapore surrendered. The Fall of Singapore shook the Government and the British Empire to its foundations.

Eventual victory of 'The Forgotten War' was brought about by air power and remarkably getting the three services to co-operate under SEAC

(South East Asia Command), although in 1942 resources were extremely stretched with reinforcements often being 'borrowed' on their way through from the Middle East. The RAF tried to counter the overwhelming strength of the Japanese, but with Hong Kong having been captured on 25th December 1941, followed by Singapore, they were forced to retreat to Burma and then supported the defence of Rangoon with Blenheims and Hurricanes but only with limited success.

Mar 42: The Japanese captured Rangoon on 7th March 1942 and Burma was abandoned. The Dakotas of No.31 Squadron were to undertake numerous supply missions as well as air evacuation, a forerunner of the vital importance of such operations in the Burma campaigns.

Air Chief Marshal Sir Richard Peirse took over control of RAF India & Ceylon but he could do little to support the retreat from Burma apart from supplying air transport. The RAF's Akyab airfield was wiped out by the Japanese and survivors sent back to Indian bases. The RAF provided air support as best they could, often operating from rough strips hacked out of the jungle, building up their strength in India during the respite offered by the monsoon with surprising speed. By this time, aircraft outputs in Britain and USA were attaining new peaks and floods of new crews were being turned out with the Empire Air Training Scheme.

Unexpectedly, the Japanese fleet was called back urgently to the Pacific to oppose an American fleet and three of its carriers were sunk by US dive bombers and torpedo planes in the Battle of Midway.

Apr 42: Mandalay in Burma fell and British forces had to withdraw from Burma across the Chindwin River into North-East India. By May, the evacuation of Allied forces from Burma was complete. But by then William D Old of the USAAF had pioneered an air route from Bengal to China known as 'Flying over the Hump': this dangerous supply route lay over the forbidding Patkai Mountains with no possibility of any landings and through very turbulent weather. 31 Squadron also took part in this hazardous operation.

CHAPTER 2

PETER'S PASSAGE TO INDIA
APR – JUNE 1942

Editor's Note:

Names of Peter's RAF colleagues have been included with the photographs wherever possible; however, there are numerous 'snaps' of colleagues that have had to be omitted. Peter's own captions are represented by italics under the photographs.

As Peter was later to tell his girlfriend Peggy, "The ship's voyage was the worst part of the War for me". Although officers fared considerably better in their cabins, my 6' 2" father and the rest of the troops were accommodated in the holds: the cramped, claustrophobic conditions must have been unbearably hot for him. No wonder he found it difficult to sleep, moving up onto deck whenever he could. He obviously didn't think much of the food either, with fish for breakfast, lunch and dinner.

RAF servicemen were often assaulted by Boers in South Africa and so, whilst on the ship, they were forewarned of the serious situation there. Durban, in Natal, was still a Dominion of the British Empire, under Prime Minister Smuts, and had only just declared war as the Boers were not keen to become involved in a 'British War'. Peter and his colleagues were warned:

> *"When in South Africa do not:*
> *Refer to the Boer War or call anyone a Boer*
> *Call anyone an African*
> *Call a Native a Nigger*
> *Mix with the Natives*
> *Call South Africa a Colony."*

Landing at Durban must have seemed a bit like paradise to my father: with its sunshine, bountiful fresh food and his generous hosts, the Fisher family, it must have been a terrible wrench to leave and continue the voyage to India through submarine and mine-infested waters. At least the Dutch vessel they boarded had slightly more room than the previous troopship.

The famous 'White Lady' opera singer gave them all a tremendous send-off from Durban. Perla Gibson sang patriotic songs in her powerful voice to over 1,000 troopships and 350 hospital ships from the Durban quay. This 50-year-old mother of three who had lost one of her own sons in the war was later honoured with a bronze plaque and a statue unveiled by the Queen.

Travelling between Madagascar and Mozambique – one of the most dangerous stretches of water in 1942 – must have been frightening, especially when they could hear ships being torpedoed in front of their convoy.

All Allied troops and supplies had to be sent around the Cape of Good Hope before heading northward along the eastern coast of Africa towards the Middle East, as none could be sent via the Mediterranean and Suez Canal. This meant the Mozambique Channel between Madagascar and the African mainland was vital for the British supply route to India, as well as for transporting oil from Iraq. By the summer of 1942 this shipping often remained without escort or air cover, and it was to prove a happy hunting ground for Japanese submarines.

On 5th June 1942, Japanese submarines sank three Allied merchantmen in the Mozambique Channel, two more on 6th June and an additional five vessels in the next few days. So it must have been a tremendous relief for Peter to sail into Bombay past the iconic Gateway of India, the monumental archway that was seen by all visitors arriving and departing India.

The *Illustrated Diary of my Overseas Tour 1942-1946* that Peter started but never finished.

Sat 11 Apr

4am. Left West Kirby for embarkation port – Greenock. Arrived Greenock 4pm and ferried by steamer to Troopship *Malaya* (displacement 21,000 tons – was previously used as an Armed Merchant Cruiser, 14 knots).

Sun 12 Apr

Sleeping accommodation very poor – 160 men sleeping in small hold; majority in hammocks, rest sleep on tables and floor. Height only 7' 6".

Mon 13 Apr

Food moderate but plentiful; usually cold when it reaches the mess table. Bought 2 boxes of chocolate (48 bars)!

Tue 14 Apr

Afternoon cruise, returned 2 hours later. Bought tin of milk, sugar, cheese, tin of fruit & jam.

Wed 15 Apr

Left the Clyde in company with numerous other troopships at 5pm. Received a letter from Mother at 38 Lemsford Road, St Albans:

Dearest Peter,

I wonder where you are? Have thought of you very many times, always last thing at night and first in the morning.

Have been very busy today with our move, all the things sent by removal van this afternoon. Where I shall put them all I do not know, but no doubt they will all find a home. I shall be very sorry to leave: I love St Albans, it has a soul.

I wonder if it it's hot with you, take care of yourself, put more clothes on in the evening if they are cooler than the day so as not to get chilled. I often picture you and your surroundings.

Fri evening: have arrived at 48 Talbot Road, Highgate. Have had a dreadful time finding a home for all our clothes, the rooms look very nice they are so large. I do wish you were here to see them. I had a postcard from Mrs Caswell; she said they had been getting about quite a lot. Peggy told me she would come in and see me Monday or Tuesday, expect to tea.

I wonder how long it will be before we hear from you? Take care of yourself.

Much love,
Mother

Thu 16 Apr

Insufficient deck space for men – officers very comfortably off.

Fri 17 Apr

Heavy Atlantic swell – numbers sea sick, felt bad myself.

Sun 19 Apr
Fine & sunny. Clocks put back one hour.

Mon 20 Apr
Saw a school of porpoises – warmer. Clocks put back one hour.

Tue 21 Apr
Heavy gale – much rain during night. Finished letter to Peggy.

Thu 23 Apr
Changed into Tropical Kit, hot & sunny. Concert in evening. SSE.

Fri 24 Apr
Hot but cloudy. Permission to sleep on deck.

Sat 25 Apr
Very hot, legs sunburnt & burning; lazed on deck most of the day.

Mon 27 Apr
Very hot. Read 'Passage to India'.

Tue 28 Apr
Slept on deck last night – slung hammock between two cargo cranes. Slept well in spite of vibration.

Wed 29 Apr
Arrived Sierra Leone midday; anchored some 3 miles off Freetown in mid river. Coast line fringed with palm trees, hills behind; no signs of cultivation. Very hot and sticky.

Thu 30 Apr
Numerous wooden bungalows dotted about the hills. Only a few brick buildings at Freetown. Very heavy tropical rainstorm came down in sheets.

Fri 1 May
Many boats paddling about around our ship; some of the negroes try to sell fruit, others dive for money. Watched an electric storm approach during night.

Sat 2 May
Very hot and sunny. Have slept on deck since last Tues – most pleasant. No blackout here, deck lights on and all port holes open. Read 'Warships at Work' and 'While Rome Burns'. Buying of fruit forbidden.

Sun 3 May
Left Freetown midday – took up different convoy positions. Slept on deck.

Tue 5 May
Heavy fall of rain soon after getting in my hammock, had to sleep on table in mess. Blackout time at 7pm.

Wed 6 May
Very hot, cloudless day, crossed the line. Read 'Pygmalion'. Windy night, took hammock down twice in anticipation of rain – however, none came!

Thu 7 May
Complaints about food. Fish, fish, fish every day! Read 'The Middle Watch'.

Fri 8 May
Detailed to clean ablutions for one week, complained to Messing Officer. Strong SSE winds – cooler, clocks put forward 1 hour. Read 'Sea Way Only' by Humphrey Jordan. Topees need to be worn.

Sat 9 May
Read 'Sailing all the seas in the Idle Hour' by Dwight Long. Lecture on Tropical Diseases. Bright night – ships clearly seen in spite of moon not having risen.

Mon 11 May
Kites flown from stern of ships, apparently for shooting practice. Strong winds, heavy swell.

Wed 13 May
Rougher – P.T. on deck.

Thu 14 May
Fish again for Breakfast and Supper!

Fri 15 May

Changed £2.00 for South African money. Part of Convoy left us for Cape Town last night. Muffled explosion heard during evening – ship shook slightly. (Heard later that one cargo ship was sunk and Corvette hit by mine. The latter was towed into port by cruiser.) Minesweeping commences.

Sat 16 May

Paravanes hoisted aboard mid-day.

Sun 17 May

Attended Morning Prayer at 11am. We were informed we had passed through an enemy mine field. Read 'The Canon in Residence'.

Mon 18 May

Land sighted 9am. Reached Durban mid-day. Disembarked 6pm; had long wait on station before proceeding to Clarewood Camp (16 miles away). Arrived there by 12pm. After a long wait and cold supper we were eventually allotted tents by 2am – 12 in each bell tent! Feet entanglement!

Tue 19 May

Taxi to 'Dead Man's Tree'. 6pm toured the city. Much impressed by its cleanliness and modern buildings. Supper at the Victoria Club – 2 eggs, 2 bacon rashers, mashed potatoes, bread, butter and tea – all for the sum of 5d!! Returned by crowded train.

One of the most popular spots for troops in Durban is the Victoria League Club, Pine Street. This photograph shows the restaurant filled with men of various fighting forces.

Victoria League Club in Durban.

Wed 20 May

Hitchhiked into Durban and we were driven around town. Lunch at Victoria Club. Saw Micky Rooney and Judy Garland in 'Babes on Broadway'. In interval, the organist played 'Till the Lights of London shine again' amidst much applause.

Thu 21 May

Train to town; Bob Wooldridge, Bill Edwards and I were picked up by a Mr Fisher whilst walking along East Street. Taken to his home for dinner. After a drink or two of gin, had a smashing meal of soup, eggs, sausage, peas, potatoes and fruit salad. Afterwards we were shown a coloured Cine film of the Kruger National Park – most interesting.

Fri 22 May

Route March in morning (ate fruit all day!). Visited Aquarium and Museum in afternoon; went for a ride on rickshaw. Large meal at St Peters Canteen.

Bob Woolridge and myself on a rickshaw, Eddie was camera shy!

Sat 23 May

Coach ride to Valley of 1,000 Hills where we visited the Zulu Reserve and inspected their kralls which are badly ventilated. They have no windows and only a small round entrance and are shaped rather like an eskimo's igloo. On the return journey, the coach engine seized whilst climbing the steepest hill (gradient 1:3)!

Sun 24 May

Sea bathe in afternoon – water very warm (76 degrees) and strong backwash. After a meal at the Victoria Club, we visited Mr Fisher again.

Mon 25 May

Mr Fisher took us to Burnham Drive where we fed the tame monkeys with bananas while he took moving pictures of us. Had drink of lager at his golf club and returned to his home for dinner and afterwards saw films again.

Tue 26 May

Visited the Botanical Gardens and took snaps there. After tea at the Jewish Club, Mr Fisher picked us up and brought us home for dinner. We were put on the 'Roll of Honour'.

Botanical Gardens Durban with Mr Fisher, Eddy Edwards, Bob Woolridge, Bill Edwards.

Wed 27 May

Visited Mr Fisher's daughter's home and met her two children, Wendy (2 years) and Peter (9 months).

Thu 28 May

Met Mr Fisher at 5.30pm and we were taken to his house, Steak and Kidney Pie for dinner. Bade farewell at 11pm and left addresses: Mr E Fisher, 7 Pincent Road, Springfield Road, Durban.

Fri 29 May

Embarked on *Westernland* at 11am (an ancient Dutch coal burning liner which does 17 knots). Given hospital fatigues.

THE
FLYING DUTCHMAN

JUNE 18th 1942

THE FLYING DUTCHMAN

COMPOSED AND PUBLISHED ON H.M.T. WESTERNLAND

EDITOR
J. J. de LEEUW
ASST. EDITORS
L.A.C. BIRCHALL
CPL. JONES

U. G. TROOPS
WNG-COMMDR.
H.F. BURTON
D.F.C.

ILLUSTRATED BY BOND AND C. Hays

CAPT. J. UEBAU

BOND

33

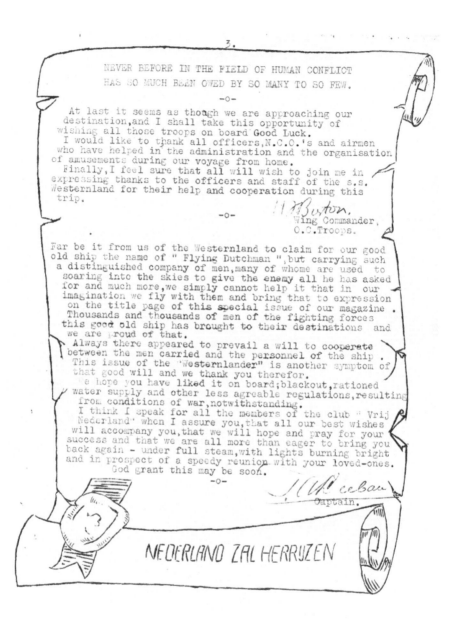

NEVER BEFORE IN THE FIELD OF HUMAN CONFLICT
HAS SO MUCH BEEN OWED BY SO MANY TO SO FEW.

-o-

At last it seems as though we are approaching our destination, and I shall take this opportunity of wishing all those troops on board Good Luck.

I would like to thank all officers, N.C.O.'s and airmen who have helped in the administration and the organisation of amusements during our voyage from home.

Finally, I feel sure that all will wish to join me in expressing thanks to the officers and staff of the s.s. Westernland for their help and cooperation during this trip.

-o-

H. Buxton,
Wing Commander,
O.C.Troops.

Far be it from us of the Westernland to claim for our good old ship the name of " Flying Dutchman ", but carrying such a distinguished company of men, many of whome are used to soaring into the skies to give the enemy all he has asked for and much more, we simply cannot help it that in our imagination we fly with them and bring that to expression on the title page of this special issue of our magazine . Thousands and thousands of men of the fighting forces this good old ship has brought to their destinations and we are proud of that.

Always there appeared to prevail a will to cooperate between the men carried and the personnel of the ship . This issue of the "Westernlander" is another symptom of that good will and we thank you therefor.

e hope you have liked it on board; blackout, rationed water supply and other less agreable regulations, resulting from conditions of war, notwithstanding.

I think I speak for all the members of the club " Vrij Nederland" when I assure you, that all our best wishes will accompany you, that we will hope and pray for your success and that we are all more than eager to bring you back again - under full steam, with lights burning bright and in prospect of a speedy reunion with your loved-ones. God grant this may be soon.

-o-

J. W. Leebaw
Captain.

NEDERLAND ZAL HERRIJZEN

'THE FLYING DUTCHMAN' special issue magazine of the Dutch troopship *Westernlander*.

Sat 30 May

Disembarked owing to refrigeration trouble, skeleton crew left. Ship put to sea for repairs. Hitchhiked into town and met Bob & Eddie at the

Victoria Club. Phoned Mr Fisher who collected us in his car and returned to his home for drinks and dinner. Was shown stool and ashtray made of Stinkwood – very expensive.

Sun 31 May
Left camp at 12am and hitchhiked into town after walking a couple of miles. Had lunch at Navy League and afterwards went to Beechwood Golf Club with Joyce and her husband. Drinks on Mr Fisher.

Mon 1 June
Were taken to docks again as advance party, only to find ship had not yet docked! Sent back to camp. In afternoon visited the snake park. Later called on the Fishers for last time and had drinks and dinner.

Tue 2 June
Reveille at 4.30am. Embarked as advance party 9am. Troopship departed 4pm. Was given a send off by an Opera Singer who had a very powerful voice and could still be heard when 200 yards away!

Wed 3 June
Reveille at 7.15am. More sleeping room than on *Malaya*. Food better and more plentiful although expensive canteen. Clocks advance one hour.

Fri 5 June
Passing between Africa and Madagascar.

Sat 6 June
Ship's concert in the evening – quite good.

Sun 7 June
Escorting cruiser comes alongside during afternoon and shouts information regarding the presence of enemy submarines. Instructed to proceed direct to Mombasa. Read 'Enter a Murderer'.

Mon 8 June
Pack of enemy submarines reported nearer. A ship is torpedoed some 15 miles ahead. Course altered again and speed increased. Zigzag course.

Tue 9 June

Mombasa reached at 10am. Strong wind blowing, cooler here than at Freetown. Vegetation very green, houses quite modern with red tiled roofs. 3 battleships in harbour and 1 aircraft carrier. Allowed ashore in evening. Clean town but sweet sickly smell in native quarters.

Wed 10 June

Short route march in morning. Ashore in evening, bought wooden doll. Walked down the Native quarters – narrow roads with peculiar lighting on walls caused by shadows thrown by leather work.

Thu 11 June

Weighed anchor midday and left with strong escort:- 1 Battleship/Merchant Cruiser, 2 Destroyers, 3 Corvette Troopships including our own.

Fri 12 June

Still continuing easterly course. Sea calm. Made some very tasty lemonade from limes.

Sat 13 June

Cape Town convoy meets us (3 more Troopships), alter course to NNE. Two Destroyers and Corvette appear to have left our convoy. Read 'I Claudius Vols I & II'.

Mon 15 June

1 troopship left for Aden. Read 'Gypsy Royal'.

Tue 16 June

Went to ship's concert in evening. Clocks put forward 1 hour.

Wed 17 June

Have slept on promenade deck most of the voyage – too hot for blankets. Strong southerly winds.

Sat 20 June

Read R.H. Mottram. Special concert for Baggage party and Captain of ship.

Sun 21 June

Arrived in Bombay mid-day. Am detailed to luggage party. After carrying out Officers and civilian baggage and dumping same on deck, the order came through to anchor in bay for a few days so all baggage had to be then returned to cabins! Made 2/6 in tips!

Gateway of India, Bombay.

Chapter 2 – Chronology of War

April 1942: Japanese submarines supported by auxiliary cruisers/supply ships were sent by Rear Admiral Ishizaki from Penang via Aden, Mombasa & Zanzibar undertaking reconnaissance and then entering Durban harbour undetected in early May but no attacks were launched.

May 1942: This was the highpoint of Japanese success in the Indian & Pacific Oceans until America won the two battles of Coral Sea and Midway when the tide began to turn against the Japanese.

Churchill realised that a Japanese air/submarine/cruiser base on Madagascar would paralyse the Allies' convoy route to the Middle and Far East so at the beginning of May Allied forces landed on Madagascar and occupied the northern portion of the island with the facilities of Diego Suarez servicing Allied vessels. But on 30th May the British battleship *Ramillies* was hit by a torpedo and had to limp to Durban for repairs and the tanker *British Loyalty* took at least one torpedo and sank.

June 1942: By 10th June the local Allied naval commander had ordered convoys and fast unescorted shipping to detour to the east of Madagascar to avoid the Mozambique Channel.

July 1942: By mid-July the Japanese forces, having damaged a British battleship and accounted for some 25 ships totalling over 120,000 tons, began withdrawing from African shores and returned to Penang in August, having suffered virtually no losses.

CHAPTER 3

DAMAGED KITES AT NO. 37 STAGING POST, BAIRAGARH
JUNE – DEC 1942

Editor's Note:

After being split up from his RAF pals at Bombay's Posting Parade, Peter was sent initially to the transit camp of Deolali (or Doolally as it was affectionately known by many). He was very pleased to find a café there where he could buy a decent meal. The meals he was able buy in India were in fact far better than the rationed food he had left behind in England. On his frequent jaunts to Calcutta (usually by 'hitching a kite'), Peter would visit Firpo's Restaurant, one of the most famous in South Asia. Its Italian owner created stunning dishes, said to number over 80 on the menu at any one time.

Peter was then sent onto the RAF's No. 37 Staging Post at Bairagarh near Bhopal in Central India and this was to be his home for the next 2 ½ years. A Staging Post was a stopping-off point for aircraft that were being ferried long distances, providing refuelling and servicing facilities. The No. 1 Armament Training Unit was formed at Peshawar on 10th March 1942 for armament and gunnery training, before moving to Bairagarh on 14th June. Peter joined it on 10th July as part of the Refuelling and Rearming (R&R) Party and this was later to be re-designated as the Repair & Salvage (RSP) Party.

Although initially being temporarily housed in the adjoining Italian Prisoner of War camp, living conditions were not too bad and Peter had his own bearer to help with washing (dhobi), cleaning, bed making and cleaning of shoes and uniform.

In the early days of the war, Bairagarh was sent bi-planes such as Hawker Harts and Wapitis, manufactured in the 1930s. Peter was able to photograph many of these damaged planes (or kites) as they called in for repair en-route to other airfields. Due to the lack of spares, everything possible had to be salvaged and repaired including aircraft that crashed nearby. One such expedition is described, travelling some distance to the village of Rheti to repair a Hawker Audax that had crashed in a field of wild cotton.

Other planes include Lysanders, a Lockheed possibly loaned from a Maharajah, one of 31 Squadron's DC2 Dakotas carrying General Wavell and a Dakota DC3 carrying Lord Linlithgow.

Bhopal was the centre of tiger hunting country and His Royal Highness, The Ruler of Bhopal, would invite many dignitaries to join him; thus Peter was able to photograph the likes of India's Vice-Roy, Lord Linlithgow, and General Wavell when they landed at Bairagarh to participate in this 'sport'.

Peter was one of those involved with designing and building their very own 'Double R Saloon' ready just in time for Christmas. In fact, for every succeeding Christmas, he was involved in organising the festivities and there are photographs for each year's event.

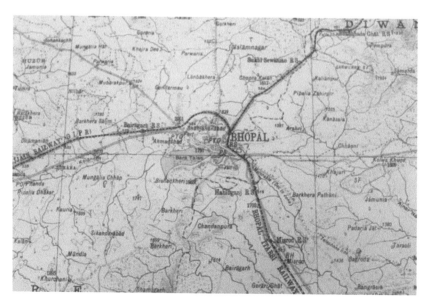

Map showing location of Bairagarh near Bhopal
(British Library Y/104/55E 1936).

40

Tue 23 June

Posting Parade. Eddie, Bob and I are split up. Eddie goes to Kancharara near Calcutta and Bob to Tempur. I am posted to Bhopal, Central India, but am sent first to Deolali, some 150 miles from Bombay.

Wed 24 June

Disembarked at 11am and marched to Bombay's Central Station. Train journey took 6½ hours. To keep cool I sat on the carriage steps with the door open and dangled my legs over the track.

Thu 25 June

Lofty billets – 'charpoys' quite comfortable at Deolali.

The Transit Camp at Deolali, often known as 'Doolally'.

Fri 26 June

Had a corn and bunion removed – cost 1 anna (1d)! Had a meal at the Chinese Victory Restaurant – chop, egg and chips, tea, bread & butter. Camp food very poor.

Sat 27 June

Walked into village and wandered around the poor quarters and saw the appalling living conditions – in some of the small dwelling places the inhabitants live with their animals. The smells are strong and unpleasant. Saw a small snake killed by village children. A town crier came round beating a drum and read out the day's news.

Sun 28 June

Church Parade – Bishop preached. Chased a chameleon out of hut.

Wed 1 July

Bloke in next bed goes to hospital with malaria.

Fri 3 July

Went to Chinese Victory Cafe for Dinner – vegetable omelette, chips, bread & butter, tea, banana fritters – 1 rupee, 10 annas.

Sat 4 July

Had lunch in Deolali: 2 eggs, chips, bread & butter, tea – 10 ½ annas.

Sun 5 July

Holy Communion at Garrison Church – heavy rain.

Mon 6 July

Digging fatigues in morning. Saw 'This Man Reuter' at the Garrison Cinema. Lunch at Deolali Cafe.

Thu 9 July

Collected films. Lunch at Chinese Victory Club with Mac and Johnnie. Marched to Deolali station at 7pm, train left at 2am. Slept on luggage rack!

Fri 10 July

Latter part of journey very interesting particularly when passing over the Vindya Mountains. Saw many baboons and monkeys on way. Arrived Bairagarh at 5.30pm. No accommodation on RAF Camp for us so we are billeted inside the Italian Prisoner of War Camp with 21,000 Ities!!

Initially billeted in the Italian Prisoner of War Camp at
Bairagarh, Bhopal.

NO. 1 ARMAMENT TRAINING UNIT FORMED AT
PESHAWAR IN FEBRUARY 1942 AND MOVED TO
BAIRAGARH (INDIA) IN JUNE 1942. IN JUNE,
CONDITIONS GRADUALLY IMPROVED WHEN WATER
WAS OBTAINED FROM A WELL SOME 3 MILES AWAY.
RAIN BEGAN TO FALL ON 23RD JUNE AND THE
SUPPLY IMPROVED. THE ROADS LEADING TO THE
RANGES WERE FOUND TO BE IN AN APPALLING
STATE. (Operations Record Air 29/602)

Sat 11 July
Serving with 1 ATU (Armament Training Unit). Billets comfortable and
airy. Our section is separated from main Itie Camp by a single barbed
wire fence. Italians take little notice of us and appear to be quite
resigned to their prison life. Beer at canteen – can get good suppers also.

Sun 12 July
Lecture by CO. Are told Bhopal is out of bounds (except cinema and
royal market) owing to outbreak of cholera. Warned about snakes and

scorpions which are numerous in this district. Also centre of tiger country.

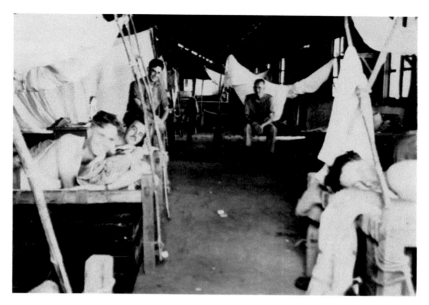

Interior of our hut, taken early morning.

Three colleagues outside Italian POW camp, RAF Bairagarh.

Mon 13 July

Reported to work 8am and busied ourselves in the workshops clearing up.

Two Ities are reported to have escaped, believed to have broken into our section and climbed over the main entrance which is unguarded at night. Both caught later. Most of these Italians have come from Abyssinia and were in the Duke of Aosta's army. Inspected a memorial built in his honour.

Bairagarh Fitter Group – Young Taff, Reg, Cyril & Chaplin.

In the workshop.

Tue 14 July

More work in the workshops clearing up. Went into Bhopal with Mac and saw 'Arise My Love' at Bhopal Talkies. Lost our way returning; found main entrance locked when we eventually arrived. Had to climb over barbed wire gates to get into camp.

Bhopal Cinema, the only modern building in the city.

Wed 15 July

Hawker Hart turns over when landing – no casualties.

Overturned Hawker Hart.

Thu 16 July

Worked on damaged Hart. Nearly stung by scorpion on elbow. Mail arrives by plane – none for me.

Hawker Hart. Chaps righting the plane using ropes, cables & manpower.

Fri 17 July

More work on the Hart. More Italian prisoners arrived.

Hawker Hart having been recovered.

Hawker Hart being repaired (note protection on propeller blades).

Italian Prisoners of War arriving at Bairagarh.

Sat 18 July

Saw 'Contraband' at Bhopal Talkies with Mac. Got lift back in bus reserved for Italian officers.

Sun 19 July

Hitchhiked into Bhopal with Mac. Interesting tour of the town: took snaps of ancient buildings, arches, tombs and Purdah woman.

Note the knife sharpener and horse-drawn trap (tonga), the fastest means of transport in these parts.

Went to 'Get Together' party in the Canteen in evening. Given many drinks by officers and had some difficulty returning to billet. Found main gate locked so had to climb over barbed wire fence once more; got caught up on top and fell into mud the other side. Was some minutes before I emerged from this sticky mess and by the time I reached the billet I was covered all over with mud!

Tue 21 July

Repaired camera, took gharri to bazaar to collect films.

Fri 24 July

Hart crashes in jungle some 20 miles away. Mac and I volunteer for night guard; we lose half our rations on way and take 3 hours de-bogging the Ambulance. Proceeded along a very rough track made of large stones and boulders about 5 miles into Jungle and returned according to instructions dropped by a guiding aircraft.

Debogging the ambulance.

RG COBLEY (GD) FLYING AUDAX AIRCRAFT K5568 WAS COMPELLED TO FORCE-LAND ON THE AIR-TO-AIR RANGE OWING TO ENGINE FAILURE. THE RANGE IS MOSTLY HILLY JUNGLE COUNTRY WITH A FEW FLAT CULTIVATED FIELDS AND THE PILOT MANAGED TO LAND IN SOME OF THESE. UNFORTUNATELY THE GROUND WAS SO SODDEN THAT AFTER LANDING, THE WHEELS DUG IN AND THE AIRCRAFT TURNED ONTO ITS BACK. NEITHER OCCUPANT WAS HURT AND THEY SPENT AN INTERESTING 6 HOURS OR SO WALKING 3 MILES TO THE RAILWAY THROUGH DEEP MUD, WITH 3 RIVERS THROWN IN FOR VARIETY. (Operations Records AIR 29/602 26TH JULY 1942)

Mon 27 July
Had a few drinks at the Canteen – Mac entertains some Wogs in their billet; he dances and sings to '4 Old Ladies', all are highly amused!

Tue 28 July
Transferred from workshops to maintenance section; working on Harts and Wapitis.

Wapiti having maintenance.

Wapiti being repaired.

Wed 29 July
Much rain, took snap of Monsoon. Sent off Peggy's present from Post Office after having same censored. Postage cost 1/8d.

Thu 30 July
Another Hart crashes – on salvage work.

Wapiti J9400 of 31 Squadron
(Struck Off Charge in February 1942).

Hawker Hart being repaired.

Hawker Hart (India) K2117 modified for hot climates.
(While the engine is being tested, one chap is holding the chocks as
there are probably no brakes; the chaps in the plane are sitting with
their heads down to withstand the blast of heat and dust.)

Fri 31 July
Take a photo of the chaps I work with.

L to R: myself, Mac, Strath, Johnnie, Taff, Eric & Dicky.

Sat 1 Aug

Johnnie, Mac and I go to Bhopal in Contractor's lorry and saw 'Buck Private'. Lorry hit a Tonga on return journey.

Sun 2 Aug

Read 'The Rubaiyat of Omar Kahayam'.

Thu 6 Aug

2 Wogs killed by a bear on road leading from camp to jungle.

Sun 9 Aug

Night guard – spent most time in unserviceable Lockheed. Large rat crawls by my head whilst lying in Lockheed! We stopped a number of Wogs crossing the Drome.

Lockheed 12 (serial no. 798), which belonged to the Indian Air Force. (A very expensive American plane, impressed from a Maharajah and taken before camouflage was added.)

Mon 10 Aug

Overslept – failed to report for work in morning.

On 18th August, I received a letter from Eddy Edwards:

Dear Peter,

I've just received a letter from Bob in which he states in no uncertain terms that he's 'cheerful'! He's way out in the Assam Jungle far from home and without a comfort in the world – not even a real job – I think he'll recover however. Speaking of recovering, I'm doing that myself, today being the last of my convalescence. I spent eight days in a Calcutta hospital with dengue fever. Though not dangerous in itself, this fever has the effect of a concentrated attack of 'flu – damned uncomfortable in fact. However, I'm OK now.

I don't think I'm much better off than Bob regarding living conditions: true I'm nearer what goes for civilisation in this country, but our billets are way out in the jungle, just mud huts, ill lit and without comfort. To be fair things have improved of late, we can even buy egg and chip suppers out here in the wilds but the basic living standard remains very much the same – poor.

I trust that you have fared better, Peter, but you always were a 'jammy' sort of bloke. I know you'll be happy if only those letters from Peggy are coming through regularly. My mail so far has consisted of one letter from home and one from Bob, hardly a fan mail is it? Do your part in keeping we three linked, Peter, Bob especially needs your aid. Cheerio and keep on beaming. Your old Pal, Eddy

P.S. I trust that by now your posting has come through – to a good station perhaps? The present one doesn't seem inviting. The crowd that were posted with me are still with me on the station though we are dispersed amongst several units. You remembered some of them? Cpls Kirby and Malt, Ginger Woods, Alec Taylor etc. The villages in this district are just as filthy as those you describe and I've a strong suspicion that this is typical of the whole of India. The emancipation of these people seems a long way off to me. All for now, I shall be writing again shortly, Eddy

Wed 19 Aug
Jungle Expedition postponed.

Fri 28 Aug
Hawker Audax makes forced landing in field near Rheti – a village some 40 miles away – airscrew broken on landing.

Sun 30 Aug
Parcelled up my Xmas presents.

THE RECORDS OF THE UNIT ARE NOT VERY CLEAR AND CONCISE AS NO PERMANENT RECORDS WERE KEPT BY THE PREVIOUS C.O. OF THE UNIT. F/O ROBINSON COMPILING THE RECORD. THE UNIT STARTED AS AN R&R PARTY. STRENGTH OF UNIT APPROXIMATELY 45, DEALT WITH APPROX 20 AIRCRAFT DURING THE MONTH, REFUELLING, DI'S ETC. (Operations Records AIR/463 Sept 42)

Setting off to Rheti.

Thu 3 Sep
Sent with repair party to Rheti to fit serviceable prop to damaged Audax. Rough journey along very poor roads. Passed through many swollen

rivers. Were held up at one river which had risen above the bridge and washed a bank of mud across the road on either side. Had to wait for coolie labour to clear same. Whilst waiting, I chased a baboon to try and get a snap but couldn't get near enough!

Passed through many swollen rivers.

Arrived at Rheti about 2pm.

Many villagers turned out to watch as we prepared tiffin.

Then we proceed to recover kite, a 2 mile walk through sea of mud carrying an airscrew between us! Took us over an hour to reach the aircraft as fields were extremely muddy and we had to cross a number of swollen streams. We had to pull one chap out who had sunk deep into muddy bed of stream.

Local inhabitant volunteered to carry propeller and act as our guide.

Eventually reached kite.

Hawker Audax crashed in field of wild cotton.
(This plane was a version of the Hawker Hart, adapted for Army Co-operation duties.)

Fitted the prop and ran up engine.

Hawker Audax after propeller is fitted.

Felt pretty weary by the time we reached the gharry as walking was most difficult through the soft mud. The village headman invited us to visit the village. Took snap of the 'main street' complete with stream running down the centre! Also snapped a Hindu effigy which, I was later told, represents their god of love.

The news was read out to some of the villagers whilst I was there.

Sun 6 Sep

Went to Railway Institute for a whist drive, dance and tombola, but soon left for the Ruby Hotel where we drank whisky, beer and gin; had some difficulty returning; searched for Morgan and found him eventually!

Thu 10 Sep

Posted by RAF to R&R (Refuelling & Rearming) Party.

Fri 11 Sep

Saw genuine demonstration of hypnotism by Professor Menzies.

Sat 12 Sep

Drinks in Canteen. Later entered the Free Italian POW Camp, chatted with some of the English speaking Ities.

Thu 24 Sep

General Wavell arrives by Dakota to carry out aerial inspection of local army manoeuvres. I service the Lysander from which the General is to inspect the manoeuvres.

General Wavell arrives in a DC2.
(This plane is from 31 Squadron.)

Fri 25 Sep

The General has much difficulty in climbing into the rear cockpit of the Lysander – he obviously isn't used to flying in one of these kites! He was leaning forward when this snap was taken.

General Wavell is leaning forward in the Lysander.
(Note the gun in the back with bomb carriers & machine gun in the struts.)

33 AIRCRAFT CALLED FOR SERVICING ETC., MOST WERE THE HUDSON AND DC3 MAIL RUNS FROM DELHI TO CEYLON. ALSO AT THE TIME VENGEANCE AIRCRAFT WERE MAKING THEIR APPEARANCE IN INDIA AND MANY OF THEM WERE CALLING TO BE SERVICED. (AIR 29/463 OCT 42)

VERY UNCERTAIN SERVICEABILITY OF WAPITI AIRCRAFT. AIR TO GROUND FIRING BY NO.9 OBSERVER COURSE USING 3 HARTS. DAILY ROUTINE ORDERS, R&R PARTY: **LAC WALKER** [& 7 OTHERS]. (Operations Records AIR 29/602 OCT 42)

On 4th October I received a letter from Mr. Fisher, 7 Pinsent Road,

Durban, Natal dated 10 Aug 1942.

Dear Peter,
It was a pleasure to get your letter and snaps.

Things are tightening up here, a permanent 'blackout' is enforced, allowance of petrol 300 miles per month, and it seems we are becoming important at last. India seems to be giving much trouble, and it all seems to boil down to the fact that Gandhi or some of his friends want to be dictators on their own. We've just read about the arrest of the leaders and it's a step in the right direction.

Business is at a low ebb and we're just plodding along in the hopes of a change for the better some day.

You'll like the snakes on the aerodrome, Peter, they are pleasant little pets though one must be careful not to tread on them – they resent that! Haven't got my films back yet as there is difficulty in processing coloured stuff, but I'm sure you fellows will come out well as my light meter is to be trusted. We shall be delighted to have you visit the Reserve with us after the War, and it could be made reasonably economical even from England. Third class on a mail boat is quite decent and not costly. Anyway, if you can manage the trip we can put you up, so make a point of it and consider this an invitation. Of course subject to anything extraordinary happening such as an invasion.

We don't feel that anything particular was done for you boys, so just forget it, Peter, we extended goodwill and hope for a kind thought in return and if we get that we are amply repaid.

My people are reasonably well and write in sending regards to yourself. We liked you well.

Yours very sincerely, ED Fisher

Tue 6 Oct
8ft viper killed in camp.

Wed 7 Oct
Played hockey for the station against Punjab Regiment and fractured hand during game. Lost 4-1.

Chaps in the Hockey Team.

Children enjoying themselves at the Fair in Bhopal,
The Muslim Festival Day of Eid.

Fri 9 Oct
Another Hart prangs beside strip.

Tue 13 Oct
Visit Bhopal City during afternoon. It is the Muslim Festival day of Eid which comes at the end of a month's fasting. Commotion caused through changing film!

Wed 21 Oct
Local saw mill caught fire; considerable damage caused to stock.

Local saw mill on fire.

Thu 22 Oct
Hawker Audax swerves off runway whilst landing, accident due to strong cross wind.

Fri 23 Oct
Lewis gun practice.

DAILY ROUTINE ORDERS BY SQUADRON LEADER E.C. FYSON. SECURITY PATROL: **707 WALKER** [AND OTHERS]. THERE WILL BE A FREE ISSUE OF

2 BOXES OF MATCHES PER AIRMAN AT BREAKFAST
TIME IN THE AIRMENS MESS ON TUES 3RD NOV
1942. (Operations Records AIR 29/602 O2 NOV)

Hawker Audax, crashed.

Hawker Audax, salvage party at work.

Hawker Audax, being recovered.

Hawker Audax, recovered.

Rifle Practice. (Considered necessary as the Quit India
Campaign had just started.)

Sun 1 Nov
Read 'Indian Harvest' by Pamela Hinkson.

Mon 2 Nov
Read 'Innocent Men' by Peter Howard.

Lysander, crashed. ('US' code used by No. 2
Squadron of the Indian Air Force.)

Lysander, crashed.

Lysander at dispersal.

Lysander (with Hawker Audaxes in the background).

Thu 5 Nov

Start building a 'shack' for the Christmas 'Bun Club'.

Our shack in the course of construction.

Sun 8 Nov

Commencement of the Hindu Feast of Dewali, Festival of Lights. New and brightly coloured cloths are worn and property including their bullocks are painted many bright colours.

HART AIRCRAFT K2091 CRASHED ON FALSE LANDING. PILOT AND OBSERVER UNHURT. (Operations Records AIR 29/602 09 NOV)

Hawker Hart K 2091 (India) crashes beside the strip.

Hawker Hart K 2091 (India).

Hawker Audax being repaired.

DESIGNATION OF UNIT CHANGED FROM R&R (REFUELLING & REARMING) PARTY TO R.S.P. (REPAIR & SALVAGE PARTY). (Operations Records AIR 29/46317 NOV)

Wed 18 Nov
Visited the Contractors Coolie Camp and took snaps of their crude dwelling places.

Were shown two leopard cubs which had been caught nearby.

H.E. THE VICEROY AND LADY LINLITHGOW ARRIVED AT BAIRAGARH AERODROME BY AIR AND WERE MET BY H.H. THE RULER OF BHOPAL AND W/CDR H.G.E. GAUBERT, DFC, AIR FIRING CONTINUED. (Operations Records AIR 29/602 21 NOV)

Sun 22 Nov
The Viceroy, Lord Linlithgow, arrived in a Dakota/Douglas aircraft for a few days' tiger hunting. He is staying with the Nawab of Bhopal.

Coolie Camp.

A friend & myself with a couple of leopard cubs.

The Viceroy, Lord Linlithgow, arrives in a Dakota DC3 (MA 925). (This is a VIP flight aircraft 'P', probably a military variation with rifle ports in the side windows.)

The Viceroy and Lady Linlithgow arriving at RAF Bairagarh.

The Viceroy and Lady Linlithgow arrive to meet
H.H. The Ruler of Bhopal for a few days' tiger hunting.

The Nawab's Palace with polo ground on the right.

Thu 26 Nov
Read 'The Son of Richard Cardin' by Neil Bell.

Sun 20 Dec
The Shack is completed: The Double R Saloon.

The 'Double R Saloon' which we built for the Christmas celebrations.

Jimmie my bearer & myself on Christmas Day.

Chapter 3 – Chronology of War:

Sept & Oct 1942: Churchill described this time as his most anxious months of the war.

Nov 1942: General Montgomery took 30,000 German and Italian prisoners in the Battle of Alamein. The code-breakers at Bletchley Park achieved another breakthrough in cracking the U-boat cipher and once more provided the Royal Navy with the means to track U-boat positions: the tide started to turn against Germany.

Dec 1942: There were now 2 RAF groups in India (53 squadrons) and 1 in Ceylon, with over 1,400 aircraft, and set for further expansion. The USAAF had also built up its strength, mainly with transport aircraft and an increase in Dakota squadrons. Streams of Dakotas were coming off the production lines – they were very reliable, easy to use and could fly in tropical conditions.

20 Dec 1942: The first of the night air raids was made on Calcutta by 8 Japanese bombers, but a number of night-fighter Beaufighters soon stopped these. The First Arakan Campaign to re-capture the RAF airfield at Akyab Island was launched on 9th December with Blenheims and Hurricanes having only limited success. The Eastern Army under Lt-Gen Irwin crossed the Burmese border to try to capture the port of Akyab but there were heavy casualties on both sides so the army retreated back to India by May.

Victor Alexander John Hope, 2nd Marquis of Linlithgow, was born in 1887 and educated at Eton. From 1936-1943 he was the Viceroy and Governor General of India, and entrusted to prepare a scheme for Federation which he believed he would have achieved by July 1941 if the war had not intervened. He strove to keep India as safe as possible by maximising the war effort and refused to be deflected by Gandhi's fast in 1943. He felt very deeply about the Bengal Famine but was criticised for not visiting the area, although his wife begged him to go. When he finished his office on 20th October 1943, his 7½ year tenure was the longest of any Governor-General, and he was succeeded by General Wavell.

Archibald Percival Wavell was born in 1899, educated at Winchester, went to Sandhurst at the age of 17 and was commissioned into the famous 'Black Watch' Regiment at 18. He served in the Boer War and the First World War. In 1940 he fought a successful campaign in North Africa as Commander-in-Chief but was replaced by Field Marshal Sir Claude Auchinleck and immediately took over the former's position as Commander-in-Chief of India. Fighting against heavy odds, he lost both Malaya and Burma to the Japanese but his reputation as a soldier stood as high as any of his contemporaries. He was a scholar as well as being a physically tough campaigner.

In **August 1942**, General Wavell accompanied Churchill to Moscow as he spoke the language (he served in Russia in 1919). Apparently, the most notable success of the evening was a speech by Wavell in Russian. Wavell succeeded Lord Linlithgow as India's last but one Viceroy in 1943.

CHAPTER 4

TREADING THE TOURIST TRAIL
JAN – DEC 1943

Editor's Note:

Although never managing to return to England on leave, Peter was able to visit much of India by hitching lifts on aircraft as well as travelling by train. He was one of a party of 40 sent for a rest in the Himalayas near Simla from 19th May to 10th June. In the days of the Raj, the British would escape the summer heat of the plains and head for the Himalayan foothills to the delightful hill stations of Simla, Kasauli and Dalhousie.

Travelling first on the crowded 'Bombay Mail' train, then sightseeing with friends in Delhi, the last part of the journey from Dehra Dun to Chakrata was by gharri along a steep, winding mountain road. But because of severe burns sustained from an accident in May, Peter ended up by spending most of his leave in the British Military Hospital and then 2 weeks' convalescence when he went walking in the Himalayas.

In October he was able to take several days' leave in Agra with colleagues, visiting the Taj Mahal, Fatehpur Sikri and other famous sites.

A variety of planes were repaired and serviced at this time including: Hawker Hurricane I & II, Vultee Vengeance, Curtiss Mohawk IV, Lockheed Hudson and Dakotas of 31 Squadron, including a rare DC2K. In fact, on 14th August Peter was able to fly in a Hudson for 3 hours on a DF (Direction Finder) Test over Bairagarh although the visibility was very poor.

Peter was again instrumental in organising the Christmas festivities by helping to build 'The Chequers Inn'.

There are constant references to class divisions within the Forces, for instance by referring to non-commissioned ground crew as the 'common erk'.

Sat 1 Jan

Had a jolly evening in 'The Double R Saloon' and later joined Mac, Strath and Johnnie in the Canteen. The company became very rowdy and tables and chairs were thrown about and broken. I stopped a table on my back! Many glasses and bottles were broken. I later saw the New Year in with Strath in the billet. We previously put Mac and Jonnie to bed! Had my wallet taken from my tunic pocket whilst asleep that night. In it was the St Christopher medal Peggy gave me.

Sun 2 Jan

Beer bar put out of bounds for a week and armed guard placed on it! I post notice in Dining Hall re loss of wallet and St Christopher.

```
F/O TIMBLE TOOK COMMAND OF THE UNIT. 29
AIRCRAFT SERVICED, MAINLY MAIL RUN. A FEW
HURRICANE REFORS BEGAN TO PASS THROUGH.

DAILY ROUTINE ORDERS BY WING COMMANDER H.P.
SIMPSON.

RELATIONS WITH INDIA: ALL RANKS ARE TO
AVOID QUARRELS AND AFFRAYS OF ANY KIND WITH
INDIANS. ANY CASE, HOWEVER TRIVIAL IT MAY
BE, IS TO BE REPORTED TO THE STATION
ADJUTANT WITHOUT DELAY. IT IS FORBIDDEN TO
LEND OR BORROW MONEY FROM INDIANS.

TONGAS WILL NOT BE ALLOWED TO PLY FOR HIRE
INSIDE THE AIR FORCE CAMP. TONGA HIRE FROM
SOUTH CAMP TO BHOPAL IS 4/- PER SEAT OR
12/- FOR FULL TONGA.

ALL GAMBLING ON STATION, CAMPS OR IN
BARRACKS IS FORBIDDEN. THIS INCLUDES
BOOKMAKING OR ACTING AS AN AGENT FOR A
BOOKMAKER.

NO INTOXICANTS ARE TO BE TAKEN INTO ANY
```

BARRACK ROOMS OR ON THE ADJOINING
VERANDAHS.

AMONGST OTHER MEASURES, FOOD TAKEN IN
BARRACKS MUST BE EATEN IMMEDIATELY AND
SCRAPS, CRUMBS, ETC. REMOVED TO RECEPTACLES
WITHOUT DELAY AS THE NUMBER OF FLIES IN THE
CAMP IS INCREASING AGAIN. (Operations Records
AIR 29/463/602 JAN 43)

Fri 8 Jan
Parcel containing silk, wooden image and 30 snaps sent off to Peggy.

A photo of Peggy on Peter's writing table.

Sun 24 Jan
Visited Bairagarh cinema with Mac, Strath and Johnnie in evening but
film stopped owing to sudden heavy gale. The first heavy gust of wind
nearly blew in one side and the cinema was soon filled with clouds of
dust. There was no pause except for a number of Wogs who rushed out
shouting.

Mon 25 Jan
Went to Bairagarh cinema again and got thoroughly wet watching the

film as an unexpected storm broke and the rain soon poured through the canvas roof. Films showing were: 'The Whalers – Mickey Mouse', 'They knew what they wanted' starring Charles Laughton and Carole Lombard.

Myself, John, Frank, Clifford, Ron D & Ron S taken outside our tent.

Tue 26 Jan
Lockheed Hudson arrived in evening bringing new CO. Refuelled same in 20 minutes.

Mon 1 Feb
Reported sick, have felt run down these last few days – have eaten little and had no sleep. I am given salt pills to take every 4 hours.

Visit the Hindu temple on top of hill overlooking camp during the afternoon with Mac and Johnnie. Felt faint and sick when climbing hill; was soon better after resting in cool shelter under large overhanging rock. Took snaps from top and inside temple. On way back we met some of our Wog cooks having a picnic who invited us to join in. We drank a homemade spirit (very potent) made from rice and ate chippaties. Mac, Strath and Johnnie leave for Trichinopoly that night.

Tue 2 Feb
Spent day in bed.

Fri 5 Feb
Went to Bairagarh cinema in evening and saw 'Song of the Musketeers'.

Sat 6 Feb
Saw 'Strike up the Band' starring Mickey Rooney and Judy Garland at Bhopal cinema. Had fortune told for one rupee outside Bhopal cinema. Was told to expect cable on March 23 which would bring me luck! I should later return home!

Tue 9 Feb
Went to flicks in Bairagarh.

Wed 10 Feb
Reported sick, have slight attack of Yellow Jaundice but feel much better now – appetite and sleep normal. Eyes and forehead turned slightly yellow. Read '39 Steps' by John Buchan.

Mon 15 Feb
Trip to Gunnery Range in jungle. Saw number of buck on way out. Later a small one was shot and we had its liver for tiffin! The Hurricane firing practice is poor; highest score is 97 out of a possible 400.

Frank and I go for a walk through the thick woods but see nothing but numerous birds of many colours. Later are informed by the headman of the village that a tiger has been seen in the neighbourhood recently!

Tue 16 Feb
Saw Ginger Rogers in '5th Avenue Girl' at Bairagarh cinema.

Fri 19 Feb
Saw 'Break the News' with Jack Buchanan. Very poor film.

Sun 21 Feb
Saw Alice Fay in 'Night in Rio'; Carmen Miranda gives poor show.

Mon 22 Feb

Went to Bairagarh flicks and saw Deanna Durban in 'Mad about Maisie' which I thoroughly enjoyed seeing a second time.

Thu 25 Feb

Trip to Sehore in gharri; ordered 1 pair of black shoes for 11 rupees.

Fri 26 Feb

Pay Parade – report afterwards re income tax. Visited Bhopal Silk Market and bought: ¼ yards of grey worsted flannel, 2 ½ yards of white poplin, slacks, open shirt, 5 salochrome films and 1 panchromatic film. Went for row on Lake for one hour for 1 rupee.

Sun 28 Feb

Took tonga to Bhopal and collected flannel trousers and poplin shirt from Tailors in Silk Bazaar. Passed wedding procession on way through City. Thousands of flies around food stalls and appalling smells everywhere.

```
47 AIRCRAFT PASSED THROUGH, INCREASE DUE IN
THE  MAIN  TO  CONVOYS  OF  HURRICANE  REFORS
AIRCRAFT   PASSING   THROUGH.   ALSO   SERVICED
AIRCRAFT   OF   U.S.A.A.C.   PASSING   THROUGH.
(Operations Records AIR 29/463 MARCH)
```

Bert & Mac.

Tue 2 Mar

Hand x-rayed at hospital and found to be OK. Plaster removed. Wrist has shrunk a little and is somewhat stiff. No. 6 IAF Squadron arrives – 6 Aircraft fail to get here owing to petrol shortage. One is burnt out and pilot killed.

Wed 3 Mar

Convoy of Hurricanes arrives, one runs into steam roller when landing and damages part of main plane.

Sun 7 Mar

Saw 'Arizona' starring Jean Arthur at Bhopal Talkies.

Sat 13 Mar

Saw 'Snow White & Seven Dwarfs' at Bairagarh cinema.

Mon 15 Mar

Peggy posted book parcel also letter containing St Christopher medallion. Sent birthday greeting by cable to Mother.

Mon 22 Mar

Shade temp 102 degrees.

Thu 25 Mar

Had hand x-rayed again and triquetrum found to be still fractured so not flying at present.

Fri 26 Mar

Saw Deanna Durban in 'Spring Parade'.

Sat 27 Mar

Frank and I cycled to other side of Bhopal Lake, 25 miles. I took a snap of a number of moored yachts belonging to the Yachting Club. Unfortunately we aren't able to hire these yachts or belong to the Club – at least not us common 'erks'! Had a glass of iced goat's milk and fruit juice on returning at the Bazaar.

Mon 29 Mar

Went for walk with Frank through barley fields and returned via Bazaar where we had an iced drink of goat's milk and fruit juice.

Tue 30 Mar

Right hand put in plaster again.

49 AIRCRAFT PASSED THROUGH. ONE HURRICANE CONVOY. GREAT INCREASE IN HARVARD TRAFFIC MAINLY GOING THROUGH TO NO. 1 F.T.S. (Operations Records AIR 29/463/602 APR 43)

Hawker Hurricane II.

Hawker Hurricane II in faded camouflage paint.
(Note long range tanks under wings.)

In comparison, this is a Hawker Hurricane I taken in its UK pre-war condition.

Thu 1 Apr

Frank and I cycled to Bhopal and hired a rowing boat for some hours. I wrote about this in a letter to my Parents:

Frank and I spent a most enjoyable day rowing on the nearby lake. We left soon after the mid-day meal and hired a couple of cycles from the local Bazaar. We were fortunate in getting two that were reasonably sound, though it's a fifty/fifty chance whether one gets back without some vital part falling off or finding oneself let down suddenly when a tyre bursts – for such is the condition of these bikes! However, they only charge 2 annas per hour so it's a cheap enough way of travelling.

We took our water bottles with us containing lime juice and also an orange and a packet of biscuits with us as we didn't expect to be back in time for dinner. The ride there was somewhat warm as the temperature was well over 100 degrees Fahrenheit in the shade; fortunately there was a strong wind blowing which cooled things off a little.

As we approached the lake down the hill I took a snapshot. It gives you some idea of its size although there is only about half of it shown in this snap. The boat house from where we hired a small zinc lined boat is just out of the picture on the left; in fact you can just see a somewhat larger boat anchored between the two trees on the left. Our intention was to explore one of the small rivers which enters the lake just to the right of that long line of hills on the opposite bank. You can see from this snap we had a longish row before reaching the mouth of this river – a distance of 2 to 3 miles. As soon as we left the shore we stripped – all but our shorts and topee – and found the strong wind blowing over the lake most cooling. However, we were rowing against the wind so what with this and the fact that the boat was leaking in a few places and consequently had to be baled out occasionally, we found travelling rather slow.

We reached the mouth of the river after 1 ½ hours rowing and after navigating between the clusters of weed we found ourselves in a somewhat shallow river with high banks of reed on either side. There is any amount of bird life on the reed banks; we saw a couple of red headed cranes standing about 4ft high. I took a snap of them but they were too far away to come out clear.

Later we passed a small Indian village on the banks of the river; their reed huts were dotted amongst the trees. As we passed further up the river we came on a herd of Water Buffalo cooling themselves in midstream. A little beyond – just past that Indian squatting on the bank – we moored and had our refreshments. We didn't stay long as we wanted to continue up the river before returning.

On our way downstream we passed a bullock cart wading across the river. Later, as we neared the mouth again, we saw a shoal of fish which skimmed along the surface of the water propelling themselves with their tails. These fish have –

according to Frank – greenish brown backs with a silver belly and long feelers. One of them jumped right over the side of our boat where it swam about in the bilge water until I caught it in the baler and threw it overboard.

Just before entering the lake we saw an Indian (a holy man I believe as he wore a rosary around his neck) punting himself across the river on a hand-made raft no larger than the top of a card table! Unfortunately I had finished the film as that would have made an interesting snap.

The row back down the lake was much easier as we had the wind behind us; we moored just as the sun was setting – the end of a most pleasant afternoon.

I also enclose a snap of me and my super comfortable, fully adjustable deck chair which I recently made! It's in the 'medium' position in this picture. By simply moving that lever, which can just be seen below my fingers, the back can be lowered into the lounging position or can be brought upright into a vertical position for reading or writing. There are twelve different positions for the back and it isn't necessary to get out of the chair when altering it! It is worked by a lever, an adjustable wedge and a spring!

The cup, by the way, was won by our Football team but the bloke who took this snap decided I deserved it for my chair-making effort!!

Hope this letter finds you all very fit – I'm extremely well myself.

Much love to all, Peter

*Me and my super comfortable fully adjustable deck chair that
I recently made.*

Mac, Johnnie & Decky, the Footballers.

Sat 3 April
Saw 'The Story of Vernon & Irene Castle' at local cinema. Bhopal and cinema out of bounds owing to an outbreak of spinal fever. Farewell Party for Sgt Brown.

Tue 6 April
Saw Ginger Rogers in 'Kitty Foyle' at Bairagarh. Heavy gale during night – am called out at 2am to re-picquet the Puss Moth.

Thu 15 April
1st Anniversary of Overseas Tour. Plaster changed.

Mon 19 April
Removing shack and suggestion of starting Club and having 'visitors night' twice weekly, organising whist drives and tombola school and badminton tournament as well as table games. Lack of co-operation of other chaps, only 3 of us erecting shack. There is a probability of fortnight's rest at hill station starting May 14th and possibility of extending leave by a fortnight and spending it at Murree.

Wed 21 Apr
Heavy dust storm strikes camp and all buildings of Technical Camp are damaged with many roofs blown off. All training aircraft are damaged except Wapitis. One Hart was blown free of picquets and carried over fence to eventually land up on its nose many yards from its original position. Verandah of shack partly blown off, otherwise little damage sustained.

Sun 25th April
Moved No. 1 Armament Training Unit (ATU) from No. 12 camp to new Domestic Camp.

> 63 AIRCRAFT PASSED THROUGH. INCREASE DUE TO 2 BATCHES OF HURRICANES AND 3 OF VENGEANCE CONVOYS RETURNING. TWO VERY RARE VISITORS: 2 P40'S OF THE U.S.A.A.C. (Operations Records AIR 29/463/589 MAY 43)

Hawker Audax
(thought to be part of 1 Armament Training Unit because of
unusual attachment behind the cockpit – believed to be cartridge
case collector, where normally there is just an exit chute).

Vultee Vengeance (AN 845) (one of a mixed batch of 500 Mk
I/IIs – quite a rarity).

DC2/3 of 31 Squadron, on the runway with a fuelling
bowser. (In the background is a Vultee Vengeance.)

Mon 3 May

Leaving for hill station on 18ᵗʰ May after working through heat of day.
Probability of moving shack again, wasted work! Long walk to cinema
(1½ miles). Ration of beer in Canteen to 3 bottles per month supplied
luke-warm. Lime juice supply with ice daily. Short walk with Frank in
jungle, frightening women at well!

Thu 6 May

Had accident in gharri on way to work; driver stopped suddenly because
of wires dangling across road and the charwallah, who was holding his
charcoal fire, lost his balance and dropped the ash tray on my leg – the
charcoal flying in all directions burnt both my hands and left arm.

IT HAS BEEN DECIDED TO APPOINT A NEW
WELFARE & ENTERTAINMENTS COMMITTEE FOR
AIRMEN. A DANCE, IN AID OF RED CROSS FUNDS,
IS BEING HELD ON THE TENNIS COURTS OF THE
RAILWAY INSTITUTE, BHOPAL ON 15ᵀᴴ MAY 1943.
THERE WILL BE A BAND CONCERT FOR ALL RANKS
ON TUESDAY 18ᵀᴴ MAY OUTSIDE THE AIRMEN'S

RECREATION ROOM (OPPOSITE CANTEEN) "GIVEN BY THE P.O.W. BAND". (Operations Records AIR 29/463 8.5.43)

Sat 8 May

Jimmy Downs, recently promoted corporal, holds party in Canteen – much beer is drunk. CO enters Canteen later and is molested by other chaps unable to get beer without coupons; numerous complaints are put before him and a voice from the crowd later tells him to "get out of the Airmen's Canteen!" Meanwhile the keys of his car have been pinched and thrown away so the CO is obliged to walk back. SPs search numerous chaps for missing keys but without success.

IN VIEW OF THE DISGUSTING BEHAVIOUR OF CERTAIN AIRMEN IN THE AIRMEN'S CANTEEN DURING THE VISIT OF THE COMMANDING OFFICER LAST EVENING, 8TH MAY 1943, ALL PRIVILEGES WILL CEASE AS FROM TODAY, SUNDAY 9TH MAY 1943. (Operations Records AIR 29/463 MAY)

Sun 9 May

All corporals and ranks below same are confined to camp owing to previous night's disturbance; beer, bar and games room are put out of bounds and everyone is instructed to stand by beds at 10.15 for roll call.

Mon 10 May

Special CO's Parade at 9.15am re Saturday night's disturbance. I have difficulty concentrating on writing letters in this heat; trying to keep cool by drinking lime juice.

THE FOLLOWING PERSONNEL ARE DETAILED TO PROCEED TO CHAKRATA FOR A PERIOD OF 14 DAYS FROM 19/5/43-1/6/43. ESSENTIAL ITEMS OF KIT, INCLUDING WARM CLOTHES, WATERPROOF CAPE AND SPORTS KIT ARE TO BE TAKEN. THE FOLLOWING PERSONNEL WILL REPORT FOR INSTRUCTIONS AT 1500 HOURS ON SAT 15/5/43:

707 LAC WALKER [& OTHERS]. (Operations Records AIR 29/463 14.5.43)

Sun 16 May

Left Bairagarh 10.15pm for Chakrata with hill party of 40. Found 3rd class carriage reserved for us in a filthy condition – many cockroaches and large black beetles on floor. Train left from Bhopal at 1am where our carriage was left until the following morning to be picked up by the 'Bombay Mail'. Frank and I slept in 2nd class compartment of another train and woke up a few minutes before it departed!

Mon 17th May

'Bombay Mail' left 7.15am. Frank and I had last minute rush to collect bedding from platform (which incidentally had been put on the train by another chap without us knowing) and were only just able to catch up train and jump on a crowded 2nd class compartment full of Indian Officers; we returned to our carriage at next stop. Passed through Agra but saw nothing of the Taj Mahal and arrived Delhi at 10pm. Booked a couple of beds in the rest room at the station which was clean, lofty and cooled by electric fans. Slept well this night!

The crowded 'Bombay Mail'.

Tue 18 May

After having Breakfast at the Station Restaurant (the Wavell Canteen was closed for alterations), we took a tonga to the Fort, Old Delhi where I had my leg and hands dressed at the M1 room of the army garrison stationed there. Then we visited Jumma Masjid, the largest Mosque in India, built by Shah Jahan during the 15th century. We were shown over by a guide whom we picked up at the station before leaving; climbed one of the large towers and took snaps. Saw the original manuscript of the Koran written by the son-in-law of Mohammed. Also saw a brown hair of the Prophet's beard and the impression of his foot in a slab of marble.

Frank Gibbs, our Guide and Tonga in front of Jumma Masjid.

After visiting the Ivory Palace where I bought a little ivory peacock on a stand, we returned via Chandni Chowk, the main street of the Bazaar. Had lunch at the Station Restaurant and afterwards took gharri to New Delhi but found majority of shops closed so took another gharri to The Viceroy Lodge where I took snaps of same and later of the Secretariat and Government House and Council House where the Indian Chamber of Princes meet. We returned to the circular arcade of shops where we had a Peach Melba milk shake, an éclair and cream cake! Returned to the station 6.30pm. Train left 7.15pm and was packed with Indians, many of whom had to stand on the running board and cling onto the windows! I promise myself that I shall travel back by myself in 2nd class.

Wed 19 May

Arrived Dehra Dun at 7am and were transported to the local RAF station where I had bacon and egg breakfast bribed from the cook. Gharri convoy left at 10.15am. Corporal breaks his wrist and is taken to Army camp (first stop). The journey from here on is controlled, the road being only wide enough for single line traffic, so we wait for the down traffic to pass. The road winds steeply along the mountain side, there being many hair-pin bends and steep precipices on one side. Our gharri breaks down when we're nearly there! The cause a faulty petrol pump, it is rectified and we arrive Chakrata at 5pm. Visit the gym in the evening and have a few bets on the racing game and a pint of Solar Beer.

On the way up to Chakrata from Dehra Dun.

Thu 20 May

Report sick and am transferred to the convalescent ward until burns heal.

Sat 22 May

Visited Bazaar and bought watch 35Rs, walking stick 1Rs and pair sandals 7Rs. Was accosted on way back for Buckshees!!

Sun 23 May

Visited Bazaar with Frank and bought Kashmir made cigarette box and ash tray and mother of pearl bracelet. Had supper at the Scotch Tea Shop.

Mon 24 May

Watched 6ft poisonous snake being skinned. Skin afterwards cured in water, alum and methylated spirits. Saw '39 Steps' at local cinema; walk back irritated leg and caused wound to give off much puss.

Tue 25 May

Transferred from convalescence to hospital. Very comfortable here – food good, nurses charming, view perfect!

Wed 26 May

Moved to another ward, later had bed taken onto balcony.

Fri 28 May

Burns improving. Read 'The Snake & The Sword'. Visited by Frank in evening, gave him Rs30 for safe custody.

Sat 29 May

Read 'Death of my Aunt' by CHB Kitchen.

Sun 30 May

Heavy thunderstorm last night; wind was unfortunately blowing towards verandah consequently my top blanket and pillow were saturated. Leg burn improving but dressing stuck fast as usual causing much pain when removing same. Powder dressing and vaseline put on this time.

Wed 2 June

Allowed out to the Flicks; saw 'Target for Tonight'. Had mango for tea.

Thu 10 June
Discharged from Hospital; granted 2 weeks convalescence. Saw 'The Big Store' at 9.30pm performance. Previously had supper at Sandy's House: salmon, egg, tomato and shredded lettuce salad; mixed fruit flan for sweet; 3 teas, bread and butter Rs1.

Fri 11 June
Presents brought up to date: silk stockings, ivory peacock, 2 ivory elephants, 1 carved wood tray, 1 cigarette fancy tin with ash tray, 1 mother of pearl bangle, 1 cigarette case, 1 sandalwood carved cow, 1 sandalwood carved camel. Still to get: Gurkha knife (Kukri), dress material, pair scissors.

Sat 12 June
Went horse-riding and afterwards had tea at Sandy's House. Later saw 'Babes on Broadway' and had a large supper at the R.C. Canteen on the way back.

Horse riding in the Himalayas.

Mon 14 June
Bought a pair of brown rabbit shoes. Played tennis with Jack Frost. Saw 'They Met in Bombay', excellent film.

Wed 16 June

Hand x-rayed and fracture found to be fully healed. Massage recommended 3 times a day.

Thu 17 June

Saw Jack Buchan in 'The Sky's the Limit', a rotten film.

Fri 18 June

Pay parade in morning. Saw Vivienne Leigh in '21 Days Together', very good acting. Found large black spider in billet and slung below its belly was a round white parcel which it later discarded; this proved to be a bunch of eggs.

Sat 19 June

2 sets of tennis with Jack; went 6-2 8-6, good games. Listened to Gurkha band play 'Retreat' in square.

Sun 20 June

Jack Frost, a friend of his, and myself climbed Deoban, the largest peak in the vicinity – nearly 10,000 ft. high – passed numerous baboons and took snaps of them; wonderful views on the way up. Summit covered with thick woods, numerous pretty wild flowers about and multitudes of small wild strawberries which were ripe and very sweet. Had a snack on summit and took a few snaps. Views of snow covered Himalayan peaks in the far distance were magnificent.

Tue 22 June

Buy pyjamas, moth balls and present for Grannie from Bazaar.

Thu 24 June

Left Chakrata. Visited Samrat Yantra Observatory built by Maharajah Jai Singh in 1710 (restored 1919).

Sun 27 June

Slept little Sat night in spite of electric fan above my bed! Left Agra 2pm and arrived Bairagarh at 1.15am Monday. Phoned station for transport but despite numerous tries could not get through. Slept in first class waiting room in company of numerous Indians.

Jack Frost and friend on summit of Deoban.

The Kyber Pass.

A Tibetan Hills Man.

Mon 28 June
Arrived back at Bairagarh camp. Water supply polluted by dead snake in well – all drinking water to be boiled in future.

37 AIRCRAFT CAME AND WERE SERVICED. TWO CONVOYS OF HURRICANES AND A FEW HARVARDS. ALSO ANOTHER P40-E AND ANOTHER STRANGER – A BEAUFIGHTER.

DISCIPLINE – DRESS: SECTION COMMANDERS ARE TO PERSONALLY ENSURE THAT ALL AIRMEN ARE DRESSED IN THE FOLLOWING MANNER DURING WORKING ROUTINE. TOPEE, SHIRT OR BUSH SHIRT TUCKED IN SHORTS, SHORTS, STOCKINGS AND SHOES. DISCIPLINARY ACTION WILL BE TAKEN AGAINST OFFENDERS. (Operations Records AIR 29/463/589 JUNE 43)

Fri 2 July
Played football in evening – position left back, very strenuous game. Shorts kept dropping down causing me to trip up once or twice!

Sat 3 July
Wrote to Peggy thanking her for sending me the new St Christopher medallion.

Fri 9 July
Special Welfare meeting held in evening; Group Welfare Officer present. Many complaints registered – poor and inadequate cookhouse food; canteen prices too high; canteen too small; no drinking water; numerous complaints made about M.O. Promised:- new large Institute with stage, cinema screen projector; new radio; better and more varied cookhouse food.

Sat 10 July
Visited Bhopal cinema and saw 'The Ghost Train' and 'Dark Streets of Cairo'.

Sun 11 July
Not overworking at present and it is a bit cooler. Mail has gone missing between Jan and June. Went for a walk with Frank along Delhi Road and back across fields – saw very large baboon and numerous youngsters.

Mon 19 July
Had tooth removed at dentist.

> NEW PEAK REACHED WITH TOTAL OF 81 AIRCRAFT. INCREASE CAUSED PARTLY BY LARGE MOVEMENT OF TIGER MOTHS AND HARVARD CONVOYS. THE OLD AND ANCIENT AUDAX AND HART APPEARS TO HAVE HAD ITS DAY AS NOT MANY PASS THROUGH.
>
> HEALTH OF STATION CONTINUES VERY SATISFACTORY. ONE CASE OF TYPHUS. IMMEDIATE MEASURES TO CONTROL CONTACTS AND AVOID SPREAD OF DISEASE. CASE DISCHARGED CURED. INCIDENCE OF MALARIA EXTREMELY LOW, ONLY 3 CASES ON WHOLE STATION. PRACTICE PARADE FOR BATTLE OF BRITAIN BIRTHDAY ON 13 SEPT.
> (Operations Records AIR 29/463 SEPT 43)

Wed 1 Sept
Watched half a dozen vultures tear to pieces a dead dog and devoured it in a very short space of time! Vultures about 3ft and had a wing span of about 6ft. Shuddered to think of the 'Towers of Silence'. Sending list of architectural books wanted to parents as interested in post-war plans.

Sat 4 Sept
Cycled to Bhopal with Frank, John and Jimmy. Bought silver chain for medallion. Frank gets puncture. We walk to lake but boatman refuses to hire boat so we pinch same! I nearly capsize in punt in underwear to reach large boat! Eat bread and apple sandwiches on boat. Offer boatman Rs1 on returning – he refuses same!!

Myself, Joe & Jimmy in residential area of Bhopal.

Tue 4 Sept

Read 'I was a Pagan' by V.C. Kitchen, very much impressed. Wrote to parents to say that I am very fit and not getting thin. Excellent news but some way to travel yet.

Fri 24 Sept

Read 'Great Argument' by Phillip Gibbs.

Tue 28 Sept

Wrote to Pegs about killing snake but little chance of getting bitten. Numerous scorpions around here; new address; defence course.

```
THIS MONTH ALL PREVIOUS RECORDS WERE EASILY
PASSED. A TOTAL OF 112 AIRCRAFT PASSED
THROUGH, MAINLY DUE TO A QUICKENING UP OF
THE HURRICANE CONVOYS. A FEW MOHAWKS CAME
FOR THE FIRST TIME AND 1 OR 2 FAIRCHILDS
CALLED, ALL HELPING TO SWELL THE NUMBER.

SEVERAL CASES OF JAUNDICE HAVE OCCURRED.
```

THIS DISEASE DUE TO VIRUS INFECTION IS UNDOUBTEDLY INFECTIOUS. OWING TO LONG INCUBATION PERIOD WITH NO SYMPTOMS IT IS EXTREMELY DIFFICULT TO CONTROL. FULL USE IS BEING MADE OF STATION SICK QUARTERS. IT IS CONSIDERED THAT THIS IS GREATLY APPRECIATED BY ALL PATIENTS, WHO VASTLY PREFER TO BE TREATED BY THEIR OWN MEDICAL SERVICE.

17.10.43 FIRST NIGHT OF CONCERT "BAIRAGARH CALLING".
NEW RAF WING AT PRINCE OF WALES HOSPITAL BHOPAL OFFICIALLY OPENED BY H.H. THE NAWAB OF BHOPAL ON 11.10.43. (Operations Records AIR 29/463/589 OCT 43)

DC2K (AX 755) 'O' of 31 Squadron.
(This was assembled in Cape Town, used by 267 Squadron in Egypt and then sent to 31 Squadron, one of the elusive DC2Ks.)

Sat 2 Oct
Sent Christmas parcel to Pegs containing artificial silk stockings, ivory peacock, cigarette container and ash tray for her parents. Sent

Christmas parcel to Parents – Mother marble dish, Father cigarette case.

Taffy Tennant malaria temp 104.2 – difficulty in persuading MO to come! Taken to BMH.

Tue 5 Oct
On special firing course, future shooting match. Having my hair cut away from a wound sustained on Christmas night! Rainy season over – warmer. But hot season not for another 6 months!

Fri 8 Oct
PAY (DROs 8.10.43)

All accounts are maintained at Base Accounts Office, Bombay. Each account will be closed at end of every four months, commencing 31.7.43 and balances notified to Units.

Airmen in India prior to 1.11.42 or who were transferred from another overseas command will not receive statement of accounts until such time as their previous accounts are transferred to Base accounts.

Tue 12 Oct
Write letter to Pegs about the recent cricket match; John Caton's commission not my line! Station variety show. John and I are to design a country inn for the Bun Club – any suggestions regarding decorations, pictures, advertisements, slogans etc. would be welcome, suggest drawing on an Airgraph.

Tue 19 Oct
Write letter to Pegs about new RAF Wing at Prince of Wales Hospital given by The Nawab of Bhopal; weekend leave to Agra; visited Taff; gadget on camera.

Cable to Pegs:

Many Happy Returns Darling, all my love Peter.

Thu 21 Oct
Few days' leave with Taffy, Jimmy, Edgar & Frank to Agra visiting:

Taj, Mosque & Jamatkhana

The Fort – Moti Masjid (Pearl Mosque), Diwan-i-Khas, Palaces of Akbar, Jahangir & Shah Jahan

Shish Mahal, Jasmine Tower, Khas Mahal, Anguri Bagh, Fish Palace & Nagina Masjid

Tomb of Akbar at Sikandra

Fatehpur Sikri, The Gateway of Victory, Jama Masjid (hornets' nests in this!)

Panch Mahal (5-storied building), Hall of Private Audience, Marganis House,

Palace of Jodha Bai, Hiram Minar or Elephant Tower.

Taffy, myself, Jimmy & Frank snapped in front of the cycle shop at Agra whilst waiting for them to repair Edgar's puncture.

Jimmy, Frank & myself in front of the Taj Mahal.

Fatehpur Sikri.

The Family Transport.

115 AIRCRAFT CALLED, MAINLY CONVOYS OF
HURRICANE AIRCRAFT BUT ONE OR TWO UNUSUAL
TYPES SUCH AS A BEECHCRAFT, A CURTISS HAWK
AND A RYAN TRAINER CALLED. THERE WAS ALSO
ONE OF THE UBIQUITOUS AUSTER AIRCRAFT THAT
CAME THROUGH. (Operations Records AIR 29/463 NOV 43)

Curtiss Mohawk IV, serial no. BT 741 (one of three of an ex-French order).

Curtiss Mohawk IV having engine maintenance.

Curtiss Mohawk IV with myself as the pilot!

Tue 2 Nov
Letter No. 97 to Pegs re changed feelings, suggest break.

Wed 3 Nov
Wrote to parents re leave not until next year but possibly another weekend shortly.

Tue 9 Nov
Wrote to Pegs: no silk stockings! But can get dress material, cosmetics, suede shoes, tea, possibility tins of cheese, beans, jam, paste etc. Books wanted: post-war plumbing in Britain, any good novels.

Wed 10 Nov
Wrote to Parents: I have plenty of money in bank and savings. I am fit and quite happy, pleasant conditions, my weight is now over 12 stone! What can I send you in parcel? Dress material, shoes for Father, tins of food etc.

Sat 13 Nov
Wrote to Parents: Construction of Old Country Inn not yet commenced through lack of material. Forthcoming pantomime and play. Off to

cinema to see 'In which we serve'. Badminton Club set up, playing badminton with woolley balls!

Wed 24 Nov
I wrote to Pegs re ideals, plans etc.

Wed 1 Dec
Letter to parents: I'm taking part in football, badminton and volleyball matches. Have heard from the two Macs. Frank is leaving next March. I am very happy and well organised.

Frank and myself in the billet. (I took this myself by means of a special shutter and thread!)

Wed 8 Dec
Went with Frank to see 'Night Must Fall'. Saw 'Reluctant Dragon' and laughed heartily. Material has been received from contractors for Bun Club.

DEC 11: A HUDSON FROM JODHPUR WITH H.H. THE RULER OF JODHPUR AND A LOCKHEED 12 FROM BIKANER WITH H.H. THE RULER OF BIKANER TO

VISIT H.H. THE RULER OF BHOPAL.

DEC 12: A WELLINGTON X CALLED FROM ALHAMBRA
STAYED THE NIGHT AND WENT ONTO DELHI, AND A
VENGEANCE CAME FROM KARACHI FOR NO. 1
A.G.S. THE OTHER VENGEANCE ACCOMPANYING
THIS ONE CRASHED AND THE CREW WERE KILLED.
(Operations Records AIR 29/463 DEC 43)

Lockheed Hudson bringing H.H. The Ruler of Jodphur to
visit H.H. The Ruler of Bhopal.

Wed 15 Dec
Letter to parents: Variety Show; played badminton; birthday cake;
having Ovaltine and toast for supper!

Wed 22 Dec
Time off for work on bar.

Wed 29 Dec
Wrote to Pegs about Christmas and Bun Club. Received your letter dated
Dec 7th – glad you hold same views; shall we wait or thrash it out now?
Present not yet arrived.

DEC 27: VERY QUIET TIME OVER CHRISTMAS, MUCH GROG IMBIBED BY ALL. A WIMPEY CAME, AND MADE TWO TRIPS FROM AND TO SANTA CRUZ, BRINGING AIR GUNNERS FROM 203 SQUADRON ON A COURSE.

DEC 30: AN AUDAX FROM GWALIOR TO NAGPUR STAGGERED IN. (Operations Records AIR 29/463 DEC 43)

Christmas Day inside 'The Chequers Inn'.

Members of my Unit together with a few Indian cooks snapped outside the 'Chequers Inn'.

I received a letter from Mother:

Dearest Peter,

We have had your Christmas letter, many thanks, you sound very fit and cheerful. Shall think of you when getting up that you are having your Christmas dinner. I hope you are able to scrounge the material for your Inn. How good forming a Badminton Club, it should give you all great pleasure. You seem to be the right type to be abroad, you have plenty of ideas which are a great help to one.

I heard from Eustace yesterday that the Whitings had their house badly damaged by a recent raid. Mr & Mrs W. were sheltering in a cupboard and were unhurt. Biddy and Eustace were at the pictures at the time. I believe ceilings and windows all down and out and a very bad crack on wall by side of house.

You certainly have put on weight, I am sure you were not 12 stone when you left England. We sent another parcel off this week. Will let you know what I decide about silk, if you can get navy blue I will have enough for a blouse, will let you know amount later. Don't worry about us as regards coal etc, we have plenty (of course we always were careful). There is still food and very hopeful. It is a cold grey morning, but soon we shall be the right side of 1944 and we all look for great things. Well all the best, my kind regards to Frank.

Much love, Mother

Chapter 4 – Chronology of War

By **mid-1943**, over 300,000 tons of concrete had been used in the construction of all-weather and fair-weather strips for the 53 Allied squadrons that were now deployed.

The RAF had 48 squadrons and the USAAF 17 squadrons, whereas the Japanese could only muster 740 aircraft in the whole of SE Asia, with only 370 in Burma.

Jan 1943: The Casablanca Conference took place, the most important Anglo-American strategic meeting of the War. Britain promised to launch an offensive in Burma after the monsoon, although a proposed amphibious landing in Burma had to be abandoned due to lack of shipping.

Churchill devoted far less attention to the Japanese struggle than to the war against Germany and British operations in Burma were chiefly to 'show willing' to the United States. 1943 was the last year in which resources severely constrained Anglo-American operations on the ground. Lord Mountbatten was made Supreme Commander in South East Asia and a huge Indian Army, supplemented by British units, pursued only limited operations against the Japanese.

If in 1940-41 Churchill had been his nation's deliverer, in 1942-43 the Americans owed him a greater debt than they recognised, for persuading their president to the Mediterranean strategy: Churchill's strategic judgement was superior to that of America's chiefs of staff. In January 1943 Roosevelt and Churchill decided to combine their bombing raids on Germany and Axis occupied countries.

By **mid-January 1943**, RAF Beaufighters were in a position to chase away Japanese bombers from Calcutta. However, the Japanese were able to cut off China's supply route: the Burma Road that ran north-east from Rangoon into China. As an added bonus, Burmese oil would be a welcome addition to Japan's economy.

Brigadier Orde Wingate lead his 'Chindits' from India into Burma (supplied entirely by the RAF), and although one group did manage to reach China and be welcomed as heroes, one third of them had to endure fierce jungle fighting and did not return. However, this set the pattern for the future: armies could be successfully supplied from the air.

General JW 'Vinegar Joe' Stilwell, an unconventional 64-year-old American with a caustic manner, successfully moved 30 miles a day with his 'long range penetration' troops.

May 1943: 275,000 Germans and Italians had surrendered on the Cape Bon Peninsula, ending the campaign in North Africa. On 17th May the Dambusters attacked the Ruhr with their 'bouncing bombs'.

September 1943: The Allies had moved to Italy and the Italians surrendered although much of the country remained in the grip of the Germans. Mass raids were launched against Berlin under Air Marshall 'Bomber' Harris when over 1,000 bombers and their crew were lost. It is estimated that 353,000 German deaths were caused by Allied bombing.

November 1943: India was renamed S.E. Asia with a joint command – RAF & USAAF – the Air Commander being Sir Richard Peirse and under him was Major General Stratemeyer of the USAAF who set the style for air operations in Burma under the slogan 'Strike! Support! Supply! Strangle!'. Strike was for close support against enemy points; Support was for casualty evacuation and troop reinforcements; Supply was for rations, ammunition, POL (petrol, oil, lubricants), medical stores and water; Strangle was for attacks on lines of communication plus troop reinforcements.

The Phoenix was adopted by Admiral Lord Louis Mountbatten (Supreme Commander) as the mascot of his command. British troops fighting in this theatre had been dubbed by the press as 'The Forgotten Army'. USA troops in Burma were led by General Frank Merrill.

The Sextant Conference took place in Cairo where much attention was given to Chinese issues. However, the British did not share the US's belief in China as an ally, nor in the massive commitment to provide aid 'over the hump of the Himalayas'. They had not forgotten that only a few months earlier Roosevelt had persuaded them to cede possession of Hong Kong to Chiang Kai-shek as a 'gesture of goodwill'.

'The Big Three' (Roosevelt, Churchill and Stalin) met at Tehran. Despite the limited success of Orde-Wingate's 3,000 men known as the 'Chindits', the numerically inferior Japanese army was still very much in control of Burma. Japanese diplomatic messages were intercepted by Foreign Office staff in Britain, Canada, India and Australia. At Bletchley Park the Japanese military section had to expand into the corridor which became known as the 'Burma Road'.

CHAPTER 5

AN 'ERK' GOES TO THE PALACE GARDEN PARTY
JAN 1944 – JAN 1945

Editor's Note:

In Feb/March 1944, Peter travelled to Bombay with his colleagues, George and Frank. He went for an interview with the Aircrew Selection Board to become a Flight Engineer. But as he feared, he was failed again due to his colour blindness, in case of difficulty in seeing red and green lights. (The red centre of the RAF roundel had been replaced by a light blue centre on all RAF aircraft in SEAC so they were not confused with the Japanese red 'meatball' markings.)

However, he made the most of his time there by visiting the exclusive resort of Breach Candy. This was the height of luxury, boasting two swimming pools, and was so exclusive that members were not allowed to invite any Indian guests, including, allegedly, Maharajahs!

Swimming was a favourite pastime of the troops and by September 1944 Bairagarh had its own pool where a popular Swimming Gala was held. Other recreational activities included their first annual Athletic Sports Meeting and a Series of Symphony Concerts.

During May it was reported that the number of sick personnel had doubled, so by the end of the month the first of the Hill or Juhu parties was sent off for a rest. Peter was included (he had just spent 5 days in hospital with gastro-enteritis) and he left Bairagarh on 29th May bound for Juhu which was situated on the coast just outside Bombay.

On 8th June, an Aircrew Medical Board passed Peter as A4B only. The 'A4' part meant he was graded as fit for air duties as a non-combatant passenger but no more, i.e. he was not deemed fit enough to be an active aircrew member; the 'B' part meant he was fit for all ground duties in any part of the world.

In October, ground crew who had worked during the summer heat were sent for their annual rest period to a hill station near Naini Tal in the Himalayas. Peter and his colleague, Jim Powell, were amongst these. He then went on to see the Taj Mahal (his second time) by moonlight: descending one of the towers, he was stung by hornets and managed to fall down the stairs!

There was great excitement when the latest York aircraft arrived in November with Air Chief Sir Richard Pierse aboard, paying a farewell visit to His Highness the Nawab of Bhopal before returning to the UK (Churchill had a York as his private plane). Besides frequent visits from VIPs, the Staging Post refuelled and serviced many different types of aircraft from the US and Indian Air Forces with the more unusual planes like the P40s and Hudsons creating quite a stir amongst the ground crew (see Appendix C for brief descriptions of the planes mentioned by Peter in his diaries and in the Operational Records).

Once again, Peter was instrumental in organising the Christmas 'Bun Club' in December 1944, having just turned 28 on 9th December.

A most exciting occasion for the base was the invitation by His Royal Highness The Nawab of Bhopal to attend a Garden Party and Sports Meeting in celebration of his 51st birthday. Sir Claude Auchinleck was there to present the prizes. He was the Raj's last Commander-in-Chief, based at Dehra Dun; also there was the youngest brigadier in the British Army at 32, one Enoch Powell.

Although no diary for this year, the many letters are able to reflect conditions in England at this time: rationing gets little mention although Peter sends chests of tea and dress material back to his family whilst Aunt Edith in South Africa regularly sends parcels of tinned fruit to them also.

JAN 01: NEW YEARS DAY – FEELING RATHER ILL. A VENGEANCE FROM AHMEDABAD TO KATNI, AND A HURRICANE FROM NAGPUR TO AGRA STAYING THE NIGHT.

JAN 07: AN ANSON FROM PALAM TO HYDERABAD CALLED WITH A/CDR CARTER AND ONE OF OUR UNFORTUNATELY VERY INFREQUENT VISITORS OF THE FAIR SEX, JUNIOR COMMANDER EVERETT. ALSO AN ANSON FROM JUHU WITH S/LDR EDWARDS.

JAN 08: THE ANSON RETURNED FROM BEGUMPET WITH A/CDR CARTER AND THE ABOVE MENTIONED FAIR VISITOR, AGAIN BRIGHTENING OUR LIVES FOR A BRIEF MOMENT.

JAN 09: A HUDSON FROM DELHI BEARING THE A.O.C. IN CHIEF, SIR RICHARD PEIRSE AND LADY AUCHINLECK FOR THE BIRTHDAY CELEBRATIONS OF H.H. THE RULER OF BHOPAL. THEN A HARLOW PASSING THROUGH FROM NAGPUR TURNED BACK AND RE-LANDED BECAUSE OF BAD WEATHER. THEN HUDSON RETURNED AGAIN FROM LALITPUR AND WENT TO JAIPUR TO PICK UP SIR CHARLES AUCHINLECK.

JAN 12: HUDSON FROM DELHI TOOK THE C. IN C. SIR C. AUCHINLECK TO JUBBULPORE, RETURNED NEXT DAY AND TOOK AWAY THE A.O.C. IN C. AND THE C. IN C. THE C.O. WAS HEARD TO REMARK THAT NEVER HAS SO MUCH GOLD BRAID BEEN WORN BY SO FEW!

JAN 22: AN ANSON CAME FROM POONA TO FETCH W/CDR BAYNE, STATION COMMANDER POSTED TO POONA. W/CDR SUTTON IS NEW STATION COMMANDER OF NO. 1 A.G.S. A DAKOTA CAME FROM ALIPORE RETURNING STORES TO STATION, PREVIOUSLY BORROWED.

JAN 23: A LOCKHEED 12 FROM BEGUMPET GOING ONTO DELHI CALLED, AND AN ANSON FROM JUHU TO DELHI CALLED AND STAYED FOR LUNCH. A LOCKHEED 12 CALLED AND STAYED THE NIGHT

WITH THE A.O.C. IN C. WHO HAD COME TO SHOOT TIGERS WITH H.H. THE RULER OF BHOPAL. (Operations Records AIR 29/463 JAN 1944)

New Year's Eve.

'The Morning after the Night Before', Jan 1st 1944.

FEB 12: ANOTHER CONVOY OF 9 HURRICANES FOR ALLAHABAD. ALTHOUGH POSTED FOR FLYING DUTIES, F/O ROBINSON MANAGED TO SCROUNGE HIS FIRST TRIP TODAY. A BLENHEIM CALLED IN WITH MORE SPARES FOR THE STATION FROM ALIPORE.

FEB 13: A MITCHELL B-25 OF THE U.S.A.A.C. CALLED TO RE-FUEL ON THE WAY TO BANGKOK. THIS IS THE FIRST ONE TO LAND SUCCESSFULLY, THE LAST TWO THAT TRIED PRANGED.

FEB 14: THE SAME B-25 CALLED AGAIN, DEFINITELY BREAKING THE HEARTS OF THE B-25 GREMLINS BY AGAIN LANDING SUCCESSFULLY.

FEB 16: A LEOPARD MOTH OF INDIA AIR SURVEY CALLED TO RE-FUEL ON WAY TO AHMEDABAD TO MAKE AIR-MAPS. (Operations Records AIR 29/463 FEB 1944)

My mother wrote to me on 4th February:

Dearest Peter,

How did your jungle party go off? How lucky to win some money. I'm so glad you seem to be having a good time, the snaps are <u>great</u>. The effort you made this Christmas for your festivities was I thought better than last year. How is the plan for enlarging the billet getting on?

You know Peter we only came to 48 Talbot Road for a year or two at the most, and houses and flats are <u>dreadfully hard </u>to get and will be for some time. Auntie Winnie heard the Westons who live at 15 Battlefield Road [St Albans] were leaving as Miss Weston is going blind; so is going to a religious nursing home near Torquay and Mr Weston is going to a hotel and they are selling their furniture. So we have been lucky to rent the house for £72 a year, but as there is a garage it will bring it to £85. We have taken it for 8 years. You will remember it has a nice garden; the garden looks very well as they have a man one afternoon a week. Father is keeping him on as we shall get the money back in vegetables. Mr Weston said they had 60 lbs of tomatoes last year so I hope we shall be as successful as you and Frank are.

There will be plenty of rooms to get all our furniture in – one does not want to sell any as you cannot buy now and the price is dreadful. The two rooms at the top of the house I shall shut up, so there are 4 bedrooms and bathroom on one floor. We hope to move on 1st May. It will be nice having the car with us again and if all well you will I am sure get it in working order. I shall get Clarks to bring it to no. 15 from Town. Mrs Wall came to tea yesterday, Auntie Winnie spent the day today. Robert is where you, John, Michael and Eustace took the car one year for a holiday we believe.

When are you going to have your fortnight's leave – shall you wait for the hot weather? I am so sorry Frank is leaving you but am glad for his sake, you might give him my kind regards. Do hope you find another nice friend. Hope you are fit and well – I am OK again. Auntie Fay said she had heard from Frank.

Much love Mother.

Letter received from Ian McGuire, RAF Station, Golden Rock, Trichinopoly, S. India, 11th Feb 1944:

Hello Pete

You will be thinking I'm a proper heel for not writing to you earlier, possibly I am but not for that reason. I have been literally swamped with Blighty mail these past few months and *just to complicate matters I decided to drop 'the pen and ink' for a month.*

I was at Bangalore on leave over the 'New Year', had quite a time and have one or two good tales to relate when next we meet. I would pen them in my reply but the censor may not have the same type of humour as you, in any case I would have to tone these down so much that they would appear commonplace. Bert was posted up Karachi way the week we were due to leave so I've carried on on my own. I have not heard from him yet, perhaps I won't either for he was the worst letter writer I've come across, but I will jab him up in a few months time. Tony is still the same, you still can't tell him anything – he knows – but I guess after a time that becomes one of his lovable qualities, or should I have said amusing.

You recall the little girl I used to pour my heart out to. I am still pouring it, I always was big hearted. For her part she writes more than ever about less and less, that is hardly fair to her. Her letters are interesting and at times nearly intimate but she can't make up her mind whether she is in love with me or not. I must be losing my grip as a salesman if I can't put across a first class commodity like me. She writes me about six times a month so I can consider myself among the probable starters and I feel that at least I am preventing her from doing anything rash, like marrying some other guy.

I was more than sorry to hear of the 'drop in temperature' of your own affair, and with your permission will go into it more fully in my next letter. I do reckon that most of us live in a 'Fools Paradise' as few mature women can do without the company of men for a period of four years. For that matter there are few men etc. etc. We all start out as idealists and finish up as cynics. I was born under the sign of Taurus the Bull, and from what I've heard Taurus was a randy old Bull, makes it kinda difficult for a well meaning guy like me, but then I suppose it would be unfair of me to let the old blighter down, but that is sufficient of bulls and bullocks.

The summer (according to the press) is nearly here, actually I have not been aware that it has been away, and as the Yank might say this is a goddam country for heat. Do you recall the long drawers the Victorians wore: the eighteen July sort with a fortnight's growth on them; if ever I see Blighty again I want to live to case my limbs in a pair of these scratchers. My blood is so thin now that when I look in a mirror I can see the back of my head and much to my surprise there is still hair there. Tony has now bought the controlling interest in 'Vitex' the hair restoring firm. It does not grow hair he says but the profits are enormous. Remind me to Nawab when next you meet, he was a great guy, the whitest man I ever knew.

Cheerio Longfella, I'll be writing you soon; when next you write enclose your home address. Bert has it with him. All the very best in the meantime.

As ever,

Ian

P.S. Have you a spare list of the second All India Series, I lost mine.

*Myself and Frank Gibbs on the roof of YMCA where we stayed
in February 1944 in front of the Taj Mahal Hotel, Bombay.*

Breach Candy, an exclusive beach resort and pools near
Bombay where George, Frank and Peter where able to relax.

A letter received from Mother, dated 18th February 1944:

Dearest Peter

As far as I am concerned, I am very glad there is little chance for you to be a Flight Engineer. Was it because of colour blindness that you were turned down? I know how welcome a change would be after so long away and we should have loved to see you, but it is a very dangerous job and I am afraid few will come through. You are all brave boys. Yes, I think I should enjoy the warmth of India but not all the dreadful animals and insects. I am even afraid of a mouse but not spiders! Martin and Francis are expected for 10 days leave, but think they will be moving soon. I hope you are fit, look after yourself. News on the Pacific is quite good. You will be losing Frank soon.

Much love, Mother.

First Annual Athletic Sports Meeting on February 19th 1944 at R.A.F. Station Bhopal.

Letter dated 20 Feb 44 from Cousin Barbara in St Albans:

Dear Peter,

It seems ages since I wrote to you and during the last week we have received your Christmas card (!!!) a trifle late, and an airgraph to Mother dated Jan 27th, so that's quite good.

Last Wed I went out to lunch with Eustace and Biddy and they are expecting to be married this summer. Biddy is really very nice although she gave me the impression of being even younger than she is. Incidentally, they have asked me to be a bridesmaid, but did not say how many they thought of having. Perhaps they will have lace or net that isn't rationed, otherwise coupons will be the difficulty. What a pity you won't be here to do your duty to Eustace and act as best man.

Robert is at present on ship and as far as we can make out, a cruiser on the Clyde. He does not appear to get off ship at all, so what on earth he does all time I don't know. He sent us some Seville oranges for marmalade so if he is as thoughtful as that, I have high hopes of what he may bring us if he goes further afield.

John is expecting a move from Paignton any day – in fact he can't go on leave until he has had his move, so obviously he is not going overseas yet. I have just spent a fortnight in Stoke, the last time I shall visit that place as the whole office is returning to London on March 18th. We shall be in a frightful mess when they all come back and to add to the trouble we have to move to a larger office on 5th floor instead of the 3rd. It is a great pity as at present we have a lovely high light room, with a French window and balcony overlooking the Mansion House corner.

John Fieling is still in Naples and is working very long hours but as the situation in Italy improves he should have a little more free time. At one point they had some very good entertainments, symphony concerts, operas and films but I think they have had to stop owing to the typhus epidemic among the Italians. As yet the Allies have had no cases reported so I imagine that by now most of the danger is over.

Fancy Auntie and Uncle coming back to St Albans and to our old house – strange really. I was glad to hear you had had a game of tennis again – the old Club (Townsend) is still just managing to get along. We had a Valentine Dance there on Wednesday which was very successful. Yesterday I played hockey at Croydon and today I am suffering from stiffness – though not so bad as when I played before with Peggy, also at the same place. This time we went through Croydon and I was surprised to see what nice shops there were for shopping. Never having had any friends or relations in South London I know very little about it, anyway I was agreeably surprised.

I had a parcel of chocolates and a letter from Cousin Edith. Both were very late in arriving and Mother's has not come yet. In her letter she said that she had sent you something so I hope you have received it by now.

Good luck to you, and may it not be long before you come home.

With love, Barbara

Letter dated 26 Feb 44 from Francis Wall based with 212/64th Med Reg RA in Felixstowe, Suffolk:

Dear Peter

Very many thanks for your letter. Sorry about your disappointments, it's rather tough on you and I expect you get pretty cheesed about things. I have been meaning to write for some time but hadn't your latest address 'til you wrote. Martin and I are home on leave again, but please don't be too envious, we're only making up for lost time, and lord knows what is in store this year! It rather savours of Front Line here as Jerry has raided London 5 out of the 7 nights we have been home and raids are pretty exciting affairs nowadays. The barrage is certainly good and centres round the planes now rather than just everywhere and rockets make a fine sight streaming up fifty or so in a bunch, bursting with large red, flashes. Everyone has their Bomb Stories again and conversation tends to centre around the new blitz. Last night was quiet, thank goodness. It's not really wise to stop in bed these days as you are better fitted to cope with emergencies if you have more on than pyjamas!

England is pretty well off – there are only a few really bad shortages – and you can take it from me there are hundreds of people who hardly know there's a war on. Everyone is anxious for the Second (so-called) Front – except those of us who feel it hanging over our future a little more intimately. Buses and taxis etc are by no means as scarce as we were led to believe when we were abroad and there are stacks of shows, films, dance halls etc running to packed houses. We're not too badly off at Felixstowe, plenty of canteens etc and two cinemas, but life there is pretty dull from an army point of view; all the old billet scrubbing bullshit that we have learnt to do without abroad!

I haven't seen much of your people this leave but will possibly see them tomorrow. Ronald is getting hitched today to Joan somewhere in Wales, and Alec [Lickorish] next month I gather, not to mention your brother in June they say! We foreigners are getting left on the shelf aren't we? Still you'd be surprised at the grand welcome you get when you return – the Africa Star and '8' helps a lot, so you must arrange for a Burma Medal or something! I haven't seen anything of Anne since returning. She appears to have cooled right off – perhaps it's just as well, as I can't say I was ever very serious.

Lin is rapidly putting on weight under the influence of marriage, baby etc! Frank Harris is much the same. General dearth of young people around home nowadays. Peggy is very fit and seems to like the nursery job OK. We have done a bit of dancing and a show with her. Mr and Mrs Caswell are well and Michael is back in the fray I believe. We are trying to carry on leave in spite of air raids but tubes and things tend to get rather disorganised and you get rather fed up trying to get home when you hang about for 35 minutes for trains! This war is hell, isn't it? Your local films sound just like the famous Shafts Circuit in the Middle East. Doesn't ENSA ever come your way? I'm busy rehearsing for our Regimental Revue to be put on in March. We have four Wrens to provide glamour, so it should be good!

It's funny to be in a position to write to pals abroad and say what a grand job they're doing out there! So many people used to write like that to me! Never mind, Peter, most of the services in Blighty have got it coming to them after four years of sweet fanny. Well best of luck and hope you fulfil your Flight Engineer eventually.

Yours from the "mashed potato and bib front",

Francis

I received a letter from Hilda Caswell dated 28th February 1944:

My dear Peter

Thank you very much for the lovely cigarette box which we received about ten days ago. It is a lovely piece of work and when the light shines on it the red colour fairly sparkles! Mr Caswell and I both like it very much. Thanks also for your letter which came earlier on the same day. Pegs and I are going to tea with your mother on Wednesday. She seems very pleased at the coming move to St Albans. We shall miss your father and mother at St Augustine's. Mrs Feiling has settled in a flat at the top of St Jude's Vicarage and cannot always manage to get up to St Augustine's on Sunday mornings. There seem to be quite a number of new folks attending and Father Martin and Francis have served the last two Sundays – on leave – and this makes it more like old times. Mick is back in Italy and recovered from his wounds. I have passed the snaps onto Pegs, they are very good. Cheerio.

With love Hilda Caswell

MAR 02: THIS WAS A GREAT DAY. TWO HURRICANES CAME FROM ALLAHABAD, AND THEN TWO SPITFIRE VIII'S. THESE WERE FOR ATP POONA, AND THERE WAS MUCH WEEPING AND GNASHING OF TEETH WHEN THIS WAS LEARNT! "SPITFIRE VIII'S TO WASTE WHILST HURRICANE II'S ARE STILL ON OP'S" WAS ONE VERY CAUSTIC COMMENT. THE C.O. WAS HEARD TO SAY HE WOULD NOT MIND RISKING GOING BACK ON "OPS" IN THESE.

MARCH 07: OUR OWN PET B-25 CREW BROUGHT ANOTHER ONE IN FOR BANGKOK, AND TWO HARVARDS ARRIVED FOR NO. 9 SQUADRON. A HUDSON ALSO CALLED TO PICK UP FERRY CREWS FOR ALLAHABAD. (Operations Records AIR 29/463 MARCH 1944)

I received a letter from Eustace dated 21st March 1944:

Dear Peter,

Biddy and I are getting married on 3rd June. I am very sorry you will not be here as I should have liked you to have been best man. I am hoping John Caton will be able to be. It will be at Crowstone Congregational Church. I am very sorry it won't be at a C.E. Church and I know you and Mother and Father will be as well. Still plenty of people who are not the same religion get along all right. We hope to go to Stratford-on-Avon for our honeymoon.

I hope you have an enjoyable leave,

Cheerio Eustace

A letter received from Barbara dated 22nd March 1944, 10 Lancaster Road, St Albans, Herts:

Dear Peter

Did you know that I am now Fire Woman Caton 897826 of the N.F.S. part-time? So far I have been very lucky in not having any sirens on my duty night; otherwise of course you have to turn out etc. In due course I have a nice (?) uniform with tin hat and respirator. We have unfortunately changed our office in the Bank and now work on 5th floor. We have a lovely view over London and see Law Courts and St Pauls quite clearly. What we complain about is our journey to get there, actually now it is nothing to walk up a hundred odd stairs – at least it should be nothing but you're winded by the time you get to the top! The reason we had to move was because the part of our office that was evacuated to Stoke has now returned to London and we had to find more accommodation.

By the way, are you hard up for films or can you get them fairly easily as I believe there is a scheme here so that we can send films out to you. If you want some I'll see what I can do for you. I know the Navy and Middle East can get them but I haven't enquired about India. John is now living at home and travels to London daily. He is working at and near the Zoo if that means anything to you. We don't see very much of him as he is out dancing most nights. It is too late for the pictures by the time he has got home so dancing is all that is left for him. Robert is up in Scotland but has only been allowed on shore once since he has been there, which is about 8 weeks. He hopes to come home for a spot of leave in April and of course we shall be a full house again for that short while.

I have just heard from Eustace that he is going to get married on June 3rd as that date is completely out as far as I am concerned I shall not be able to act as bridesmaid. As a matter of fact if the coast ban is kept on, I suppose no-one will be able to go to it. I don't know whether your Mother and Father can get permission, but of course it is a long way ahead even now.

I heard you had a game of tennis the other month. We are going to be quite well off for balls this year as Dunlop recover them for you and on an average you get back 10 for every 12 you send them. Last year there were no new balls at all so this will be marvellous. Last Sunday I spent the day trying to re-putty the greenhouse and paint it. We were short of both so I had to leave the puttying only half done and the paint had to be put on and almost taken off again. Still I'll finish it next weekend I hope and give it another coat later on. Do you ever hear from Edith Easley now? We all had parcels of tinned fruit etc from them for Christmas, though they arrived late. I also had a box of chocolates which of course were very useful and went like hot cakes. Last week I went to a W.F.S. dance and strangely enough thoroughly enjoyed myself – there were plenty of males to go round which of course is something unusual nowadays. Have all your old friends given up writing to you or do you hear from Michael Caswell, the Walls, John and Ronald, just to mention a few.

With best wishes and love, Barbara

APR 01-07: DURING THE FIRST WEEK, THERE WERE VERY FEW AIRCRAFT PASSING THROUGH:

ONLY AN AVERAGE OF ONE PER DAY OF ASSORTED TIGER MOTHS, ANSONS, ETC. ONE SPITFIRE VIII LANDED AND DAMAGED A FLAP AND IS NOW WITH A.O.G.

APR 15-21: AGAIN WE AVERAGED THREE PER DAY IN THE THIRD WEEK. WE HAD SOME MARTINETS, FIRST TIME SEEN, AND A NOW INFREQUENT I.N.A. CALLER SHORT OF PETROL ON HIS WAY TO DELHI. ONE DEFIANT WAS REFUELLED, AND AFTER TAKING OFF UNFORTUNATELY DEVELOPED AN OIL LEAK AND THE PILOT ON RETURNING TAXIED INTO A TRENCH DRAIN, DAMAGING THE AIRCRAFT BADLY. THIS AIRCRAFT WAS HANDED TO 140 R.S.U. [REPAIR & SALVAGE UNIT] FOR DISMANTLING. A B-25 ALSO CALLED WITH G/CAPT LEATHER AND AN AMERICAN CREW, ON WAY TO KARACHI.

P/P BOYCOTT AND HIS "GANG SHOW" ARRIVED AND GAVE A PERFORMANCE. (Operations Records AIR 29/463/589 APR 1944)

A letter received from Mother dated 4th April 1944 from 48 Talbot Road, Highgate:

Dearest Peter,

Your letter from Bombay was very interesting, so glad you had a change before the heat. Very many thanks for the blue silk, a most useful birthday present. I am having it made into a dress, it will save quite a number of coupons. Also Father was pleased with his pyjamas – his birthday is 5th Sept.

I expect you have heard that Eustace & Biddy are getting married on 3rd June (Sat) at the Congregational Church (Chapel) at Westcliff and reception at Hall afterwards. As you can guess I was very upset to think Eustace would not have the blessing of the Church. Biddy of course could not be married in Church as she is not a Baptized member. I pray she may come into the Church later. Eustace says it will make no difference to him. Biddy is such a dear girl, not too modern, and I think will make him a good wife. Mrs Caswell says she does not think I should mind the Chapel Wedding! They will live with her people until after the War.

We shall ask the Caswells, but no one else from St Augustine's. I hope we shall have got to St Albans by then. I do wish you could be with us all; will let you know the time later on. It will be a white wedding and 3 bridesmaids. John Caton may be best man in officer's uniform as Eustace, Mr Whiting and Father are to wear morning coats and top hats. I think, and also Father, that lounge suits would have been more suitable but the Bride usually chooses. The Ban on Southend Biddy said would not stop guests for the wedding, thought you would like to hear all news.

Hope you are fit, we all are, much love Mother

A letter received from Mother dated 11th April 1944:

Dearest Peter

We have been lucky and received two letters from you in 3 days. So glad you enjoyed your stay in Bombay, it must be lovely to be in a civilized town again and would do you good. Breach Candy sounds a delightful place.

I am so glad you do not think it very dreadful Eustace getting married in a Chapel. I have quite got used to it and realise it is Biddy's faith. You take the same view as Auntie Doll and Auntie Nell, they both admire Biddy to sticking to her faith and as you say we pray she may come into the Church later. The wedding is at Crowston Congregational Chapel and the reception at a *hall in Westcliff. They hope to go to Stratford-on-Avon for their honeymoon if they can get in, but places are so crowded now inland. I am going to St Albans for the day Friday. We hope to move sometime in May but it is not definite the date yet. Am looking forward very much to being at St Albans again. Father has gone to the Walls for bridge. Mrs Wall has just started playing; they asked me to go and talk to Mary, but I hate being out after blackout in case the Warning goes, although it has been very quiet the last 3 weeks.*

Much love Mother

I received a letter from Cousin Edith Easley of Cape Town, South Africa dated 27th April 1944:

My dear Peter

I was sorry not to be able to send you the monthly service booklet this month as there were very few for sale. It was a pity because it was an interesting one but I hope to get one next month. I am sending you a short history of South Africa. It is very concise but may be interesting to you. It is so difficult to get books in South Africa at present. There have been letters from your Mother, Auntie Mary & Barbara since I last wrote. It is sad your Mother has not been well, but no doubt the milder weather and return to St Albans will suit her and she will soon be quite herself. Highgate must have altered considerably since she lived there; it is depressing to return to a place you know well and find big changes.

So Eustace has decided to be married next month. Everybody seems to like the fiancée but thinks she is rather young to face the responsibilities this age has thrust on young people. But if they are really in sympathy and fond of each other they would know that life may not be too cosy at first but may be very happy and prove the little difficulties at the beginning were worthwhile. After all, young people must have plans – a vision of some kind of future, the future they will work for.

Barbara does send such interesting letters – she seems a busy, energetic young person. She was thrilled at the thought of joining the Fire Fighting Service. I hope she will not have any very realistic work to do and will not be over-taxed. The raiders are frequent visitors but they always pay for their curiosity. The arrival of the Dominion Prime Ministers in London has helped to provide a topic of conversation. Distance scarcely exists these days. By the time you are an "old gentleman" planes will be as popular as cars are today. The little children all seem to have an air of mechanical sense. Hope you are well and busy and not having a very gruelling time.

With love from Edith Easley.

In April I drafted a reply to Cousin Edith:

Dear Cousin Edith

Yesterday I received a letter, the souvenir booklets and the South African book from you – very many thanks indeed. It was strange they should all arrive on the same day considering they were posted at varying intervals! The souvenir booklets of the special monthly services are very interesting. It seems there is a strong religious feeling in Cape Town and I hope and pray it continues because I feel certain that true happiness and lasting peace can only come through Christianity. What we need is a great Christian revival; people must be made to realise that until we learn to be less selfish and start to consider the needs of others, we shall never get any great social improvement.

We are fortunate in having a very energetic Padre who visits our camp regularly. He and a few others have been doing our best to swell the numbers at the Sunday services though I am *sorry to say we haven't had a great deal of success so far.*

I'm glad Mother and Father have moved out to St Albans. I am sure Mother will be happier there and hope her health improves. It was lucky they moved before the flying bomb raids started though I imagine Father must have some difficulty in getting up to Town each day. I have just received a letter from Barbara who mentions they carry on working during the raids but doesn't say whether she has been called out on her Fire Fighting duties. I hope they overcome this menace quickly.

At the beginning of last month I was down at Bombay on an aircrew selection board. As I feared I was failed again on the colour test and therefore have no further hopes of becoming a Flight Engineer. I was down there for about a week and enjoyed the change. Of course I spent a lot of time swimming as it was very hot just then.

Father tells me Eustace is expected home on a fortnight's leave and wonders whether or not it's embarkation leave. It will be hard luck if he has to go overseas now; as it is I believe he has been posted far up north. The monsoon is upon us now and we have had plenty of rain during the first few weeks but I much prefer this to the hot summer as it is naturally much cooler now. I have seen quite a few snakes lately and killed a couple last week though they were both very small – only about 18 inches long! Scorpions too are rather numerous as the rain has driven them to take shelter, sometimes in our billets!

Yours Peter

MAY 15-21: THE THIRD WEEK WAS A BIT BETTER, 12 AIRCRAFT PASSING THROUGH. WE GOT THE FIRST CONVOY FROM SANTA CRUZ FOR A LONG TIME, ONLY 4 HURRICANES, BUT MAYBE AN INDICATION OF BETTER THINGS TO COME. IT IS

TO BE HOPED SO AS THE UNIT IS BEGINNING TO
STAGNATE WITH HAVING NO WORK TO DO.

MAY 22-31: THE LAST WEEK SLACKED OFF AGAIN,
ONLY 8 AIRCRAFT PASSING THROUGH, A FEW
ASSORTED ANSONS, AND THE NAWAB OF BHOPAL
WENT AWAY IN A LODESTAR. SGT. CHARLTON NCO
I/C WAS POSTED TO MAURIPUR, AND SGT HEAPS
CAME AS A REPLACEMENT, FROM MAURIPUR TO
HERE. F/O ROBINSON WAS PROMOTED TO FLIGHT
LIEUTENANT AND IS POSTED W.E.F. THE 26TH OF
MAY, BUT NO RELIEF IS YET FORTHCOMING. THE
FIRST OF THE HILL OR JUHU PARTIES WENT OFF
TODAY, THE 29TH, AND WE SHALL SEE SHORTLY
WHAT KIND OF A PLACE THIS IS FOR A REST.
NUMBER OF PERSONNEL REPORTING SICK HAS
DOUBLED. (Operations Records AIR 29/463/589 MAY
1944)

Letter received from Frank Gibbs, Mansfield, Nottinghamshire, dated 5th
May 1944:

*Well, here we are, safe and sound back in the old Island after a
pleasant and uneventful trip. I am just completing my first
week's leave, having been granted three weeks as expected
which as you can well imagine is going down very fine. It is
certainly great to be in the old home town once more. Much to
my surprise and I am pleased to say that conditions back here
are better than we were led to believe they were. Of course,
don't misunderstand me, but as you know some of the new
arrivals gave Blighty a rather dismal outlook.*

*I might just add a point for Geordie's benefit and that is the
quality and quantity of the English "BEER". We were able to get
very well refreshed during our four day stay in Morecambe, in
private billets by the way, prior to our dispatch for home, and
now although there are limits to many things, life in England is*

still far from being a bind. I have not as yet been notified of my posting; but expect to get it during my leave period, so as soon as it comes through Pete, I will drop you a few more lines.

All is well at home, things being much the same as when I left in 41, except of course the Kiddie who I hardly recognised, but made a great fuss when I stepped off the train, and has since been an endless source of entertainment.

I trust you returned safe and sound to the old unit after our spot of leave together and here's to a pleasant continuation of your life on the RSP [Repair & Salvage Party] and may you have the good fortune of a speedy return to your home life.

All the best for now, cheerio Frank.

Letter received from Ian McGuire, RAF Station, Golden Rock, Trichinopoly, South India, dated May 8th.

My dear Pete

I have some rather distressing news for you. The other day word came through from Karachi that poor old Bert had passed away on the 21st April to be exact, after a brief illness of four days. He reported sick on the Tuesday with pains in the head and heavy sweating. On Wednesday he was on the Serious List, on Thursday on the Danger List, on Friday he was dead and so the quartet that had agreed to meet after the War has now become a Threesome. I must say this news has been very upsetting to me, happening some four months after our first separation in two and a half years. I can't help but feel if I had been along with him it might not have happened, but I suppose we can't argue logically along those lines, it is just a hunch.

Somehow it is difficult to visualise Bert as dead, he took no chances in life – always played safe – most careful with his hygiene, but there I go telling you things you already know. This is not intended to be a letter, Pete, just a short note to pass on the sad news. If you see McAuley, give him the "gen", I'll be dropping him a note later. Keep well old boy, I'll try and settle down to a half decent letter to you one of these fine days. That statement is becoming a stock phrase of mine but next time I'll try and justify it. Tony and I are still jogging along; we have our usual dog fights to keep us in trim, otherwise life is pretty dull. Give my regards to Peggy, that is if she is still single and sending you oodles of mail. The next time you drop me a line, send your home address; if you recollect the last time we exchanged addresses it was Bert who took a note of them and I forgot to take a copy of them.

About books, the best I've read of recent was "The Way of a Transgressor" by Farson – keep it in mind, it is worth reading. Until my next attempt, cheerio and all the best. Look after yourself. I had another evening similar to Xmas 1942.

As ever, Ian B.

Letter received from Lieut R F Lickorish, London, dated 14 May 1944:

My dear Peter

I thought you might like to have the enclosed photos of me and the missus – we have managed to spend quite a few weeks together and need I say, been hopelessly happy. Joan is great fun and always full of mischief and we usually do the most mad things and thoroughly enjoy the doing of same.

Now I hear that Eustace and Biddy are getting spliced very shortly – I forget whether or not you have met her, if not I liked her very much if that is any guide and I think they should make a good do of it.

Up till now the letter seems to be all about weddings but there is just one more although I expect you have heard that Alec [Lickorish] was married some three weeks ago. Heather, his wife, is very nice though perhaps a bit spoilt and used to plenty of everything – anyway you shall judge for yourself and I hope in the near future too. Their wedding was apparently a great success – very much to our regret neither Joan nor myself were able to get there.

Well, I don't think that there is very much more news for you at present old man – I haven't been home for quite some time but mother writes saying all your people are fit and well, and I do hope it is the same with you. I hope to get a Captaincy very shortly – it will mean more money but a lot more work so I am not greatly bothered. Still at the moment it is still in the balance and we await news from the War House. Look after yourself and here's hoping the old war gets finished very soon now and you can come and pay Mr & Mrs R.F.L. a state visit – boy oh boy do I promise you a binge!

All the best, Ronald

JUNE 01: TODAY WAS A SLACK DAY BUT THE MONOTONY WAS RELIEVED BY THE ARRIVAL OF AN ANSON CARRYING AIR VICE MARSHALL D'ARCY POWER – P.M.O. HIS MACHINE REQUIRED MINOR SERVICING AND HE LEFT FOR AURANGABAD AFTER A SHORT DELAY.

JUNE 05: F/LT C.G. ROBINSON LEFT THE UNIT TODAY ON POSTING TO KARACHI AND THERE WERE FEW SORRY FACES AT SEEING HIM GO. F/O R BRIGGS, S.P. SIGNALS OFFICER, ASSUMED CONTROL OF THE UNIT, WHILST SGT HEAPS WILL BE RESPONSIBLE FOR THE HANDLING AND SERVICING OF AIRCRAFT. A BLENHEIM V LANDED LATE THIS EVENING AND SINCE IT HAD AN

ELECTRICAL DEFECT, THE STAGING POST WORKED UNTIL 2200 HOURS TO RENDER THE AIRCRAFT SERVICEABLE.

JUNE 08: TODAY A VISITING ANSON AND HUDSON CALLED. THE ANSON CARRYING TWO REGULAR VISITORS: W/CDRS ARNIE AND COULSON. **LAC WALKER RETURNED FROM AN AIRCREW MEDICAL BOARD, HAVING BEEN PASSED A4B ONLY.**

JUNE 09: THERE WAS MUCH EXCITEMENT TODAY WHEN 3 LIBERATORS WERE SCHEDULED TO ARRIVE FOR THE PURPOSE OF CONVEYING NO. 1 A.G.S. PUPILS TO H.C.U. THEY TOOK OFF WITHOUT A HITCH, BUT THE THIRD WAS UNABLE TO START ITS OUTER STARBOARD ENGINE DUE TO A FAULT IN THE MESHING GEAR.

JUNE 25: THE E.W. RUNWAY, HAVING BEEN CLEARED BY THE P.W.D. IS NOW IN DANGER OF BEING RE-OPENED. IT IS HOPED THAT THIS STAGING POST WILL BECOME VERY MUCH BUSIER WHEN THIS OCCURS. (Operations Records AIR 29/463 JUNE 1944)

Letter received from my brother Eustace on his honeymoon at New Place Hotel, Stratford-on-Avon, dated 8th June 1944:

Dear Peter

Biddy and I thank you for your cable of 3rd June. We were both very sorry you were not with us. I was married in uniform. Sgt Kerr, he is a friend of mine in our company was my best man. I was granted 7 days leave, I was lucky to get that. I was not allowed to see the Bride-to-be on Saturday morning so I was invited to her Aunt's place in Westcliff. I went from there by car with Bill (best man) and arrived at the Church about 12.10. We were married at 12.30 and the service was over about 1 o'clock. We had 3 group photos taken, there were also 3 rolls of film taken there and at the reception, will send you them later.

The Reception was held at Dossett in Westcliff; it went off very well, at least Biddy and I thought so. There were the usual speeches, Bill read out about 20 telegrams. Biddy sung to us afterwards, she has a grand voice. We changed there and caught the 4.10 train to London, we had a car booked to take us to Paddington and just had time to catch the 6.10 train to Leamington, where we caught a train to Stratford. We have had a lovely time here on our honeymoon. The weather has not been too good, but fairly dry. We have been rowing on the Avon twice. Tonight we went to the theatre and saw "The Taming of the Shrew". Do you remember, we all went before the War? I want you to meet Biddy, she is the sweetest girl in the world (at least I think so).

What do you think of the invasion? I hope the war will be over soon so we can all meet. Cheerio, Biddy sends her love, Eustace

Letter received from Father dated 19th June 1944:

My dear Peter

This is my first letter from 15 Battlefield Road to you and I am glad to say the move has been a great success – Jones Bros brought down the things last Thursday and Friday and I was at home all the time from Business looking after the things as they came in – it was great fun and of course I made some mistakes and got some of the things wrong – anyway we are much straighter now and Mother is ever so happy. Auntie Nell came on Friday night for a couple of days and did any amount of washing and polishing. Auntie Winnie managed to find several women who came in and did scrubbing and general cleaning –

yesterday (Sunday) we went to the Catons for tea and previous to that we went to the Abbey for the Annual Rose Day Service, when everybody goes in Procession and take roses to the Shrine of St Albans. Mother did not go as she needed her afternoon's rest but she came round to the Catons for tea. P.S. Mother suggested you might like me to keep the car for your return provided you help me a little with the expenses as it will cost something to bring it from Highgate if it can be moved.

How about your leave? Has it come off yet? I do hope so because it would mean some respite for you from the great heat. Hope to write again on Friday.

Cheerio and all the best, love Father

Letter from Auntie Doll dated 20th June 1944:

My dear Peter

Expect by now you have heard about the Pilot-Less Planes that have been coming over since last Thursday. So far have not seen one but have heard one explode which was quite enough for me. Wasn't it strange your Mother and Father should have moved just when this trouble started again. So far St Augustine's, 48 Talbot Road and 97 have been spared.

To get to Austin's wedding on Saturday at 1015, Auntie Nell and I are staying at the Euston Hotel as we have to catch a train at Fenchurch Street Station at 9.30. Auntie Amy is much better and quite expects when the doctor comes tomorrow he will let her go downstairs but she will not be able to live an active life just yet. Molly is coming home for the weekend.

Much love Auntie Doll

Letter from Father dated June 26th 1944, 15 Battlefield Road, St Albans:

My Dear Peter

We are beginning to get nice and straight now here — there is a lot to do in the garden. This evening, as it was wet, I have been tidying up the greenhouse. Austin Westwood was married on Saturday. Auntie Doll and Auntie Nell were the only two able to go — it was a pretty Wedding and everything went off well. Auntie Winnie called round this morning for a chat and Mother is now talking to Auntie Mary on the phone.

I expect you are now back at the Camp after your visit and rest to Bombay — I do hope you feel all the better for the change. Bye the bye, in your last letter you spoke about being advised to take a Commission. Mother and I are both in favour of your doing that and know you would make an admirable Officer and have the right character for it. I wonder what you will finally decide to do.

We have just had a call from a Lady, who is a School Mistress, to put her up here as she has been bombed out of her Flat in London — I expect she will have to come for a time as it is only right we should do what we can.

I've had some new potatoes and green peas out of the garden yesterday, they were very nice; there are a lot of lettuce which are very welcome and save money as they cost about 6d each in the shops. Last evening I went to the Abbey for Evensong, it was lovely.

Cheerio, and all the best, love from all, Father

Ron Ayres on Juhu Beach.

*L to R: Jimmie Pride, Reg Salter, myself, Calcroft & Ron Ayres
all eating bananas!*

Letter from Frank Smith, RAF Juhu Bombay, dated 27th June 1944:

I hope you don't think that I have forgotten you or your hospitality during my stay in Bhopal. The reason why I couldn't contact you earlier was that I was away, shortly after you left, so the first opportunity I got of writing to you I have grabbed it. I am sorry I couldn't come to see you off at the station as I had planned to, was because the blooming work that piled on in the last minute, cleaning the Big-cheese's kite and getting it ready for the next day, and what do you think happened. He phones up the next day telling us to cancel the trip as he won't be taking off. I wish one could speak one's mind out very frankly. I would shake some of these school tie blokes honest I would!

Peter, you know the night you left Juhu, the people at the Sanatorium had an E.N.S.A. Show with just three people in it, it was a damn good evening's pastime. We had the old favourites, as usual, and the dame that played the piano gave us a turn on the Piano Accordion (or the Squeeze Box) and she came out with some good community songs, you know the ones that are generally heard when the lads are a bit tight and I met the lad that accompanied you down to our hanger. I spoke to him for a little while and he had told me that you had gone.

Well Peter I do hope we meet again and under better circumstances. I shall be waiting patiently to hear from you. By the way I shall be sending you one of the snaps I had taken outside the billet. I hope you will like it, at present it is at the photographers being printed. The rains are taking their time to come to Juhu while I am penning this it's drizzling very slightly.

All the best Peter Boy, hoping to hear from you.

Best wishes, Your Pal Frank

Sitting in the deckchair I made.

Letter dated 30ᵗʰ June 1944 from Barbara:

My dear Peter

It seems a long while since I wrote to you so I had better make up a little leeway. Glad to hear you are still getting on OK but I do suggest that you apply for a commission if you can. No harm can be done by trying and you might just as well come back to England even if only for the course and return afterwards. Still that's up to you.

I've read your letter about the Indian and it honestly amazed me. I know there is a little feeling but I didn't realise it was quite so strong. I don't know if you remember an Indian at the Tennis Club but there is always a certain amount of feeling, even after 3 years, personally I find him very nice.

I have just returned from a week's holiday in Wales, at Criccieth, not far from Pwellhi, and I think you know that. We had the most perfect weather and lived in bathing suits. The water was on the cold side owing to the lack of sun earlier to warm it. After the first few days, boats and canoes were allowed out at sea so we enjoyed canoeing – very good for your arm muscles and very tiring. Now I am back at work with the doodle bugs buzzing around, though it doesn't seem to make much difference to us. As a matter of fact I never know whether the 'Alert' is on or not. I had a letter from Edith Easley the other day, she said she had been sending you some books but was afraid that some had been lost, she hoped you were alright.

I hope we shall have some good weather soon as I am longing to get in some more swimming. I lived in the sea at Criccieth. By the way do you ever see bathing caps? I was fortunate to borrow your Mother's but as it is pre-war I feel it may give up any time and with it goes my last hope.

John Fieling is still at Naples. I'm not sure whether he said he had heard from you lately or not. Someone surprised him with a long letter and I think it may be been you. Robert is due for leave in August and John is still at home though working harder. Good luck and best wishes. With love, Barbara

JULY 02: 11 VENGEANCE IV'S WERE HANDLED TODAY, BEING THE LARGEST NUMBER IN ONE DAY THIS YEAR.

JULY 22: AIR MARSHALL SIR J.E.A. BALDWIN ARRIVED IN A B-25 AIRCRAFT OF THE U.S.A.A.F., AND AFTER VISITING THE NAWAB OF BHOPAL, LEFT ON JULY 23RD.

JULY 29: A VENGEANCE IV AIRCRAFT NO. FD238 CRASHED ON TAKE-OFF AT 1450 HOURS. THE CREWS WERE UNINJURED, THE ACCIDENT APPEARED TO ORIGINATE FROM A SWING TO STARBOARD WHICH THE PILOT OVER-CORRECTED, CAUSING THE AIRCRAFT TO SWING VIOLENTLY TO PORT INTO VERY SOFT GROUND. THIS RESULTED IN THE AIRCRAFT TIPPING ON ITS NOSE AND COLLAPSE OF THE STARBOARD UNDERCARRIAGE LEG.
(Operations Records AIR 29/463 JULY 1944)

Letter from Auntie Doll dated 4th July 1944:

My dear Peter

I said I would tell you if anything happened, well a Doodle Bug fell at the back of Fuller's House and killed May Brown (Dot March's Sister) and of course damaged quite a lot of the surrounding houses including the Gillis but I do not know if the Caswell's caught it. Anyway Peggy would tell you. Friday was a very bad day so we didn't open 97 Mount Street [W.R. Walker Ltd], it was my turn on so I was not sorry I didn't have to go up. Yesterday and today have been much quieter. Given fine weather the RAF will get the better of them; they certainly are very beastly things, naturally it has slackened things at 97 very much. Much love, Auntie Doll

Letter from Auntie Doll dated 11 July 1944:

My dear Peter

Have just had an airgraph from Frank and in it he said he has just finished seeing all the usual sights in Rome and was looking forward to going the round in Florence. Rome was more expensive than Cairo; what a lot you Boys will have to talk about when you all meet again.

We have heard several Doodle Bugs drop at 97 but so far not near enough to do any damage but quite near enough for my liking! One fell Sunday morning at the back of Coleridge Buildings, Shepherds Hill; guess they heard it alright in St Augustine's. We had one Saturday night about 5 miles away (south) and the one this afternoon was about 5 miles away (north) on a Common. I told you I would tell you, so I have done so.

Much love, Auntie Doll

Letter received from Francis from Northern France dated July 1944:

Dear Peter

Just a line from one of us "beach-head veterans" to tell you how things are going. Everyone is very optimistic here in France and things seem to be going the right way. So far the weather has been pretty bloody most of the time and on the chilly side for summer, particularly at night. This part of France does not seem representative of the starving millions of occupied territory, as there's plenty of grub about – cheese, butter, eggs etc. I saw a cartoon in the paper rather like an H.M. Bateman "The Soldier who offered to share his rations in Normandy". All the civvies were standing round laughing, and tucking into great plates of food! The people generally seem well disposed to us liberators, though quite a lot don't seem to care tuppence one way or t'other. We have been pretty well protected from the weather by living in farm buildings but it must be pretty deadly for the P.B.I. The farmer here is a rather gruff individual and not one of those generous ones we read of in the papers of lashing out of the scoff or nosh.

We are kept pretty busy most of the time and have had a good many semi-sleepless nights since we came over, but so far things have luckily not lived up to my somewhat dubious imaginings! In fact it's quite on the cards that the people at home have had more shit slung at them than we personally have. Jerry aircraft haven't worried us overmuch; the usual night raids, which cause more damage from ack/ack barrage "unexpired portions" than anything else. A few ME's or FW's have come tearing across in the day, but two or three have "had it" in so doing already. You should see the Typhoon racketeers going in to attack. They do dead vertical dives on their targets. Thank heaven I'm no Jerry. It must be hell — bombing and our weight of artillery! These robot bombs sound a bit of a bastard at home, but I don't see how they can have very large supplies of them.

Mother went to Eustace's wedding and apparently everything went off OK. I gather Ronald has gone to an unknown destination, so perhaps I'll see him, though I don't suppose he'll come up into our areas much! Well, Peter, best of luck and don't get too brassed off!

Cheerio, Francis

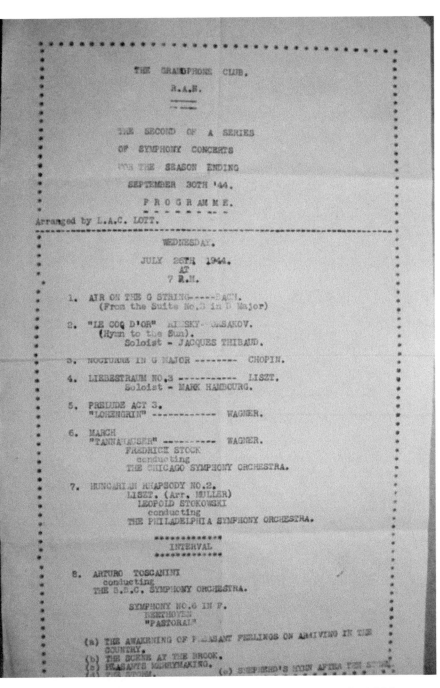

THE GRAMOPHONE CLUB.

R.A.E.

THE SECOND OF A SERIES

OF SYMPHONY CONCERTS

FOR THE SEASON ENDING

SEPTEMBER 30TH '44.

P R O G R A M M E.

Arranged by L.A.C. LOTT.

WEDNESDAY.

JULY 26TH 1944.
AT
7 P.M.

1. AIR ON THE G STRING------BACH.
    (From the Suite No.3 in D Major)

2. "LE COQ D'OR" RIMSKY- KORSAKOV.
    (Hymn to the Sun).
        Soloist - JACQUES THIBAUD.

3. NOCTURNE IN G MAJOR -------- CHOPIN.

4. LIEBESTRAUM NO.3 ----------- LISZT.
        Soloist - MARK HAMBOURG.

5. PRELUDE ACT 3.
    "LOHENGRIN" ------------ WAGNER.

6. MARCH
    "TANNHAUSER" ----------- WAGNER.
        FREDRICK STOCK
        conducting
        THE CHICAGO SYMPHONY ORCHESTRA.

7. HUNGARIAN RHAPSODY NO.2,
        LISZT. (Arr. MULLER)
        LEOPOLD STOKOWSKI
        conducting
        THE PHILADELPHIA SYMPHONY ORCHESTRA.

        ****
            INTERVAL
        ****

8. ARTURO TOSCANINI
        conducting
        THE B.B.C. SYMPHONY ORCHESTRA.

        SYMPHONY NO.6 IN F.
            BEETHOVEN
            "PASTORAL"

    (a) THE AWAKENING OF PLEASANT FEELINGS ON ARRIVING IN THE
         COUNTRY.
    (b) THE SCENE AT THE BROOK.
    (c) PEASANTS MERRYMAKING.   (e) SHEPHERD'S HYMN AFTER THE STORM.
    (d) THE STORM.

The Gramophone Club Symphony Concert on 26th July 1944.

Letter received from Frank Smith, RAF Juhu, Bombay dated 31st July 1944:

Dear Peter

I must agree with you regarding mail, I got a letter from the girl which took 8 days to reach me and it was from Calcutta – this mail run normally took 4 days, now its doubled.

I have given up hopes of going to Blighty for my Aircrew course. I thank you for that open invitation, Peter, of going to your place when I go to England. I do hope everything is OK at home from flying bombs. I have been to a few ENSA Shows during these few months. I have been to a good many shows, I mean the pictures. While I am penning this letter to you the rains and winds are simply playing havoc with trees and houses – there is a mad breeze on.

On Tuesday I went to the Yank pictures, they always put up a good show. They had two pictures namely "The Miracle of Morgans Creek" and "No Time for Love" – both were very good indeed. The latter was a good laugh and bags of fun. On Thursday I saw "San Francisco" starring Jeanette MacDonald, Clarke Gable and Spencer Tracey – a good picture all round. She sang one verse of Jerusalem, oh it was marvellous, and when she sang "Nearer my God to Thee", there was a blooming lump as big as a football in my throat. And then I saw "The Black Swan" starring Tyrone Power, Maureen O'Hara and George Sanders, it was very good indeed. Have you seen any more pictures of late? Well, Peter, everything is OK this end by the Grace of God!

Best of luck always, Frank

AUG 10: AIR CHIEF MARSHALL SIR R.E.C. PEIRSE, KCB, DSC, AFC ARRIVED TODAY IN A

DAKOTA FD879 TO VISIT THE NAWAB OF BHOPAL. HIS VISIT WAS OF SHORT DURATION AND HE LEFT AGAIN ON THE MORNING OF THE 11TH AUGUST.

AUG 15: A WELLINGTON IC BB479 LANDED HERE FROM ARMADA ROAD EN ROUTE FOR POONA. ON MAKING ITS APPROACH, THE AIRCRAFT HIT A HEAVY BIRD, DAMAGING THE SKIN AND 2 GEODETICS. CLOSER EXAMINATION REVEALED THAT THE WHOLE OF THE FABRIC NEEDED REPLACING OWING TO THE RAVAGES OF MONSOON CONDITIONS IN BENGAL.

AUG 20: A D.C.S. PASSENGER AIRCRAFT OF THE INDIAN NATIONAL AIRWAYS CONVEYING MANY VIP'S CALLED FOR REFUELLING. THIS WAS UNUSUAL SINCE THESE AIRCRAFT HAVE NOT LANDED HERE FOR MANY MONTHS.

AUG 28: A NEW TYPE OF AIRCRAFT, VIZ AN EXPEDITER MB190, WAS REFUELLED TODAY. IT PASSED THROUGH FROM POONA EN ROUTE TO DELHI CONVEYING HIS EXCELLENCY SIR JOHN COLVILLE, THE GOVERNOR OF BOMBAY.

AUG 31: DURING THE MONTH, THE WEATHER HAS BEEN VERY BAD, HEAVY RAIN, HIGH WINDS BEING EXPERIENCED. THIS WAS REFLECTED IN THE FLOW OF AIRCRAFT, ONLY 59 BEING HANDLED, COMPRISING 12 HURRICANES AND THE REMAINDER A MIXED BAG OF ANSONS, SPITFIRES, DAKOTAS, HARVARDS, CORNELLS, MARTINETS, VENGEANCES, WELLINGTONS, BEAUFIGHTERS, THUNDERBOLTS AND EXPEDITERS. (Operations Records AIR 29/463 AUG 1944)

Dakota DC3 with a damaged propeller.
(The ladder would give Health & Safety some concern!)

DC3 Dakota having maintenance. (This one appears to be a
VIP flight aircraft 'P', probably a military variation with
ripple ports in the side windows.)

Letter received from Eustace, Egypt, 11th August 1944:

Dear Peter

I am now in Egypt. The trip out here was calm and I was not sea sick. The weather here has been dry and hot. There is plenty of sand about here, we are sleeping in tents. There are several canteens here, also a camp cinema which I have been to several times. We are quite a long way from a town. I miss them all at home, shall be glad to get back again. After the War Biddy and I hope to have our home at Westcliff. I have done some training since being here, we do most of it in the morning and evening.

Cheerio Eustace

Letter received from Ian McGuire, RAF Station, Golden Rock, Trichinopoly, dated 22/8/44:

My Dear Pete

Thanks for your letter of May 30th. Yes, it was all very sad about Bert. I have been writing to his mother pretty frequently but it is some time since I last heard from her. I believe she has been ill which is not to be wondered at after the terrific strain she has come through.

I was sorry to hear about your tummy trouble and trust that you are once more six feet two inches of glowing health. I've had the most hellish run of prickly heat this year. I managed to lose it for a few weeks when I visited the Nilgiris, a range of hills in Southern India where I spent an enjoyable rest leave, but the prickly has caught up on me again and my back is more tender than a baby's what's for. Tony and I are still drifting along in much the same old way, pulling each other to pieces when we can get the opportunity. We are going to have a small celebration on Sept 5th on which date we will have been three years together in the RAF which I am sure must be pretty near a record. I've had my fair share of beer since I came down here and if not for it I am sure I would have been well round the bend. I still write my little popsie, recently having completed my hundredth letter. If she does not marry me, I'll sue her for postage and with the money I get I'll return and settle down in India, what a thought!

I was interested to hear about your trip to Bombay but it is to the far side for me. I hate travelling in this country having already seen more than my share of it. Had a letter from my pal who did three years in Gibraltar, he is now in Normandy and has seen enough war to last him the rest of his life; he was only eleven weeks back in Blighty, then off again. The news from all fronts is indeed most encouraging but don't get too excited about an early trip home, we'll be out here for a long time yet, worse bloody luck.

I have taken a note of your shop address and if sometime in the distant future a wizened decrepit creature comes to your counter, don't call the police, it might well be me. Since last I saw you there has been a few little incidents which I am sure would bring a smile to your lips, but these must keep until I see you in person. I was glad to hear that you still correspond with Peggy, but this cardboard lover stuff is certainly an unnatural business. If I can't land a job after the war, I might have a dabble at the priesthood, do you think I'd be a success? Ere I forget could you send me a list of the Second All India Series. I believe I could rustle up a few who are interested, if you think it is worth it let me have your quote by return. Regards from Tony.

As ever, Your old friend, Ian B.

Letter received from Mother dated 25th August 1944:

Dearest Peter

Many thanks for your cheery letter dated Aug 7th.

Your Grandparent's house at 48 Talbot Road has been blasted again at 5.30am Wed morning. The flying bomb fell on No. 30, seven people in the house were killed, Miss Whitwon was one of them. There are about 20 houses condemned including 48. So Mary and Cyril are putting their furniture in the two top rooms and living with us until the end of the War which I hope will not be very long. Cyril, Mary and Phyllis were in the cellar and unhurt. All Saints is badly damaged. I wrote to Eustace yesterday and just remembered I did not put RASC, I did that once before and got it returned. I had a chat to Biddy on the phone yesterday and give her a ring once a fortnight. I picked beans for our dinner this evening. The Hillman has arrived, it managed the journey alright!

Hope you are keeping fit and the weather is cooler with you now. Eustace said it is very hot with him but is getting used to it.

Much love Mother

SEPT 16: A BEECHCRAFT PASSED THROUGH THIS MORNING CONVEYING THE MAHARAJAH OF BARODA.

SEPT 19: A BEECHCRAFT ARRIVED TODAY CARRYING AIR VICE MARSHALL D'ARCY POWER AND GROUP CAPTAIN CANON DIGGLE. THE AIRCRAFT WAS REFUELLED AND ATTEMPTED TO FLY TO HAKIMPET BUT HAD TO RETURN DUE TO BAD WEATHER. THE DISTINGUISHED VISITORS STAYED WITH US FOR 2 DAYS BEFORE THE WEATHER CLEARED SUFFICIENTLY FOR THE AIRCRAFT TO DEPART.

SEPT 22: TODAY, THE DAKOTA FD879 RETURNED BRINGING THE NAWAB OF BHOPAL BACK AGAIN AND THIS TIME HE WAS ACCOMPANIED BY THE MAHARAJAH OF JODPHUR.

SEPT 30: DURING THE MONTH, THE HIGHEST NUMBER OF AIRCRAFT SINCE FEBRUARY LAST HAVE BEEN REFUELLED AND SERVICED. THE TOTAL WAS 89, COMPRISING 39 REFORS AND 50 COMMUNICATION AND CASUAL VISITING AIRCRAFT. THE TYPES HANDLED WERE AN EXTREMELY MIXED BAG OF EXPEDITER, VENGEANCE, HURRICANE, CORNELL, SPITFIRE, MARTINET, DAKOTA, PUSS MOTH, ANSON, LIBERATOR, HARVARD, ARGUS, PROCTOR, BEAUFORT, OXFORD, BLENHEIM, HUDSON, DEFIANT AND STINSON L-5 AIRCRAFT. (Operations Records AIR 29/463 SEPT 1944)

Bristol Beaufort DW 804. (This was with 22 Squadron, S.O.C. (struck off charge) on 13 December 1944.)

Bristol Beaufort DW 804 (a very rare aircraft in India).

Letter received from Francis Wall, Med Reg RA, B.L.A. (North East France) dated 11th September 1944:

Dear Peter

Very many thanks for your letter of August 23rd which came pretty quickly considering recent events! Glad you are OK and you didn't sound so browned this time, though how you can be much else in your place I don't know.

Things have certainly been moving at our end, and we feel pretty bucked because as a direct result of our mad dashes, the doodlebugs are now more or less extinct, and we're hoping they're sleeping upstairs again at home now! We have had a really amazing reception in this country, far better and more amazing than I ever dreamed possible. Normandy was frigid in comparison. Following along behind the tanks in our jeep we were pretty accessible for kissings, embracings and general mobbing! We got completely swamped by pears, apples, tomatoes, flowers, beer etc and cigars, showered on us from all directions. The girls here are very attractive and can they kiss? I'll say! There is a tendency towards blondes, not synthetic, but really fair haired. "Liberating" has been pretty exciting and interesting, I can tell you. One felt next best thing to Royalty driving along between cheering multitudes. A lot of the people speak either French or English so it's not too difficult to get along.

We had some pretty exciting times, picking up prisoners en route and hoping all the time the pinging of snipers wouldn't get any louder! A good guide as to whether the Jerries had been long gone was whether the flags were out or not. Often we were personally first in, as I assist in the chasing of gun positions and at one place the patriots rose in full force from the hedges thinking we were Jerries. It was a tense moment! A lot of the time fighting was going on miles behind us which is rather disconcerting! The patriots have done pretty good work hunting up snipers but I'm more afraid of the way they brandish their small arms all over the place in their excitement.

At home everybody thinks the War is as good as finished judging by the papers. Relaxing blackouts, home guards and everything. A bit previous I think as there's still loads of work to do out here! I have now been given a third stripe so have reached the same exalted position as Martin! Well, Peter, best of luck. We're trying our best to get this damn thing over.

Cheerio, Francis

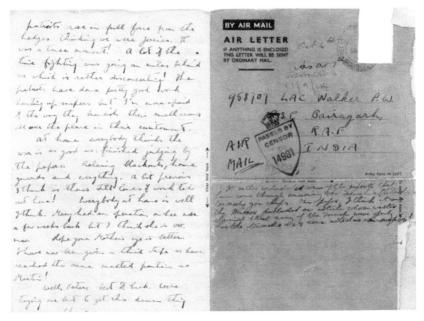

Letter from Francis Wall to Peter dated 11th September 1944.

Letter received from Mother dated 16th September 1944:

Dearest Peter

Many thanks for your air letter dated Sept 3rd, received 14th. Many thanks for the £30 it is very kind and thoughtful of you and will be a great help to Father. Yes, we are looking forward to our holiday at Bournemouth and are going to a modern hotel which I shall enjoy. I am very fond of this house and have coffee when shopping at the Barn or Black Cat, it is like a holiday living here. I have a very good daily, a nice person who can cook well, she comes every day except Sat & Sun from 9.30-1.00 o'clock, twice a week stays until after lunch, so am lucky as help is hard to get.

The Hillman I think we shall keep until you return and see what you and Eustace will be doing. Father gave her a good clean last Sunday. The Flying Bombs are much less but here we are quite quiet. Shall enjoy seeing the photos of Swimming Gala, so glad there were so many at the services Sept 3rd, you must be a great help to the Padre. Mary and Auntie Winnie got to North Wales, they travelled all night. Many thanks for sending the parcel of Glucose, it will be much appreciated as only certain people can buy it. Father has gone to 97 Mount Street this am, the first Saturday since the end of July as he felt more people are returning so he should open. Am feeling myself again, it is so nice after so many months not feeling fit. Had a letter from Eustace, we get one each week, he is getting on quite well and does not seem quite so homesick as I thought he did at first (but it might have only been my fancy).

What joy to know we are at the end of the War. Glad you are keeping fit, each day nearer to seeing you. Much love, Mother

Swimming Gala at Bairagarh, 2 September 1944.

The Blighty Boat Race!

Letter received from Edith Easley, Cape Town, 1st October 1944:

My dear Peter

A few weeks ago your welcome, very interesting letter and snapshots arrived. Thank you for spending the time to write. Judging by the snaps you look well. You seem one way and the other to be having a busy and pleasant time. I am so sorry the result of your visit to Bombay was disappointing but do trust and hope your interest and efficiency will bring some other reward. I am glad you have received the book and booklets. I am afraid Cape Town is not more religious than other towns. The War has stirred the conscience of a few, some churches have better congregations. In many the RAF have been very noticeable. The City Hall Service on the first Sunday in the month is inspiring, it was arranged during the Great War – then Mary and I went regularly. It was revived for this War – of course it is conducted on interdenominational lines. The address is often given by a layman but this afternoon it was given by a Royal Navy Chaplain, who at one time was attached to the Parish Church Kensington, St Mary Abbotts I presume. Have you ever heard of it? I went once on a Sunday morning. It has many socially interesting associations – no doubt ecclesiastical too. I listened in to the sermon for that is what it was, very helpful too. It will probably be published in next month's booklet.

There was an airgraph letter from your Mother a few days after yours; since then there has been one from Auntie Mary. Your Mother does seem to have had a bad time. I am glad she is progressing. Hope to hear that she is well and feeling more like her old self. It was a comfort to hear she had moved to St Albans and that your Granny was with her. When the first news of the flying bombs was announced I was so sorry to hear 48 Talbot Road had suffered damage. What a mercy nobody was in at the time! I think your Mother will be happier at St Albans.

She had lost touch with Highgate – the War must have made it very different to the place you all left a few years ago. Except for those flown by aeroplane, the robot planes have been much affected by the capture of the launching sites. News was announced today of the fall and capture of Calais. Those German soldiers are fanatically loyal to Hitler and have held out the extra hours. Arnhem was one of the saddest episodes of the War. The position was so bravely clung to with the outlook so hopeless. But we try to console ourselves by thinking there was something attained, we cannot understand.

Winter has gone and the Spring will soon give place to early Summer. The oaks are in various shades of green and are lovely and gardens are pretty. Those who have been fortunate enough to get to the country say the wild flowers are beautiful and prolific. Petrol is being strictly rationed from today being more than seventy five miles from your home town in a motor car or vehicle will be an offence in the eyes of the law. Cousin Elizabeth has just had a month's leave but spent it in the Transvaal visiting friends. So we may not see her for another year unless the longed for Peace is proclaimed before then and we fervently pray it may be. With love and best wishes from us all, your affectionate cousin,

Edith Easley

OCT 17: A U.S.A.A.F. MITCHELL 253415 LANDED FOR REFUELLING EN ROUTE FOR RATMALANA AND DELHI. THE PILOT WAS MAJOR GENERAL MCCONNELL AND AMONG THE PASSENGERS WERE GROUP CAPTAINS HUNT, YORKE AND HILLIER.

OCT 20: THE FIRST BARRACUDA TO BE SERVICED AT THIS UNIT LANDED TODAY AND CAUSED GREAT INTEREST AMONGST THE OFFICERS AND AIRMEN ON THE STATION.

OCT 31: THE GREAT IMPROVEMENT IN THE WEATHER HAS NOT CAUSED ANY INCREASE IN THE NUMBER OF AIRCRAFT HANDLED. ON THE CONTRARY, THE TOTAL NUMBER OF AIRCRAFT HANDLED DURING THE MONTH TOTALLED ONLY 47.

THE PERSONNEL SITUATION HAS EASED TO SUCH AN EXTENT THAT IT HAS BEEN POSSIBLE TO SEND THE AIRMEN WHO HAVE WORKED IN THE HEAT OF THE LAST SUMMER TO A HILL STATION FOR THEIR ANNUAL REST PERIOD. (Operations Records AIR 29/463 OCT 1944)

Jack, Jim & myself on Matra station on our way to the hill station; note 'beastie' (water carrier) laying the dust on the platform.

Dorothy's Seat, Naini Tal, myself with Jim Powell.

Myself in a Dandy at Naini Tal.

Letter from Mother dated 23rd October 1944:

My dear Peter

Many thanks for your letter dated October 8th, received this morning. You will have received by now our letter re our holiday. Yes, it was a great success and we feel much better for it. Our hotel backed onto the Central Gardens, as you mentioned the colour of the trees at this time of year was lovely. Strangely, the gardener who worked for Mr Weston came today and said if we liked he could give us each Monday from 1-5 for the garden. Father was very pleased as it is really more than he can manage now they are busier at business and the vegetables out of the garden are cheaper and much nicer than bought at a shop.

Mrs Wall spent last Tuesday with me, she enjoys coming out here. Martin and Francis are in Holland and were well when she last heard. I told you Alec [Lickorish], his wife and Jim called last week when Alec was home on leave from Aachan. He really looked none the worst for the dreadful ordeal. Many thanks for the parcel of food – it will be a most acceptable present. I wondered if you could get some more material cotton or like you got before for some pyjamas – I wonder where you will go, I am sorry Ron cannot get his leave at the same time.

John Caton is home on embarkation leave only 3 days. I believe he applied for the job, he of course does not know where he will be sent (Liaison Officer). We hear from Eustace each week, he sounds quite cheerful, has been bathing in the Mediterranean quite a lot. Did Father tell you Mrs Whiting and Biddy called at Mount Street last week, they were in Town for the day as Biddy had the day off. Father has just come in from the War Prayers – Auntie Winnie was also there. Auntie Mary and I went this morning. Must close.

Much love, Mother

Letter from Barbara, St Albans dated 27th October 1944:

My dear Peter

Many thanks for your letter which arrived in 10 days, very quick. I seem to have missed the boat on Christmas posting so don't know when you'll receive my gift. I have sent off a book called "This Is London" – I think a better title would be "This Was London"; however, it is still very interesting. Also done up separately is a pack of cards, you may find them useful, otherwise I feel sure some of your pals will be able to.

You will probably be surprised to hear that John has been home on embarkation leave. He came home on last Sunday night and returned to Morecambe on Wednesday. We haven't yet heard from him, nor do we know where he is going. He rather thought it might be America – anyway he is definitely taking over a job of a man who has been abroad sometime – his job will be liaison officer. Naturally, he was very pleased, as the mere thought of being demobbed and having to return to the Bank made him annoyed. I think he absolutely loathes the idea – so what he will do when the time comes I can't imagine.

Your bangle has come in for some very pretty compliments – everyone admires it and now that I have no watch at the moment it is in daily use.

Robert hopes to come down to Chatham in Dec, for his first board, he was unable to get down to see John. I walked home with Uncle tonight and heard all about you and the hornet's nest. I do hope you didn't suffer too much inconvenience – must have been horrible trying to get down those stairs. Maybe you'll take notice next time they try and warn you. By the way did I tell you that my wireless is now in full working order – no one else uses it now as the conditions on which it is borrowed are that you pay for the damage incurred. This may be anything, so they all steer clear of it. I have been going out quite a lot recently. We had a dance at tennis last Sat. Week and I went to a social and dance last Sat. And there is an A.F.S. dance on Wed. They all seem to come at once.

By the way, have you changed your job now that your address is different? It sounds rather as if you are on an aerodrome on some route to England or the near East maybe. We had high hopes of having the car out again but the latest news tonight seems to say not before next summer at the earliest. All good wishes to you,

Love Barbara

Letter from Francis, Med Reg RA BLA dated Oct 29th, 1944:

Dear Peter

Very many thanks for your letter of 7th Oct and all your news. Things should be looking up out your way after the terrific fleet engagement recently – a smashing job of work. Things are going "according to plan" here which is an easy non-committal way of describing things! The weather has improved a little and we have had several very fine days after a very wet spell. I am now on a so-called 48 hours leave in Brussels, a very fine name for it owing to it taking five hours to get there, our time was very much curtailed and we spent only a day and a half actually there. This is not much after over four months of continuous action, but it was better than nothing. There is no food to be had except at a rather crowded NAAFI and the beer is like water. We saw Rita Hayworth in "Cover Girl", a technicolour musical with bags of oomph! ENSA have taken over a smashing cinema for the purpose. Everything is still very festive and be-flagged, but underneath there's an undercurrent of half-starvation! We've certainly got a job on trying to feed all these de-occupied peoples.

We've had quite a few jet-propelled ME262's [Messerschmidt 262 jet fighters] around; it's a job to see them at all, they come and go so quickly. Bofors guns are hopeless for tackling them unless they're lucky. A strafing ME got shot down, however, by a Bofors slap on our gun position sometime ago. A few weeks ago FW's [Focke-Wulf planes] were appearing in swarms, but not so much lately. I'm glad Alick Lickorish managed to get out of Arnhem OK – an unpleasant area to say the least of it!

How does Eustace like Egypt? I gather Cairo is US these days. He should have been there in the pioneering days of Christmas '40!

Well Peter, the very best of luck, and all best wishes for Christmas and peace next year we hope and pray. Cheerio Peter,

Yours Francis

NOV 04: A VENGEANCE CREATED A LITTLE EXCITEMENT TODAY, ITS PORT TYRE BURST ON LANDING. THE AIRCRAFT CAME TO A GENTLE REST AND THE CREW CLIMBED OUT UNHURT.

NOV 10: F/O BRIGGS LEFT THE UNIT TODAY AMID MUCH HANDSHAKING AND MANY LONG FACES. F/O GOULD ASSUMED COMMAND. SGT HEAPS IS STILL TO BEAR THE RESPONSIBILITY OF SERVICING.

NOV 12: SGT HEAPS AND CPL DONALDSON LEFT WITH THE HILL PARTY FOR A WELL-EARNED LEAVE AT THE REST CAMP, BOMBAY. CPL ARGENT IS TO BEAR THE RESPONSIBILITY OF THE UNIT'S SERVICING WHILST SGT HEAPS IS AWAY.

NOV 16: H.H. THE NAWAB OF BHOPAL RETURNED IN DAKOTA KG795 FROM CHITTAGONG WHERE H.H. HAD BEEN INSPECTING THE FORWARD AREAS.

NOV 24: TODAY WAS A GREAT DAY IN THE HISTORY OF THE NO. 37 STAGING POST FOR IT GAVE A ROUSING WELCOME TO THE FIRST YORK AIRCRAFT TO BE SERVICED AT THIS UNIT. THE YORK HAD AIR CHIEF MARSHALL SIR RICHARD EDMUND CHARLES PIERSE, KCB, DSO, AFC ABOARD. THE COMMANDER-IN-CHIEF WAS PAYING A FAREWELL VISIT TO HIS HIGHNESS THE NAWAB OF BHOPAL, BEFORE PROCEEDING TO THE U.K. WHEN THE COMMANDER-IN-CHIEF HAD BEEN DRIVEN AWAY, THE CAPTAIN OF THE YORK (S/LDR MATHEWS AFC) GAVE PERMISSION FOR THE SWARMING THRONG OF OFFICERS AND AIRMEN TO INSPECT THE AIRCRAFT. (Operations Records AIR 29/463 NOV 1944)

Letter received from Father dated 2nd November 1944:

My dear Peter

Very pleased to hear you have been enjoying your holiday so much – it must have been thrilling to see the Taj Mahal by moonlight, everybody of note says that it is the most impressive time to see at night time. I expect you feel that even the fall on the stairs was worthwhile, even though you may have got one or two bruises. By now I expect you are back again at 37 Staging Post and no doubt plenty of exciting tales to tell the other fellows about.

Mother went shopping this morning, popped into the Barn for coffee and met Robert there so they chatted away for half an hour or so. The Rathbury Company have started a new train this week – leaves St Pancras at 5.17 and gets to St Albans at 5.48, just about half an hour's run. I thus get home by six o'clock – very good for the dark nights. Uncle George was in bed yesterday with a cold – but was alright this morning and went to Business as usual. The flare up on the Western front again has renewed our hopes the War will be over sooner than we thought – how lovely if Peace was to come by Christmas! One never knows. If this letter arrives just about Christmas time, I hope you have a very happy day and that before long we shall have the joy of joys of welcoming you back again. Cheerio and all the best from us all, love Father

Letter received from Reg Salter, 59 S.P. Nagpur, RAF India, dated 8th November 1944:

Dear Peter

First, I must apologise for not writing before and the only excuse I can give is I have been kept busy during the past few weeks and never realized the time had gone by so quickly. But, thanks for your letter and I am certainly glad to hear that you are still keeping fit and well, and don't get overworking, as that has never done anybody any good, especially in the RAF. Gee, it must be a bit of a blow to you not to be able to write letters at work anymore and I suppose that means that the "carrion" board is no longer in use. I bet you are far happier working than you were when I was there and nothing to do. By the way, has John Godfrey been lucky yet with regards to a posting? I had a letter from Paddy O'Rourke and he said that John was still binding about his posting. Poor old John, I don't think he will ever get away now. I think I boobed by not going with Willy Parr, as civvy billets in "Cal" would have suited me down to the ground, not forgetting the swimming pool either.

I supposed you are busy with the preparations for Christmas. It doesn't seem a year ago that we were busy in the billet for the "bun club". What a Christmas, believe me, Peter, it was one of the best I've spent. I don't think I shall have such a good time this year, as very few of the chaps here seem interested in a "booze up". I shall certainly miss Geordie and Paddie this year. The beer situation is pretty grim, as the ration is only 1 bottle per man, per month (perhaps). Of course, I usually manage to scrounge a few bottles from the non-drinker, so I don't do so bad. But, you know me, don't you Pete.

I expect you welcomed the opening of the swimming pool but it must be too cold for swimming now, down there. There is a swimming pool here, and it is still warm enough for swimming as the temperature is still around 85 degrees in the shade. We had "friend Joe" to visit us, a couple of weeks ago, and I clicked for the job of driving him around and he was in a really good mood. We had quite an interesting conversation, and something he told me put me in a good frame of mind. I will certainly pay you a visit in the West End whenever I am up that way, and if I go back to my old job, that will be quite often. So don't be surprised if I pop in someday.

Well, Peter, I'm afraid I've nothing more to say this time. Please remember me to everyone, and wish them all a happy Christmas for me. And just in case I miss you, let me wish you a very Merry Christmas and all the very best for the New Year. So, cheerio for now, your old Pal,

Reg.

Letter from Charlie Clark, No. 607 Squadron, RAF India, dated 10th November 1944:

Dear Peter

I promised to write to you, and I feel I must do it now or never. I suppose you have thought of me from time to time, and wondered how I am faring. Well, to speak quite truly, it is not so very much different here, although the climate is normally a little more trying, and the countryside more "jungly". I do not regret the change as I feel that I spent too long a time at Bhopal, and despite the fact that there are many stations a lot *worse, I am glad I moved on.*

I do not wish to imply that I am glad to have lost the company of the fellows in the billet. That is one loss that I deeply regret. No "flannel" is intended. How is Martin keeping? I liked him a lot, and admired his efforts to widen his range of talents – poetry, music, cooking and so on. Does he still laugh heartily at his own jokes? I liked him for that too! Pass on my best wishes. Give my respects to Cairns, to Taffy and even to Cpl Pride! Remember me to the others.

How is the Padre getting on, and what success have you had with the latest talks? Here I have not got organised in that direction, as climatic conditions etc make it much more difficult. It is nice to be able to visit the City, although the journey there and back is rather irksome. I remember you saying to me just before I left that you would like to see me after the War. I feel that way too, so who knows that we may just meet again in London? All my respects, and write a note to me if you feel like it. Your friend, Charlie

DEC 01: THE MONTH OPENED WITH THE DEPARTURE OF HIS HIGHNESS THE NAWAB OF BHOPAL TO DELHI. EXPEDITER HB133 WHICH CARRIED HIS HIGHNESS WAS THE ONLY ONE HANDLED THROUGHOUT THE DAY.

DEC 06: THERE IS TREMENDOUS CHRISTMAS SPIRIT RUNNING THROUGH THE UNIT AND EVERYONE IS EAGERLY COUNTING THE DAYS. **LAC WALKER WHO IS ORGANISING THE UNIT'S BUN CLUB HAS BEEN RUNNING AROUND SCROUNGING AND "BORROWING" EVERYTHING HE CAN GET HIS HANDS ON.**

DEC 08: THE COMMANDING OFFICER, F/O L.R. GOULD DFM RETURNED FROM DELHI TODAY. ON HIS

WAY BACK THE C.O. CALLED ON 227 GROUP WELFARE OFFICER AT AGRA AND COLLECTED 1 WIRELESS SET, 1 GRAMOPHONE AND A DOZEN FOOTBALLS, ALL OF WHICH WILL BE GREATLY APPRECIATED BY THE MEN ON THE UNIT AS THEY SWEAT AWAY THEIR OVERSEAS TOUR IN THIS LAND OF FANATICAL FEASTING AND FASTING.

DEC 10: THE SERVICING PARTY WHICH IS TO HANDLE THE COMMANDER IN CHIEF'S AIRCRAFT AT INDORE LEFT AT 1000 HOURS THIS MORNING. THE PARTY WAS MADE UP OF THE FOLLOWING AIRMEN: CPL WOODFORD, LAC BRYCE J, **LAC WALKER P, F11E**, LAC WATERS C, ACI SMITH B. (Operations Records AIR 29/463/589 DEC 1944)

Letter from Mother dated 9th December 1944:

Dearest Peter

Today is your birthday, I can't believe you are 28. Yes, we have thought of you a lot and wondered whether you would have a cake like last year – I hope so. It is nearly 8 o'clock with us so expect you are in bed, I wonder how you spend the evening – no doubt we shall hear in one of your letters. I am pleased you think there is a chance you may be back in 1945. Fancy Eustace is in Greece and all this trouble going on – I do trust he will be kept safe, I am rather anxious. Biddy was very worried when she rang me up on Thursday. We had a letter from Eustace on Thursday telling us where he was, he seemed quite happy and said Athens was a very clean city and the people friendly. Countryside rather like Wales but not so green, more rocky, but the trouble had not happened then.

Please Peter don't go to that smellie Royal Market to get Father some material, I would rather you did not. Eustace said he had received no mail for 3 weeks poor boy! I think it is dreadful that you both have had to go through with this dreadful war, it is going on for too long, but you are all so cheerful. It is wonderful and can't be easy at times. I have given Auntie Doll 15/- for your birthday and Christmas.

Much love, Mother

My 28th Birthday Cake, 9th December 1944.

Letter received from John Godfrey, RAF India dated 15th December 1944:

Dear Peter

Just a few lines, pal, hoping things are going along with you fine, and all the boys at the old "dump". I'm glad to say things are really wizard up here, plenty of work in our shop. Doing pretty much the same as I was down south. We're having marvellous grub and living on fruit salad, trifle, blancmange. I'm afraid if Xmas dinner is anything in comparison, the Xmas I had in South Africa won't be so good! I'm really looking forward to it now. We've got a wizard crowd and NCO's and officers and I might say everybody seems fairly contented up here. By the way, the most bewildering thing up here is the cold weather! We're wearing blue all the day and that's including pullovers. You see a white frost in the morning when you walk (or march I should say) down to work so we can't complain at all. The canteen is a pretty cosy place too, well decorated by some "erks", wizard piece of work. There's a wood fire burning in the grate. I had a stroll down to the Cinema on Sunday evening and I was surprised to see so many decent roads and also a spot of civilian life about the place.

I haven't had a chance to get into the town yet, hoping to have a trip on Sunday and spend the day down there. Everybody seems to have a cycle up here and I think I'll be hiring one too – cost Rs7 per month or Rs10 for a new one. I guess you'll be feeling pretty wealthy tonight eh? India's day of days I should reckon! Anyhow they won't make so much out of me for I'm afraid somebody's slipped up and I haven't had any at all never mind back pay (just as we used to say Cash Trades eh?). We're on our own up here though I haven't to argue in that respect. Is the workshop still as grim as ever?

Anyhow Pete I'll have to be saying cheerio, give my regards to all the old boys especially and also to everybody else. By the way, has anybody arrived in my place yet? Between you and me, I doubt it but hope so for your sake! So keep smiling and here's wishing you all the best in the world for Xmas and the New Year.

Yours sincerely, John

Letter received from Barbara dated 17th December 1944:

My dear Peter

At the moment it is pouring with rain and I had arranged to go out hollying. Eunice and I were going yesterday but it was also wet, anyway we still have next Sat and Sun to go, after that we give it up as a bad job and go without. I understand that Eustace has been to Greece and back to Egypt, so he may see John yet. As a matter of fact we have written to tell him off as we haven't heard from him since his arrival in Cairo.

The St Albans Hockey and Cricket Club had a dance at the Barn on Tuesday. It was a 'dress' affair and it seemed very strange to be wearing an evening frock again – also to see men in evening dress and dinner jackets. Rather nice for a change – though I was glad it was a fine evening as there were of course no cars to go in. Robert has passed his board and starts on his commission course at Brighton on January 3rd. Before that he comes home on leave for 14 days. I hope you managed to get the fellows interested in their Christmas activities in the end. I quite agree with making the best out of everything. Auntie Frances said something about your Padre leaving so I wonder if you will have one with you on Christmas Day.

Wishing you all the best for 1945 and perhaps you'll be lucky enough to be home before that is finished.

Love Barbara

DEC 15: THE STATION COMMANDER (W/CDR S C SUTTON) GAVE PERMISSION FOR TEMPORARY ELECTRIC LIGHTING TO BE LAID ON TO THE UNIT BILLET FOR USE IN THE BUN CLUB. **LAC WALKER, BUN CLUB ORGANISER, HAS STARTED "BORROWING" THE NECESSARY EQUIPMENT.**

DEC 23: WORK HAS SLACKENED OFF CONSIDERABLY AS CHRISTMAS DAY APPROACHES. A BAND SHOW WAS PRESENTED BY THE STATION BAND AND BY VARIOUS MEMBERS OF NO. 1 AGS. IT RECEIVED A ROUSING WELCOME AND WAS THOROUGHLY ENJOYED BY ALL WHO ATTENDED.

DEC 25: AN EXCELLENT DINNER WAS PROVIDED OUT OF ADDITIONAL CHRISTMAS MESSING GRANT FOR THE PUBLIC ACCOUNT, ASSISTED BY A GRANT FROM THE STATION PSI. MOST SECTIONS HAD ARRANGED THEIR OWN BUN CLUB AND THESE PROVED GREAT ATTRACTIONS DURING THE EVENING.

DEC 27: THE UNIT WAS VERY LUCKY IN AS MUCH AS THAT NO AIRCRAFT LANDED DURING THE TWO DAY CHRISTMAS HOLIDAY. MANY ARE OBVIOUSLY SUFFERING FROM THE RESULTS OF IMBIBING TOO MUCH GROG!

DEC 30: THE SPITFIRE WHICH HAS BEEN AWAITING A NEW HOOD AT THE UNIT SINCE 30.7.44 AND WHICH HAD BEEN LOOKED UPON AS THE UNIT'S FAMILY HEIRLOOM, WAS TAKEN AWAY TODAY BY A PILOT FOR NO. 8 FU AND DELIVERED TO 308 MU ALLAHABAD. (Operations Records AIR 29/463/589 DEC 1944)

JAN 03: A GREAT AND MOMENTOUS EVENT TOOK PLACE AT 1030 HOURS THIS MORNING: THE INAUGURATION OF WORK ON THE UNIT'S AERODROME LATRINES.

The Christmas Bun Club.

Myself at the Christmas Bun Club.

JAN 09: THE STATION COMMANDER (W/CDR SUTTON) GAVE PERMISSION FOR THE UNIT TO KEEP ITS "BUN CLUB" AND RUN IT AS A SOCIAL CLUB. THIS IS TO BE KNOWN AS "THE THIRTY SEVEN CLUB". F/O GOULD (UNIT COMMANDER) IS TO BE THE HON. PRESIDENT AND CPL WOODFORD HAS BEEN APPOINTED CHAIRMAN OF THE COMMITTEE, WHICH IS MADE UP OF THE FOLLOWING AIRMEN:

TREASURER – LAC WATERS; SECRETARY – LAC OUSBEY; COMMITTEE MEMBERS – LAC SPRINGFIELD, AC2 COX, LAC MACMILLAN, **LAC WALKER**, SGT BURNS.

THE HURRICANE (LD 839) WHICH WAS HELD UP BY BAD WEATHER YESTERDAY LEFT AT 1400 HOURS. (Operations Records Air 29 Jan 45)

The Palace Garden Party, January 1945.

JAN 10: STATION HALF HOLIDAY. H.H. THE NAWAB OF BHOPAL IS PROVIDING THE AIRMEN OF RAF STATION BAIRAGARH WITH A GARDEN PARTY AND SPORTS MEETING AT THE OLD PALACE IN CELEBRATION OF HIS 51ST BIRTHDAY. SIR CLAUDE AUCHINLECK IS TO PRESENT THE PRIZES. THE UNIT IS WELL REPRESENTED IN ALL EVENTS AND IT IS HOPED TO FURTHER INCREASE THE HONOUR OF THE UNIT BY GIVING NO.1 A.G.S. A SOUND BEATING.

THE FOUNDATIONS OF RAF STATION BAIRAGARH SHOOK AND QUAVERED WITH THE LOAD OF BRASS AND AIR MARSHALL'S BRAID WHICH LANDED TODAY. THE FIRST AIRCRAFT TO LAND HAD H.H. THE NAWAB OF BHOPAL AND AIR VICE MARSHALL SHARPE. OUR NEXT VISITOR WAS W/CDR KIRKPATRICK FROM NO. 226 GROUP IN EXPEDITER HB154. LATER IN THE AFTERNOON W/CDR CLEGG FROM NO. 227 GROUP ARRIVED IN HURRICANE LE737. BETWEEN THE ARRIVALS OF AIR MARSHALLS, AIR VICE MARSHALLS AND WING COMMANDERS, TWO NEW LIBERATORS FOR NO. 1 A.G.S. LANDED. AS EVERYONE EXCEPT A SKELETON CREW FROM THE STAGING POST HAD GONE TO THE PALACE TO WITNESS THE SPORTS, THE LIBERATORS HAD TO BE HANDLED BY THIS UNIT. THE COMMANDING OFFICER (F/O GOULD) WAS RATHER SHAKEN WHEN ONE OF THE PILOTS FROM THE LIBERATORS PUSHED A FORM INTO HIS HAND AND SAID "SIGN FOR THESE TWO LIBS, OLD BOY". (Operations Records AIR 29/463/589 JAN 1945)

The Nawab's Palace Grounds on Sports Day: Bill Ouseby, Ron Ayres & myself.

'The Palace Tea Party'. L to R: Geordie Metcalfe, Bill Ouseby, Jake Woodford, Jock Boyce, Trumper, Geordie Martin, myself, Ron Ayres, Bill Bassett.

Letter received from Auntie Winnie, St Albans, 15th January 1945:

Dear Peter

Thank you so much for the chest of tea, it is very kind of you. I always remember when you were all here that last Christmas you were in England, how you enjoyed the tea and I told you it was pre-War.

Your parents seem very happy in Battlefield Road, what a blessing we got your Mother's eye put right, the poison must have got into her system after having it all those years. She seems a different person. Grannie is wonderful, we have had a lot of snow so she has been indoors a week and has been out today as the snow has gone. I shouldn't wonder if you are home this year. You will have plenty to tell us. 120 of us from St Saviours went to the pantomime at Watford on Sat, it was great fun going in a crowd. We went by train at 5.25 and had to get the 10.00 back and we all walked home from the Abbey station. Robert was not St Joseph in the Nativity this year as he did not expect to be home, but he was after all, so was stage manager with the Vicar. We had a lovely Christmas Cake, a real pre-War one as John Fieling got Barbara some nuts with plenty of almonds among them, so we borrowed a nutmill and ground them for almond icing.

What a lovely collection of snaps you have, still the same old Camera I expect. John has not taken one with him.

We have had quite a lot of skating here but hope now it is over for the winter, as I don't like extreme cold. I do hope you will be home soon, this war is making us all so tired.

Best wishes and thank you very much.

Your affectionate Aunt, Winifred Caton

Letter received from Francis Wall, 212/64th Med Reg RA, B.L.A. dated 12th January 1945:

Dear Peter

How did you fare for Christmas this year? No too bad, I hope. We had a very unsettled time altogether but managed to get a good dinner and a bit of a binge! It was a white frosty day with the sunshine and would have been lovely under better circumstances. We have had a continuous freeze now for three weeks and quite heavy falls of snow which make the countryside quite pretty, but make going out rather hard for the P.B.I. [Poor Bloody Infantry] *and the roads very treacherous for us. Martin's lads are under canvas at the moment, but I am lucky enough to be in a house of sorts and we keep a large wood fire going. On the guns they keep fires going as much as possible to keep warm, but it is no joke firing guns all night this weather. Some of the boys have now gone on home leave, but so far Martin and I haven't drawn lucky for it, so we won't be going for several weeks at least. This recent Rundstedt 'Do' has been a bit of a b-----, but perhaps in the long run it may help — who knows?*

We are getting a pretty comprehensive Western European tour over here. We have been all up to Nijmegen, where we did a lot in support of the airborne boys, for which we have been given their Pegasus to wear as a mark of thanks! I'm glad Alec Lickorish got out of there OK, they must have had a hell of a time there. In those days we used to see F.W.190's [Focke-Wulf fighter planes] *come over in batches of forty or more! Now he slings his wretched buzz bombs all over the area! I'm afraid they're still having a thin time at home with them.*

Best of luck Peter. How long have you been in India now?

Cheerio, Yours Francis

Received letter from Barbara, St Albans dated 20th January 1945:

My dear Peter,

I heard from Auntie Frances that you have been enjoying swimming – you made me quite jealous of your hot weather! On and off we have had quite a lot of snow, especially today and there's still more about. I shall look forward to the snaps you took then. Incidentally, haven't you nearly completed three years out there now and aren't you due to return? You'll be wanting to hit the high spots I expect when you do come home. By the way is 'OY' licensed in your name or Eustace's because if it is in your name, you are entitled to petrol on your leave, otherwise I believe you can't get it – that's just to set you thinking of course.

Your tea chest arrived safely, many thanks, but Mother has written to you I believe. At the moment I am leading a life of leisure, having contracted a very mild form of impetigo on my face, due I think to the dirty blankets at the N.F.S. I have been at home over a week and the impetigo has gone but the Doctor still thinks I need the rest so I am to see him next Thurs again. Just as well as I have a lovely cold today and am therefore stopping indoors. Being at home I have been able to do quite a lot of sewing and if I can find some nice material I hope to start on a summer frock next week. There seems quite a good chance that John and Eustace will meet in Palestine – Eustace talks of going to Haifa which we think is John's local town, so they may be stationed quite near each other and not know it.

Next Saturday I am hoping to go to see Bobby Howes in 'Cinderella' at the Winter Garden Theatre in London. Whether I'm back at work or not I should be well enough for that as it is only a matinee so I shan't be home late. As you have been in the jungle shooting I take it you'll be bringing home a tiger skin when you come. You must have something to show for it don't forget. All good wishes to you, love Barbara

Chapter 5 – Chronology of War:

4th February 1944: The second Battle of Arakan was launched. On 14th February, British and Gurkha troops suffered heavy losses near Mandalay. Fighting side by side, the British and Indian soldiers encountered fanatical and at times suicidal resistance but still managed to enter the town on 6th March.

March: A strong 'Chindit' force, led by Major General Orde Wingate, was moved by glider following the construction of an airstrip deep behind enemy lines, although Wingate was killed in a US plane in a storm on 24th March before he saw the full success of his operations. The Chindits had regular supplies dropped in by aircraft and thus had an advantage over the Japanese. Glider borne troops hacked out airstrips for the US Dakotas which then towed gliders with troops, guns, ammunition, stores and bulldozers over mountainous ranges to clearings in the jungle 40 miles SW of Myitkyina, the main Japanese base in NE Burma. They were then able to meet up with Stilwell's long-range penetration group and the Chindits. One of the most dramatic demonstrations of Allied air supremacy in Burma was the delivery by air of most of Wingate's forces in 'Operation Thursday'.

The Japanese commander in Burma, General Ranjya Mutaguchi, decided to launch an attack against the British in India after the successful Chindit offensive. On 6th March 1944, 3 Japanese divisions set off for Kohima and Imphal, high in the Assam Hills of India, in order to oppose the British, Indian and Gurkha forces, with both sides suffering from exhaustion and disease. The Japanese attempt to take Imphal, the gateway to India, had stalled at Kohima in the spring monsoons of 1944. Both Kohima and Imphal were under siege and the greatest battles of the war in Burma took place there. General William Slim's Burma Corps, composed of British and Indian troops, held back General Mutaguchi's division in fierce fighting.

The Allied defenders had the benefit of airlifts from both the RAF and American Air Force and transport aircraft were withdrawn temporarily from the 'Hump Run'. By comparison, the Japanese had scant supplies. By 23rd April, British and Indian troops had advanced over 300 miles as Tokyo ordered a general withdrawal to the coast in response to American successes in the Pacific. It had taken a staggering 80 days before the Japanese were forced to withdraw, with only a quarter of their original force left.

By the end of the battles of Imphal and Kohima, the RAF had flown 19,000 tons of supplies and 12,000 men and flown out 13,000 casualties and 43,000 non-combatants. During the three month siege of Imphal, 8,000 supplies sorties were flown bringing in some 850,000 gallons of petrol, 1,300 tons of grain, 400 tons of sugar, 12,000 bags of mail and 43 million cigarettes. Parachuting stores was no easy task and aerial supply was operated by a joint Army and Air Force Command. The Allies, helped by American General Stilwell, were successful in re-opening the 'Burma Road' allowing supplies in from China.

April 1944: Morale amongst the British was described as 'poor', with apprehension over invasion casualties and strikes by thousands of miners and aircraft factory workers.

6th June 1944: D-Day landings took place. One of Churchill's finest achievements was in postponing D-Day (code named 'Overlord') to June from 1942 or 1943 as the Americans had wished. Both the Prime Ministers of Canada (Mackenzie King) and South Africa (Jan Smuts) paid tribute to this. At an operational level the US and British armed forces worked adequately together, with much of the credit for this due to Eisenhower. "The D-Day landings of 6th June represented the greatest feat of military organisation in history, a triumph of planning, logistics and above all human endeavour."

June 1944: The first pilotless flying bombs (the VI) began falling on London and SE England, causing heavy damage and casualties but the danger decreased as the Allies overran the German launch sites in Northern France. Between June and early September 1944, it was estimated that nearly 7,000 of these 'doodlebugs' were launched, although luckily over half were destroyed before reaching their targets.

Late June 1944: The 14th Army advanced in Burma, reinforced in numbers and with massive artillery backing. They rooted out the enemy and over 50,000 of the best Japanese troops were killed and 700 guns destroyed. By July, the Japanese had to fall back as they were starving and low on ammunition.

July 1944: British troops had reached the Chindwin River and in the Autumn another attempt was made to seize the vital air bases on Akyab Island. The IJAAF in Burma, comprising 4, 5 & 12 Air Divisions, had a strength of 161 aircraft, compared to the 1,500 RAF and USAAF aircraft operating at this time.

20th July 1944: There was an attempt to assassinate Hitler by a group of German officers placing a bomb under his table at HQ in Eastern Prussia. Unfortunately, he escaped virtually unhurt and the generals were executed.

24th August 1944: France, including Paris, was liberated.

August 1944: Admiral Lord Louis Mountbatten gave an address to the press: "Burma is going extraordinarily well as an Allied effort. We do not want a lot of limelight, in fact we do not want any, but I go round and talk to men in the Command and what worries them is that their wives, their mothers, their daughters, their sweethearts and their sisters don't seem to know that the war they are fighting is important and worthwhile, which is most assuredly is... The front on which we are at present fighting extends some 700 miles and is second only in length to the Russian Front... It is Japan's land route to India and more important, the Allies land route to China... The Japanese control Burma's rivers, railways and roads and, since they are a rice-eating army, they live off the fat of the land. We, on the other hand, are fighting from the most difficult lines of communication imaginable. Parallel with the developments on land, we have gained a major victory in the air, we have practically swept the Japanese air force from the Burma skies. Since May 1944 alone we have carried by air just on 70,000 tons and 93,000 men, including 25,500 casualties, accomplished under the worst flying conditions possible... I should like to take this opportunity of paying a tribute to the Government of India and the India Command. The importance of India as a base from which operations are launched in SE Asia cannot be over emphasised."

Allied forces in Burma were to suffer 10,000 killed, 2,000 missing and 27,000 wounded; in excess of 50,000 Japanese were killed. Allied forces had nearly 250,000 casualties from sickness – mostly malaria and dysentery. (Peter's cousin, Major Billy Haughton, was one of those killed.)

September 1944: The V2 long-range rockets attacked London, fired from sites in territories still occupied by the Germans.

October 1944: The Japanese air force in Burma had reduced to less than 125 aircraft. RAF strategic and tactical squadrons resumed intensive air attacks as the worst of the monsoon came to an end. The Allies had not achieved complete air supremacy in all areas but had bombed bridges, strafed trains, cut Japanese supply routes and destroyed fuel depots. Transport aircraft continued their colossal undertaking of maintaining air supplies to the Allied armies over ever-increasing distances.

November 1944: The British 14th Army traversed the rain-soaked jungle to cross the Chindwin River but Vice Admiral Lord Louis Mountbatten, commanding officer of South East Asia, was forced to divert troops and supplies elsewhere, allowing the Japanese to withdraw across the Shwebo Plain and behind the Irrawaddy River under their new commander, General Hyotamo Kimura. For the allies, the objectives of Mandalay and then Rangoon lay ahead. Air Command of South East Asia was further strengthened with Liberators to replace Wellingtons in strategic squadrons and more Mosquitoes also.

December 1944: An Allied attack on the Arakan area was followed by the capture of the port facilities and airfields at Akyab.

January 1945: The RAF could again use Akyab Island as a base and amphibious assault on the mainland. Ramree Island was also recaptured with about a thousand Japanese trapped in the swamps there and many devoured by crocodiles.

CHAPTER 6

OFF TO JOIN 31 SQUADRON AT HATHAZARI
FEBRUARY 1945 – MAY 1945

Map of Burma showing locations of RAF Hathazari, Akyab &
Ramree Island.

Editor's Note:

Burma, situated on India's eastern boundaries, runs from its northern Chinese boundary for 1,000 miles to its southern coast where the capital, Rangoon, is situated. Most of the land is jungle-covered mountains through which flow the rivers of Irrawaddy, Sittang, Chindwin, Manipur and Salween. Burma had long been a half-forgotten corner of the British Empire before Allied soldiers there called themselves the 'Forgotten Army'.

The Japanese invaded in December 1941, their soldiers quickly adapting to jungle warfare, and they used local elephants to force paths through the dense vegetation. Malaria and dysentery flourish in the monsoon season from mid-May to mid-September when valleys flood and thick cloud, thunderstorms and turbulence make flying extremely hazardous.

As from 14th February 1945, Peter was officially posted to No. 31 Squadron (Transport) which had only just moved on February 6th from Comilla to Hathazari in India, close to the Burmese border. Hathazari airfield had an all-weather strip of steel mat construction and new records were set that month by the squadron, flying to every part of the Burmese front from the Singu Bridgehead north of Mandalay to the Ru-Yua Roadblock in the Arakan.

Formed in 1915, the first 25 years of 31 Squadron's history were spent on India's North-West Frontier, hence the motto 'First in the Indian Skies'. During World War 2, the squadron was based in North Africa and the Middle East before moving to Burma for the remainder of the war. Following post-war operations in Java and India, the squadron returned to the UK in 1948 to perform communication duties. In 1955 it joined the Cold War in West Germany operating in reconnaissance and strike/attack roles. In recent years, the squadron has carried out operational assignments during the Gulf War, the Iraq War, in Kosovo and in Afghanistan with operations recommencing in 2014 in Iraq against ISIS forces.

Peter was fortunate to be able to hitch a lift with Air Marshall Hollinghurst in his Expediter from Bairagarh back to Delhi, before continuing onto

Calcutta for a week's leave. Then started a somewhat tortuous rail journey from Calcutta to Chittagong: crossing the Brahmaputra, showering off continual soot from the train's engine and running out of rations.

Being stationed with No. 31 Squadron was to be quite different than Peter's period of duty at No. 37 Staging Post in Bairagarh: he was now in the thick of cholera and malaria infested jungles where the Japanese fought their deadly guerrilla warfare. Over-crowded bashas prey to snakes, scorpions and termites with almost non-existent washing facilities were the norm here. Both the air and ground crews had to work in appalling wet and muddy conditions which meant that dysentery and prickly heat were common place.

Parts for planes at this time were in very short supply. In Peter's diary for May 1945, he devoted six pages to drawings he made of improvised parts (see Appendix B). Ground crew had to use their ingenuity all the time due to lack of spares for the planes.

Peter was able to photograph the notorious cyclone that hit Hathazari, blowing down the newly-built officers' mess and guard room. The camp was left with no food or water and a field canteen had to be set up by the Royal Green Jackets and servicemen had to build new bashas.

With very primitive facilities and little in the way of entertainment, this was a far cry from the relative civilisation of Bairagarh. In a letter to Peggy he described it as "grim here, busy but not overworked". When joined by the Americans, the RAF airmen were at least able to use the cinema at their nearby airbase and were astonished at the amount of equipment and luxury items the Americans brought with them.

31 Squadron operated Dakotas, firstly the DC-2 in 1941 and then the DC-3 from April 1942 with the military version known as the C-47. This extremely robust aircraft produced by the US Douglas Aircraft Company became an icon. General Eisenhower summed up the Dak's contribution to winning the Second World War by including the C-47, the others in his list being the Jeep, the bazooka and the atom bomb.

No. 31 Squadron had achieved record operations during February so no wonder they needed additional ground crew to join them. In 1942 as well as airlifting some 4,000 people out of Burma, they also played a substantial part in assisting the Americans with the formidable flights over the 'hump' from north-east India into China. In 1944 the squadron evacuated wounded and sick from deep inside Burma during the second Chindit campaign, assisting at both Imphal and Kohima. By 1945, they had aircraft flying throughout Burma, with loads carrying anything from petrol, rations, money and mail to barbed wire.

Peter was able to fly on several operation sorties assisting with supply dropping near Mandalay and Myitcha (see Appendix A).

Following the capture of Meiktila and Mandalay, General Slim's congratulatory message to the Fourteenth Army included the following:

"There could not have been any victory without the constant, ungrudging support of the Allied Air Forces. The skill, endurance and gallantry of our comrades in the air, on which we have learnt so confidently to rely, have never failed us. It is their victory as much as ours."

FEB 13: THE UNIT AGAIN LEAPT INTO THE LIMELIGHT WHEN AIR MARSHALL HOLLINGHURST ARRIVED IN DAKOTA FD879 AT 1415 HRS. THE DAKOTA PUNCTURED A TYRE WHILST TAXIING TO DISPERSAL. THIS MEANT THAT A COMPLETE WHEEL HAD TO BE FLOWN FROM WILLINGDON. AMH'S STAFF OFFICER ARRANGED THIS BY TELEPHONE. EXPEDITER KT478 LANDED AT 1630 HOURS WITH ALL THE NECESSARY SPARES FOR THE DAKOTA WHICH DEPARTED FOR WILLINGDON AT 1800 HOURS IN COMPANY WITH THE EXPEDITER.

AS THE EXPEDITER WAS GOING BACK EMPTY, THE PILOT WAS ASKED TO GIVE LAC WALKER AND LAC FLEMING, BOTH OF WHOM HAD BEEN POSTED TO NO. 31 SQUADRON BENGAL, A LIFT TO DELHI.

FOR SOME UNKNOWN REASON THE PILOT OF THE EXPEDITER - S/LDR ARNSWORTH - WAS UNABLE TO DO SO BUT ASKED A.M. HOLLINGHURST IF HE WOULD TAKE THEM. MUCH TO EVERYONE'S AMAZEMENT, THE A.M. AGREED. (Operations Records AIR 29/463 FEB 1945)

Tue 13 Feb

Left Bairagarh at 6pm in DC with Air Marshall Sir Hollinghurst. Pleasant trip though bumpy over mountain range. Arrived Delhi 8.30pm. Spent night at RAF station and stayed at Wavell Canteen the following night. Visited Delhi Fort; Kashmir Gate and Church of St James.

Church of St James, Old Delhi (the church of the Viceroy of India). This church sheltered many women and children during the Mutiny days.

Thu 15 Feb

Left Delhi Midnight.

Sat 17 Feb
Arrived Calcutta 9pm, proceeded to 35 PTC.

Sun 18 Feb
High Mass & Evensong at St James, Calcutta.

Mon 19 Feb
Met Underwood (medical orderly at Bairagarh). Obtained export licence from Customs authorities.

Tue 20 Feb
Saw 'Ten Little Nigger Boys' at ENSA theatre, Calcutta. Sent off 'Personal Effects Parcel' (weighed 20lbs) contained numerous books including *Beautiful India* and *South Africa* and 2 pairs of shoes.

Wed 21 Feb
Evensong at Cathedral, spoke to Canon afterwards. Visited Queen Victoria's Memorial – dirty building covered with scaffolding.

Fri 23 Feb
Dinner at Firpo's. Saw site of 'Black Hole'.

Sat 24 Feb
Sent to 5 BSU to escort lorries. Spent afternoon checking equipment. Supper at Firpo's Restaurant. Wrote home in evening. Excellent billets here – food good also.

Sun 25 Feb
Drove gharri to goods yard some miles away and loaded same onto 'low loader' trucks (rather like riding on a switch back). Obtained some provisions (bread, sugar, tea, tinned milk, hard boiled eggs). Left late afternoon.

Mon 26 Feb
Arrived Santahar that afternoon. Had shower and change. Got shouted about a lot.

Tue 27 Feb

Obtained 4 days rations. Visited Bazaar. Had tiffen in canteen. Shouted about again. Party split up – three of us transferred to other gauge railway but not sufficient low loaders for others. Divided rations and ate the large tin of fruit that night. Left about 11pm.

Wed 28 Feb

Arrived at ferry junction about 7.30am. Kept waiting until 2pm when trucks were individually run into ferry barge. 'The Porpoise' ferry boat towed us across – the crossing of the Brahmaputra taking about 1 hour. Reached other side about 5pm but weren't finally unloaded until late evening.

Crossing the Brahmaputra.

Thu 1 Mar

Arrived Menisinge in morning and obtained bread. Arrived at a large junction that night and left some hours later. Our trucks got split up here, mine next to engine now. Plenty of soot during night – pillow and sheets covered in it. Breakfast of beans, tomatoes and soot! Able to have a shower when engine refilled with water.

Having a shower behind the engine!

Crossing the King George VI Bridge over River Surma near Chittagong.

Fri 2 Mar

Within 11 miles of destination but train held up in siding – probably be stuck here for 12 hours or more. Run out of bread and sugar. Hoping to obtain rations.

Sat 3 Mar

No rations sent – have been stuck in this siding for over 24 hours. Living on chappatties and jam which the Indian soldiers kindly gave us. Left late afternoon and arrived Chittagong one hour later. Unable to unload lorries that night as ramp is in use.

Sun 4 Mar

Unloaded gharries in morning. Had accident whilst driving second lorry off low loaders. The metal strip between tracks slipped and front near side wheel dropped through gap; took a couple of hours to jack it up. Arrived 31 Squadron, Hathazari late afternoon.

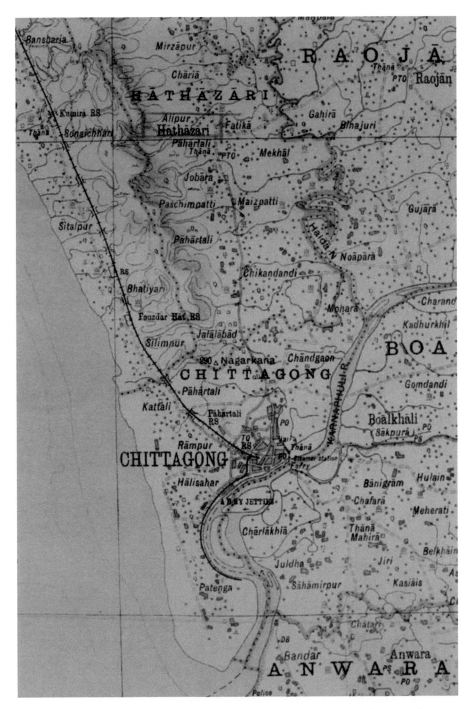

Map showing location of Hathazari, near Chittagong, close to the Burmese border. (British Library Y/104/79N 1926)

NO. 31 SQUADRON MOVED FROM COMILLA TO HATHAZARI ON FEB 6TH WITHOUT INTERRUPTION TO OPERATIONAL COMMITMENTS. THE MOVE WAS CARRIED OUT BY AIR AND ROAD; NEARLY ALL PERSONNEL WERE TRANSFERRED BY AIR. THE AIRFIELD AT HATHAZARI HAS A SINGLE ALL-WEATHER STRIP OF STEEL MAT CONSTRUCTION. THE LOADING BAYS HAVE BEEN ALLOTTED TO THE SQUADRON AT THE NORTH END OF THE RUNWAY. UNTIL THE END OF THE MONTH, ONLY ONE WAS AVAILABLE AND THE OVER-CROWDING WAS A HANDICAP TO QUICK LOADING. ALL SECTIONS ARE LOCATED NEAR THE STRIP.

THE DOMESTIC CAMP OF BASHA CONSTRUCTION WAS ONLY COMPLETED AT THE END OF THE MONTH, AND TENTED ACCOMMODATION HAD TO BE PROVIDED FOR SOME OF THE PERSONNEL ON THEIR ARRIVAL. THE CAMP IS LOCATED A FEW HUNDRED YARDS FROM THE SOUTH END OF THE RUNWAY; THE ADVANTAGE OF BEING SO CLOSE TO THE STRIP IS OUTWEIGHED BY THE NOISE AND DUST. IT IS COMPACT: ALL THREE MESSES ARE SERVED BY ONE KITCHEN. FURNITURE FOR BOTH OFFICES AND MESSES IS IN EXTREMELY SHORT SUPPLY. CHARPOYS ARE THE ONLY FURNITURE ISSUED FOR QUARTERS, BUT INGENUITY, BAMBOO AND STATIC LINES HAVE MADE GOOD MANY DEFICIENCIES.

WITHOUT DOUBT, THE SQUADRON HAS NEVER BEFORE IN ITS HISTORY EQUALLED THE RECORD OPERATIONAL EFFORT MADE IN THE MONTH OF FEBRUARY 1945. IN 28 DAYS OUR AIRCRAFT FLEW A TOTAL OF 3,700 HOURS, MADE 1,703 OPERATIONAL TRIPS, DROPPED 223.8 TONS OF SUPPLIES AND LANDED ANOTHER 1,383.4 TONS, INCLUDING THE WEIGHT OF 1,046 TROOPS.

IN SETTING THESE RECORDS, THE SQUADRON HAD A NUMBER OF UNUSUAL ISSUES TO CONTEND WITH. IN THE FIRST WEEK, MOVING PERSONNEL AND EQUIPMENT IMPOSED A STRAIN ON MAINTENANCE. OWING TO THE LARGE NUMBER OF AIRCRAFT POSTINGS IN JANUARY AND FEBRUARY, A HIGH PERCENTAGE OF THE CREW WERE UNFAMILIAR WITH THE WORK AND THE ROUTINE. REPLACEMENTS FOR AIRCRAFT WERE NOT IMMEDIATELY AVAILABLE AND THE AVERAGE STRENGTH OF AIRCRAFT HELD ON THE UNIT FELL FROM THE NORMAL 19.9 TO 18.4. NO. 31 SQUADRON HAD AIRCRAFT FLYING TO EVERY PART OF THE BURMA FRONT FROM THE SURGU BRIDGEHEAD NORTH OF MANDALAY TO THE RU-YUA ROADBLOCK IN THE ARAKAN.

31 SQUADRON DROPPED MONEY, RATIONS AND MAIL. WITH FEW EXCEPTIONS, LOADS CONSISTED OF PETROL, RATIONS, ORDNANCE STORES. THE A.S.O. AT HATHAZARI PACKS TINS OF PETROL IN FLIMSY BAMBOO BASKETS, WHICH ARE ROUNDLY CURSED BY THE DROPPING CREWS ON ACCOUNT OF THE SPLINTERS CAUGHT IN HANDLING THEM. BARBED WIRE IS ANOTHER UNPOPULAR LOAD.

REPLACEMENTS WERE NOT IMMEDIATELY AVAILABLE FOR AIRCRAFT WRITTEN OFF FOR ENGINE CHANGES OR OTHER REASONS. AS A RESULT, THE AVERAGE STRENGTH OF AIRCRAFT AND DAILY SERVICEABILITY FELL BELOW THE 2 PRECEDING MONTHS.

PERSONNEL WERE IMMUNISED AGAINST CHOLERA. THERE WAS ONE CASE OF MALARIA, ALL BILLETS BEING SPRAYED WITH DDT, 5% IN KEROSENE, TWICE WEEKLY AND THERE HAS BEEN A MARKED DECREASE IN THE NUMBER OF MOSQUITOES. STATIC WATER IS BEING OILED TWICE WEEKLY;

DRAINAGE CHANNELS HAVE BEEN DUG BY THE ANTI-MALARIAL UNIT ON THE STATION; THE MAIN DRAINS, HOWEVER, HAVE NOT YET BEEN DUG OWING TO THE AMOUNT OF HIGHER PRIORITY WORK WHICH THE G.E. HAS IN HAND.

HATHAZARI OFFERS FEW WELFARE FACILITIES. 117 SQUADRON HAS ESTABLISHED A FOOTBALL FIELD AT THE SOUTH-WEST CORNER OF THE RUNWAY, AND GENEROUSLY OPENED IT TO OUR PLAYERS. THREE WELL CONTESTED GAMES BETWEEN THE TWO SQUADRON'S TEAMS WERE PLAYED.

THE GARRISON ENGINEER SET UP A SMALL OPEN-AIR STAGE FOR VISITING ARTISTS. PATRICIA AND MARIA BURKE WERE THE FIRST WELCOME GUESTS TO USE IT, AND ON FEB 27 & 28TH A RAF GANG SHOW PRESENTED 2 EXCELLENT EVENINGS OF ENTERTAINMENT. A VISITING PROJECTION UNIT SHOWED ONE CINEMA.

A CANTEEN WAS IN OPERATION SOON AFTER OUR ARRIVAL. A BASHA IS BEING BUILT TO TAKE THE PLACE OF THE MARQUEE WHICH NOW CONTAINS IT. WITH SO MUCH HIGH PRIORITY WORK DEMANDING HIS ATTENTION, IT IS UNLIKELY THAT THE GARRISON ENGINEER WILL BE ABLE TO PROVIDE MORE SPORTS FACILITIES OR RECREATION BUILDINGS FOR SOME TIME.

AIRMEN'S BASHAS WERE IN MOST CASES GROSSLY OVER-CROWDED AND WASHING FACILITIES ETC. BEING ALMOST NIL; ONLY 2 WATER-PUMPS WHICH WERE USUALLY IN AN UNSERVICEABLE CONDITION BEING AVAILABLE FOR USE AMONGST 400 MEN.

THE DISCIPLINE ON THE SQUADRON AS A WHOLE WAS EXCEPTIONALLY GOOD.

A LEAVE AIRCRAFT WAS ALLOTTED TO FLY PERSONNEL PROCEEDING ON LEAVE TO CALCUTTA ONCE A WEEK, AND DURING THE MONTH A GOOD NUMBER OF OFFICERS, NCO'S AND AIRMEN PROCEEDED ON LEAVE.

AN AMERICAN AIR FORCE UNIT BASED AT HATHAZARI WAS IN POSSESSION OF A 1ST RATE FILM PROJECTOR AND UP-TO-DATE OPEN AIR SHOWS WERE GIVEN NIGHTLY, AND SQUADRON PERSONNEL WERE PERMITTED TO ATTEND THESE SHOWS.

THE GANG SHOW PRODUCED BY RALPH LEADER WAS VERY GOOD. SQUADRON WEEKLY NEWS SHEET WAS PRODUCED FOR THE FIRST TIME. SERIES OF CLASSES RUN, INCLUDING BIBLE CLASS AND DEBATING GROUP. AN INDIAN CANTEEN IS BEING RUN ON CAMP FOR THE USE OF SQUADRON PERSONNEL AND IS PROVING TO BE A SUCCESSFUL INSTITUTION. (Operation Records AIR 27/352-356 FEB/MAR 1945)

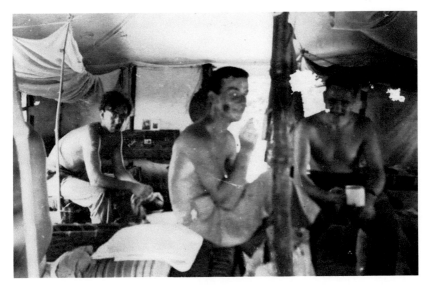

Interior of my Basha.

Sun 11 Mar

Wrote letters to Peggy & Parents: News good, work interesting, settling down here. Living conditions poor, no showers, have to pump all water. Water situation grim.

Sun 18 Mar

Wrote to Parents and Peggy: walked to village where I bought cushions for the chair I've made.

Interior of my Basha, note chair I made!

Received letter from LAC John Godfrey, c/o 307 M.U. (E.R.S.), S.E. Asia Air Forces, dated 19th March 1945:

Dear Peter,

I must say you've certainly surprised me by going and getting yourself posted, you can't let them get away with that can you, not much chance I guess so why worry? Anyhow pal, I do sincerely hope you're getting along fine and are keeping in the best of health. Many sincere thanks for your welcome letter and the three snaps which arrived last Saturday. I really am very settled up here and count myself very lucky to be here! I'm feeling more like my old self again and maybe you'd hardly recognise me for I'm now as fat as a ---- (you know!), actually I'm just over twelve stone so you see I'm not being starved to death like I reckon I used to be! Anyhow things are going along fine up here, like yourself we aren't overworked but at least they keep us out of any mischief and the days and weeks slide by so quickly and that's all that really matters eh?

I was really shaken by the news of Frank Gibbs losing his wife – terrible for him isn't it? You just can't understand his feelings and it's to be hoped he doesn't take it too badly, but heck what a shock after being apart for so long. It's so hard on the children too. Anyhow let's hope they can find some happiness together in life and may time help to heal and ease their feelings. I just can't get over it Pete and yet similar things are happening to so many thousands of people in these times; it certainly does make you count your blessings and you realise just how lucky you really are to be alive and kicking and to live and plan for the future.

Anyhow pal I do hope you are nicely and comfortably settled down by now, certainly sounds a fairly 'quiet' place you're at. Does make Bhopal sound like a rest camp too, still if you're happy! The lads are a good crowd, it's worth a lot in this country – you certainly travelled in style eh? Think you must have given the 'Old Boy' the wire about wanting a 'kite' when you were posted! I'm surprised to hear you were pushed for cash in town when you were in Calcutta – squashes the nickname we gave you eh? Yes, it is a good job you could take a joke Pete, or else we should all have been walking around with black eyes and broken noses!

Hope all the folks at home are keeping fine. Do you still hear from your "girl friend" – suppose you'll go and get married in the end eh? We'll have to wait and see.

From yours truly, John.

Sun 25 Mar

Wrote letter to Peggy: have a good holiday at Lorna Doone; grim here but am glad of posting; busy but not overworked, sunburnt; Chittagong – very poor road there; 2 days off work; Father becoming Church Warden; tour reduced to three years.

Fri 30 Mar

Trod on a snake when walking to evening service at 117 Squadron!

Mon 9 Apr

Wrote letter to parents: heat no worse than Bhopal – same latitude; trod on snake on Good Friday; saw 'Song of Bernadette'. Jungle non-wooded; work quite hard.

Tue 10 Apr

Wrote letter to Pegs: her holiday and nursery where she works; are there any young innocent girls left or must I remain a confirmed bachelor?! 2 old friends here. Remember me to Ma & Pa.

Thu 12 Apr

Terrific storm breaks at 7am. Roofs of most billets blown off. Kit and bedding of many chaps is saturated. Our billet is saved though on one occasion roof lifted about 3 feet.

Taken during the lull between the storms.

Inspecting the storm damage.

22 Apr

Wrote to Parents: 2 days off a week, work hard; wash in 3 gallons. Don't worry about me – few wild animals, only walk in built up areas. Am trying to fix up leave.

Tue 24 Apr

Flew to Taungtha [near Mandalay] on supply trip.

Received letter from Biddy, 22 Retreat Road, Westcliff, dated 27th April 1945:

Dear Peter

Thank you very much for your letter and the greetings. Yes! I miss Robert more than it is possible to say but the news is so good I do not think it will be many months now before our attention can be turned to the Japs. However, life is very serious at the moment. When the end of the German war is reached I don't see that there can be too much jollification. There will be such a lot of sober work to do. So many homeless, so many sick, both mentally and physically. What a terrific task in view. The news from those camps in Germany was appalling was it not? It is hard to realise that the captors were human beings at all. Even the survivors will be scarred for life both mentally or otherwise.

I was very interested in the last part of your letter about the united front. I agree entirely that united Christian fellowship is absolutely essential. What a lot of practical work there is waiting to be done by Christians. What a frightening experience you had with that snake. I think I should have stood still and got bitten.

We are all looking forward to meeting you at home. To me, you are the most "unreal" person. I cannot get used to the fact that I have got a brother-in-law. I expect it seems absurd to you that you have got a sister-in-law.

The news at nine o'clock was very good was it not? The Americans and Russians joined up, Moscow captured, etc. Very good.

All best wishes Biddy

Letter received from Mrs A E Samuel, Mayfair, London dated April 1945:

My dear Peter

I was ever so pleased to hear from you again, although I don't agree with you that you have been guilty of neglect. On the contrary, I am afraid I was enjoying your letters and not answering them regularly – not because of forgetfulness really, but because I thought I had so little to say that I thought would be of interest to you. Life is very changed for me in every way, and it is sometimes with difficulty I can persuade myself that I am the same person. Now to answer your letter: I am keeping fairly well – the various kinds of bombs and rockets have not affected me very much, but for all shall I be thankful when the war comes to an end. We have been having an early spell of hot weather which has brought things out too soon, and now it has turned quite chilly again and it will put things back. Still it was a nice break, although rather sudden.

Your snake experience was most unpleasant. How lucky you were not bitten. I keep the photos you send, and I am always interested in them. I realise all you say about Christianity – I am afraid that things have become very slack and will get worse after the war has finished for a time, like it did in the last war. Goodness knows what peculiarities we shall develop: may they be for good and not for bad. 'Jazz' came after the last war. I have heard of the books of E.J. Lewis but I haven't read any so far. I expect you are beginning to long for home. Last night the blackout restrictions were raised and lights were pouring out of the windows into the streets! A strange, but welcome sight.

I often feel I would like to send you a book. Do let me know if there is anything special you would like – I think you like history, but I don't know if you have kept the same taste since you have been away. Little Carlo sends you his best regards. He takes great care of me, dear little soul, and he keeps very well. I hope to be seeing your Aunt soon and before long let us hope we shall be meeting again. Write soon again. Yours very sincerely, AE Samuel

Tue 1 May
Flew on afternoon sortie to Myitcha (on west bank of Irrawaddi).

The cramped interior of a Dakota flying an 'op'.

Wed 2 May

Wrote letter to Peggy: have received no letter for 5 weeks; busy flying – not all joy flights. Leave may be cancelled.

Fri 4 May

Wrote letter to Rev Rowland – Ron and I unable to come this month. Ron to Naini Tal, mine postponed; shall put in for month's leave and spend fortnight at Bangalore with my cousin Siddie.

Sat 12 May

Wrote letter to Parents: why not temporarily licence the Hillman for when I return as might be cheaper to use it for work – I could share expenses. Railway fares must be expensive.

Chapter 6 – Chronology of War

Feb 1945: The 'Big Three' – Churchill, Stalin and Roosevelt – met at Yalta in the Crimea. With Allied success very likely, they were discussing plans for Japan and Germany. Formation of 'Tiger Force' for operations in the Far East.

March 1945: Aerial supply operations had reached their peak with 78,250 tons of stores delivered and 27,000 military personnel transported. The effectiveness of these operations was, however, dependent upon the speedy construction of all-weather airfields, which was due to the 14th Army Sappers who were able to build 200 airfields in only 6 months. Airfield strips were constructed using a variety of innovative techniques ensuring good drainage so they could keep operating in the monsoon periods. The soil was stabilised using oil and then brick, with concrete and pierced steel planking (PSP) being put down on top of the compacted soil.

"Supply-dropping is itself an art. The aircraft must fly at a minimum height and speed during the process (which, when serving front-line troops, brings it within periodic small-arms fire of the enemy). To complete an accurate drop it must make at least eight circuits over the dropping-zone. During this half-hour the pilot must keep his heavy ship trim. Or else the parachute will get tangled in his rudder as the loads tumble out of the doorway. For the crew it means a violent and unceasing effort to haul the crates and sacks the length of the 'hold' as far as the open door, poise and push them clear. In Burma the job was complicated by the lie of the land, which placed dropping-zones in narrow valleys, jungle clearings and hollows in the hills. These sharp contours set up air turbulences, which are intensified in the monsoon: on one occasion a Dakota emerged from a cloud upside-down. When the drop took place at night, with the enemy using counterfeit signals to decoy you off course, the fun really began." (*The Campaign in Burma*, Lt Colonel Frank Owen.)

According to Sergeant Douglas Williams, a Wireless Operator and

Gunner with RAF 194 Squadron, "Flying conditions in Burma were atrocious. There was always tremendous turbulence because of the heat. The bouncing up and down made it difficult moving supplies to the door to despatch them. We often flew through lightning." (*We Gave Our Today*, William Fowler.)

"The Dakota was a marvellous aircraft, light on the controls, with very reliable engines and you can land it on a five-hundred yard long strip at night." (Warrant Officer Deryck Groocock of RAF 194 Squadron).

"Even in monsoon storms when you had very little say in what happened to you, plunging down three thousand feet and up again two thousand feet in torrential rain and lightning, the Dakota was a wonderful aircraft. It had one snag: the cockpit leaked badly in heavy rain and we used to put oilskins over our knees to keep the water off our laps." (Pilot Officer James Thirlwell, RAF 194 Squadron.)

Towards the end of air operations against the Japanese, the RAF received Hurricanes, Wellingtons, Blenheims and Spitfires, whereas the USAAF had the more modern aircraft such as Liberators and Mitchells.

20th March: Mandalay was recaptured, aided by Burmese soldiers who decided to change sides. They had previously joined the new national army fighting with the Japanese invaders as they had been unhappy about British colonisation of their land. The Burmese people had initially welcomed the Japanese as liberators from British rule but became thoroughly disillusioned by their new masters' conduct. Allied air offences were very successful with air bases seized throughout Burma and the Japanese were driven back towards Rangoon.

12th April: The Allies found themselves in a bewildering new world following the enormous shock of Roosevelt's death. Churchill then had to work with the wholly unknown figure of Harry Truman.

29th April: General Slim launched final attacks against Rangoon at the end of April so that by 29th April Rangoon was left by the Japanese with looting and general lawlessness breaking out.

Slim's 14th Army was engaged in finishing the fighting of Japanese troops in Burma, and then preparing for an amphibious assault on Malay, scheduled for September. Churchill, however, remained preoccupied with the fate of Europe: his heart was never deeply engaged with operations in Asia. The fighting across Burma and the Pacific was brutal and the Japanese resorted to suicidal tactics: the Allies unleashed every type of weapon available to them. In May and June 1945 the rest of Burma was being cleared of the Japanese ready to re-take Malaya and thence Singapore, but these plans were cancelled when the Japanese surrendered on 2nd September.

1st May: Royal Navy seaborne forces together with Gurkha parachute troops were dropped at Elephant Point near the mouth of the Irrawaddy to seize Rangoon while 26th Indian Army Division came ashore on both sides of the Rangoon River. The city was deserted: the Japanese had withdrawn and the local population turned out in force to cheer the Indian troops as they moved into the heart of the city.

Tue 8th May: VE Day was proclaimed. Germany's unconditional surrender was made official at General Eisenhower's HQ in Rheims, France on 7th May, to take effect on the 8th. There were great celebrations in Britain, with many street parties. Apparently, there was very little mention of VE Day in Burma.

CHAPTER 7

FLYING OPS IN BURMA:
RAMREE ISLAND, AKYAB, RANGOON & SINGAPORE
15 MAY 1945 – DEC 1945

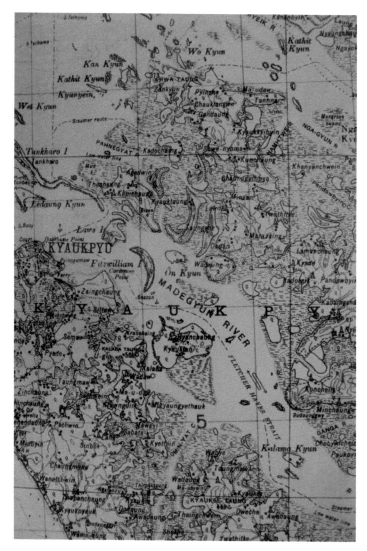

Map showing location of Kyaukpyu, Ramree Island.
(British Library 10RY/85E 1928)

Editor's Note:

Operations were flown in support of the 14th Army with the actual business of dispatching the loads being risky and back-breaking. Mixed loads including mules were particularly unpopular as out-of-control beasts had been known to wreck Dakotas. Dangerous sorties were flown in incredibly difficult flying conditions, looking for landing strips hacked out of the jungle in order to drop much-needed supplies or to pick up wounded soldiers. Toungoo, with its metalled runway, was captured before it could be destroyed and this became the busiest airport in Burma.

31 Squadron's sphere of operations was very wide ranging, from Myitcha to Mingaladon, and also to Meiktila where fierce fighting was encountered. Whilst cut off from outside communications during the siege, aircraft from this unit flew at all times carrying stores and equipment to the beleaguered troops and evacuating the seriously wounded. Several aircraft never returned from these sorties, as reported in the Operations Records.

This was an epic campaign for which 31 Squadron was awarded several battle honours. Summed up in Roger Annett's book:

> "Each day the 14th Army alone had needed 2,000 tons of rations and that in an area of mountains, jungle, swamp and dust 1,000 miles long."

The main problems were caused by bad weather and constantly having to fly through thunderstorms: a combination of lightning flashes, extreme turbulence, heavy rain and hail rattling against the aircraft. From Meiktila to Mingaladon, the aircraft had to unload and be airborne in less than nine minutes and were constantly fired at by the Japanese, with many failing to return to base, some just lost forever in the jungles and swamps.

Peter was to move around a lot with No. 31 Squadron in the next few months starting on 15th May 1945 when he moved from Hathazari in India to Burma – RAF Kyaukpyu on Ramree Island, which had at last been recaptured from the Japanese.

The conditions on Ramree Island were even worse than at Hathazari: it took 8 days for men stripped to the waist, working in appalling conditions, to even clear the jungle before a camp could be made. No wonder Peter's leave was postponed in May. At least the beach was nearby: swimming was so popular with the men that up to 3 trucks a day ferried them to the beach despite the sharks and dangerous currents. Shopping trips were arranged to Calcutta: Peter enjoyed these excursions, especially the interesting flight over the Ganges Delta. Peter recalls the ingenuity of his colleagues in collecting rainwater and making improvised showers as well as chairs and tables. As he said in a letter to Mrs Samuel, "Heath Robinson has got nothing on us!"

In June/July Peter was involved in maintenance and repair of the aero-engines. It must have been gruelling work as ground crews had to work in pouring rain for weeks at a time with no shelter available. One of 31 Squadron's ground crew, Stan Walker, recalled that:

> "Our crew was the finest propeller changing squad in the whole RAF. We could change an airscrew on a Dak III from start to finish in eight minutes flat, and there was no lifting gear."

By August, Allied forces had mainly driven the Japanese from Burma and No. 31 Squadron was split into 5 locations: Tilda (Central India), Akyab, Ramree, Toungoo and Mingaladon (Rangoon). About the same time as the atom bomb was dropped on Hiroshima on 6th August, Peter was promoted to Acting Corporal. It is extraordinary how the end of six years of war is so casually dealt with by the servicemen in Burma; all that is mentioned in Peter's diary is that he heard there were 'Japanese peace rumours'.

31 Squadron was sent to Tilda in East Central India to regroup and train for coming operations clearing the Malayan Peninsula and retaking Singapore: 'Operation Zipper' was for training in para-dropping and glider towing. Peter was sent to Tilda via Calcutta on 9th August and whilst there, much to his delight, the CO let him fly a Dakota part of the way back from Bilaspur to Tilda.

His stay there was cut short as he was deemed to be part of the Advance Party to Rangoon and had to return to Calcutta, Ramree Island and then onto Rangoon where he was fortunate to witness the surrender of Japanese forces in Indo China and the Malayan Peninsula headed by Lt General Numata and Rear-Admiral Chudo.

Peter eventually received two weeks' compassionate leave in early September when any redundant aircrew were posted off. He had a great deal of trouble arranging his leave since 31 Squadron had moved about between four different locations and Peter ended up flying over 800 miles in order to get his pass stamped! He was able to visit his cousin Siddie, a Sister at Bangalore Hospital in Southern India, staying at the popular hill station of Ooty and visiting the nearby impressive Kolar Gold Mines.

From Ramree Island Peter flew back to Akyab in November – this had been 31 Squadron's first Burmese base in early 1942, sent there to defend it following Pearl Harbour. Accommodation was mostly in bamboo bashas although Peter slept at first in the old canteen.

Peter was then part of the Advance Party sent to Kallang airfield in Singapore on 12th November whilst the Squadron's HQ remained at Akyab and a small servicing party was left at Ramree Island. Peter was able to fly as Second Pilot on 26th November over Singapore taking photographs of the docks, town and the Cathay Building. The situation in Singapore at the end of the war was said to be chaotic. Peter was able to visit the 'Great World Amusement Park' and together with many of the other troops was warned by the squadron that brothels were out of bounds due to the VD epidemic. There is anecdotal evidence, however, that the squadron hierarchy encouraged the medics to establish a vetted 'clean' brothel exclusively for squadron use.

31 Squadron's priority now was to rescue prisoners of war and internees and flew some interesting trips. Australian ex-POWs were flown from the River Kwai region and Bangkok all the way down to Darwin. General Sukarno (later President of Indonesia) was flown from Batavia to Surabaya, whilst so-called 'Chinese Comfort Girls' were flown from Penang to Medan

(still a controversial issue today between China, Japan and other South East Asian countries).

Operational Records makes a short mention that 'W' crashed on 23rd November but this hides a big story for 31 Squadron – the notorious 'Bekasi Massacre'. A Dakota was forced to land just 4 miles from the Batavia airbase and all 5 crew and 20+ Indian troops survived but were then taken to a nearby village and overnight brutally murdered.

All the squadron's popular Commonwealth servicemen were now recalled: Canadians, Australians and New Zealanders made their way home.

Captain Alec Lickorish was a good friend of Peter and his family, mentioned several times in the family's correspondence: it was he who found Lord Haw Haw in Germany in May 1945. Lord Haw Haw was the nickname given to William Joyce, a prominent Nazi propagandist, who used to give the famous 'Germany Calling' broadcasts. He was the last person to be convicted of treason in this country, being executed at Wandsworth on 3rd January 1946.

> *"Statement of Captain Alexander Adrian Lickorish, dated 23 June 1945, describing meeting the odd tramp-like figure who turned out to be William Joyce while collecting wood on the German-Danish border. He also explains how he and his colleague recognized Joyce's voice and how Joyce was shot during his detention." The M15 Documents on William Joyce (KV 2/248/39a).*

THE SQUADRON MOVED EN-BLOC TO KYAUKPYU (RAMREE ISLAND) FROM HATHAZARI ON 15TH MAY 1945. A SMALL ADVANCE PARTY (F/L A.H. MCEWAN RAAF C/O) HAD ARRIVED PREVIOUSLY ON THE 8TH MAY TO CLEAR A SITE AND ERECT TENTAGE FOR APPROXIMATELY 700 MEN AND ALSO TO UNLOAD AIRCRAFT AS THEY CAME IN FROM HATHAZARI WITH UNIT EQUIPMENT. THIS MOVE AT THE PEAK OF OPERATIONAL COMMITMENTS CAUSED ONLY A LOSS IN OPERATIONAL FLYING TIME OF HALF-A-DAY.

THE SITE CHOSEN FOR 31 SQUADRON WAS A VERY POOR ONE INDEED BEING COVERED ENTIRELY IN DENSE UNDERGROWTH, THERE NOT BEING EVEN A SMALL CLEARING. WORK WAS COMMENCED IMMEDIATELY ON THE MORNING OF THE 8TH (V.E. DAY) AND A CONCERTED EFFORT WAS MADE TO RID THE SITE OF ALL TYPES OF SCRUB. IMPROVISATION WAS THE ORDER OF THE DAY WITH BAYONETS, KUKRIES, AN AXE AND ANYTHING ELSE WITH A CUTTING EDGE BEING USED.

IT WAS A LONG AND SLOW PROCEDURE OCCUPYING ALL OF EIGHT DAYS, WITH THE MEN WORKING STRIPPED TO THE WAIST UNDER GRUELLING CONDITIONS. CLEARINGS WERE MADE, TENTS ERECTED AND AIRCRAFT UNLOADED AS THEY CAME IN, ALL MORE OR LESS AT THE SAME TIME AND MUCH WAS ACCOMPLISHED WHEN THE MAIN PARTY ARRIVED. ALTHOUGH CONDITIONS TO SAY THE LEAST WERE TRYING AND MUCH INCONVENIENCE CAUSED THROUGH THE MONSOONS, THE DISCIPLINE AND MORALE OF THE UNIT WAS EXCELLENT AND NO SERIOUS OFFENCES WERE COMMITTED DURING THE MONTH.

ON ARRIVAL AT KYAUKPYU WELFARE FACILITIES WERE NON-EXISTENT AND STEPS WERE TAKEN TO ORGANISE A CANTEEN, TWO EPIP TENTS BEING PROVIDED FOR THIS SO ESSENTIAL AMENITY AND SOON A 'CHAR SWINDLE' WAS ORGANISED WITH TEA BEING PROVIDED AT ALL TIMES OF THE DAY. THE CANTEEN WAS WELL STOCKED WITH COMMODITIES OBTAINED FROM CALCUTTA AND THE CBID. YMCA BUILDINGS WERE ERECTED ON THE FORMER SITE OF KYAUKPYU TOWN, NOW NON-EXISTENT, AND QUITE A FEW OF THE PERSONNEL WERE TO BE FOUND THERE OF AN EVENING ENJOYING THE GRAMOPHONE RECITALS OR MUSIC

OF THE RADIO, ALL TYPES OF TABLE GAMES WERE ALSO TO BE HAD.

TOWARDS THE END OF THE MONTH THE SQUADRON WERE ALLOTTED TWO CINEMA PROJECTORS WHICH HAD BEEN DEMANDED ABOUT SIX MONTHS PREVIOUSLY. A LARGE NISSEN HANGAR WAS ALLOTTED TO THE UNIT BY THE GARRISON ENGINEER AND STEPS WERE TAKEN TO PROVIDE IT WITH SEATS MADE OUT OF METAL STRIPS AND A SCREEN MADE FROM SHEETS. LIGHTING WAS PROVIDED BY A MOBILE POWER PLANT AND ON OPENING NIGHT EVERYTHING WAS IN ORDER, THE UNIT NOW BEING IN POSSESSION OF A FIRST-RATE CINEMA.

SHOWS WERE GIVEN NIGHTLY TO A LARGE ATTENDANCE SO MANY SEATS BEING ALLOTTED TO UNITS OTHER THAN 31 SQUADRON AND THE QUALITY OF FILMS WHICH WERE OBTAINED FROM THE CANADIAN AND NAVAL UNITS ON THE ISLAND WERE EXCELLENT. THREE TRUCKS WERE PROVIDED FOR PERSONNEL WHO WISHED TO GO BATHING, NEEDLESS TO SAY THESE TRUCKS WERE ALWAYS FILLED AS BATHING WAS THE CHIEF ATTRACTION WHILST THE UNIT WAS AT RAMREE. HOUSEY-HOUSEY OR TOMBOLA CONTINUED TO BE PLAYED TWICE WEEKLY WITH FULL-HOUSES AT EACH SESSION.

ONCE AGAIN AS IN PREVIOUS MONTHS ALL 31 SQUADRON OPERATIONS WERE FLOWN IN SUPPORT OF THE 14TH ARMY WHICH LATER WAS SPLIT UP INTO TWO GROUPS, 12TH AND 14TH, AFTER THE FALL OF RANGOON ON 8TH MAY 1945.

IN THE FALL OF RANGOON, CAPITAL OF ALL BURMA, WHICH WAS THE COG-IN-THE-WHEEL AS IT WERE OF JAPANESE STRATEGY, BEING THEIR MAIN

SUPPLY DEPOT HAVING A SEAPORT WHICH ALTHOUGH BADLY SHATTERED BY RAF ATTACKS WAS USABLE BY SHIPS OF MEDIUM TONNAGE, THE ENEMY SUFFERED A MAJOR LOSS. RANGOON BESIDES BEING THEIR MAIN SUPPLY DEPOT WAS THEIR GHQ BURMA HEADQUARTERS AND CENTRE OF THEIR LINES OF COMMUNICATION.

THIS VICTORY OVER THE ENEMY WAS THE CLIMAX OF ONE OF THE QUICKEST ADVANCES IN THIS WAR THROUGH THE WORST CAMPAIGNING COUNTRY IN THE WORLD FROM THE PLAINS OF IMPHAL SCENE OF BLOODY FIGHTING TO THE "OBJECTIVE", RANGOON.

THE SQUADRON'S SPHERE OF OPERATIONS WAS A VERY WIDE ONE, RANGING FROM MYITCHA TO MINGALADON WHERE AIRCRAFT OF THIS UNIT WERE AMONGST THE FIRST TO LAND, AND INCLUDING MEIKTILA WHERE SOME OF THE FIERCEST FIGHTING IN THIS THEATRE WAS ENCOUNTERED. AIRCRAFT FROM THIS UNIT FLEW INTO MEIKTILA AT ALL TIMES DURING THE SIEGE WHEN IT WAS CUT OFF FROM OUTSIDE COMMUNICATION, CARRYING VARIOUS TYPES OF STORES AND EQUIPMENT TO THE BELEAGUERED TROOPS, AND EVACUATING SERIOUSLY WOUNDED PERSONNEL.

ON MANY OCCASIONS OUR AIRCRAFT WERE FIRED AT BY JAP S/A WHILST IN CIRCUIT PRIOR TO LANDING AND OFTEN WHILST ENGAGED IN UNLOADING THE A/C, THE ENEMY WOULD OPEN UP WITH MACHINE GUN AND MORTAR FIRE IN AN ENDEAVOUR TO INTERRUPT UNLOADING AND IF POSSIBLE DESTROY THE MACHINES. NEEDLESS TO SAY A FEW AIRCRAFT RETURNED TO BASE WITH HOLES IN VARIOUS PARTS OF THEIR STRUCTURE BUT NO SERIOUS DAMAGE WAS SUSTAINED. ONE

A/C LANDED, UNLOADED AND WAS AIRBORNE, ALL IN LESS THAN NINE MINUTES (QUITE A FEAT) DUE TO THE FACT THAT THE ENEMY HAD INFILTRATED INTO THE PERIMETER TRACK AND WERE TRYING TO FIRE ALL GROUNDED AIRCRAFT AND RECAPTURE THE STRIP. USUALLY AS AIRCRAFT APPROACHED MEIKTILA, A RUNNING COMMENTARY WAS GIVEN BY THE FLYING CONTROL OFFICER OVER THE R.T., DESCRIBING THE JAP GROUND ACTIVITIES IN A HUMOROUS MANNER, HIMSELF OFTEN BEING SURROUNDED BY THE ENEMY AND UNDER FIRE HE WOULD CARRY ON UNDAUNTED.

OCCASIONALLY IT WAS FOUND IMPOSSIBLE TO LAND SUPPLIES AND AN ALTERNATIVE COURSE HAD TO BE ADOPTED I.E. DROP THE LOAD FREE IN THE MEIKTILA AREA OR RETURN TO BASE WITH LOAD, THE FORMER COURSE WAS USUALLY ADOPTED.

LARGE QUANTITIES OF FREIGHT WERE FLOWN TO MYINGYAN, TAUNGTHA, TOUNGOO, PEGU PYAGGYI AND MINGALADON WHERE AIRCRAFT OF 31 SQUADRON WERE AMONGST THE FIRST TO LAND, EVEN SHWEBO AND KALEYWA FAR AFIELD AS THEY WERE, WERE VISITED THIS MONTH.

THE JAPANESE MAIN OBJECTIVE AFTER THE FALL OF RANGOON WAS TO EXTRICATE THEIR CONSIDERABLE FORCES (APPROX. 85,000 MEN) FROM TWO MAIN AREAS, (1) RANGOON AREA TO MOULMEIN WHICH THEY HOPED TO REACH BY FERRY FROM MOCKPALIN AND BY SMALL RIVER CRAFT, (2) FROM THE PEGU PYAGGYI AREA WHERE LARGE NUMBERS OF THEIR FORCES WERE TRAPPED. THE JAPANESE INTENTION HERE AS FAR AS CAN BE ASCERTAINED WAS TO EVACUATE THEIR FORCES THROUGH A SMALL ESCAPE CORRIDOR NEAR PEGU

ITSELF THROUGH INTO THE PEGU YOMAS AND THUS INTO THE SHAN HILLS.

AT THE TIME OF WRITING THIS NARRATIVE, ONLY MERE CONJECTURE CAN BE USED AS TO WHETHER OR NOT THE ENEMY'S BID WILL BE SUCCESSFUL IN EXTRICATING THEIR ILL-EQUIPPED, UNDER NOURISHED AND DEMORALISED REMNANTS OF THE IMPERIAL JAPANESE ARMY IN BURMA.

DAKOTA AIRCRAFT "Z" FL 594 OF 31 SQUADRON, TOOK OFF FROM BASE KYAUKPYU (RAMREE ISLAND) AT 0600 HRS ON 22ND MAY ON A NORMAL SUPPLY DROPPING MISSION TO PEGU. THE AIRCRAFT FAILED TO RETURN AND, ALTHOUGH SEARCHING A/C SCOURED THE AREA KYAUKPYU TO PEGU, NO TRACE OF THIS AIRCRAFT OR CREW COULD BE FOUND AND IT MUST NOW BE PRESUMED THAT ALL THE CREW WERE KILLED. (Operations Records AIR 27/354 1-2 May 1945)

Our tents on Ramree Island.

Sun 20 May

Wrote letter to Parents: re living conditions, tent erecting, rain, clearing undergrowth, means of collecting water; given news of demob plans.

Sun 27 May

Wrote letter to Parents: re Squadron's activities in Burma; flown on 2 ops into strip near Mandalay and second to banks of Irrawaddi. We flew fast, bumpy through clouds, climbed 1500 feet.

Thu 31 May

Wrote letter to Parents: Don't expect to be demobbed before next March. Visited Idol Temple with Bill. Sea bathe most refreshing, compensates for all discomforts.

Outside the Idol Temple.

ALTHOUGH RANGOON HAD FALLEN TO OUR TROOPS DURING THE PREVIOUS MONTH, THE LACK OF HARBOUR INSTALLATIONS AND DAMAGE DONE TO THE DOCKS THERE, AND THE LACK OF TRANSPORT (DUE TO THE BOMBING OF THE RAILWAYS BY ALLIED AIR FORCES, COUPLED WITH THE EFFECTS

OF THE TORRENTIAL MONSOON RAIN ON THE DIRT ROADS) MADE IT IMPERATIVE THAT AIR TRANSPORT STILL BE USED.

THESE REASONS, COMBINED WITH THE FACT THAT OUR TROOPS WERE CONCERNED WITH CONSOLIDATING AND SUPPLYING THEIR POSITION ALONG THE TOUNGOO-PEGU RAILWAY, AND WERE ALSO ENGAGING THE JAPANESE FORCES IN FIERCE BATTLES AS THE NIPS TRIED TO WITHDRAW THEIR MEN FROM THE PEGU YOMAS, ALLOWED NO LET-UP IN THE COMMITMENTS OF THE SQUADRON.

OVER 1,000 OPERATIONAL SORTIES WERE FLOWN, INVOLVING MORE THAN 3,400 HOURS FLYING. LITTLE SUPPLY DROPPING WAS DONE EXCEPT AT SANDOWAY AND TOUNGOO, BOTH ABOUT HALF AN HOUR'S FLYING SOUTH OF BASE. THE OBJECT OF MOST OF THE SORTIES WAS TO LAND MEN AND MATERIALS AT STRIPS IN THE CENTRAL PLAIN OF BURMA. SO MANY SORTIES WERE FLOWN TO TOUNGOO AND MEIKTILA, THAT THEY BECAME KNOWN TO THE AIRCREWS AS THE TOUNGOO OR MEIKTILA 'MILK RUN'!

THE WEATHER THROUGHOUT JUNE CONTINUED TO BE OF THE TYPICAL MONSOON TYPE, BUT NOT WITHSTANDING THIS, EXCEPTIONALLY GRAND WORK WAS DONE BY THE GROUND CREWS WHO OFTEN WORKED IN THE POURING RAIN (AND IT LITERALLY POURED FOR WEEKS AT A TIME) WITH NO SHELTER AT ALL. THE EXCELLENCE OF THEIR WORK IS SHOWN BY THE HIGH SERVICEABILITY OF AIRCRAFT FOR THE MONTH OF 80%.

AIRCREWS WERE FLYING AROUND 100 HOURS OR MORE A MONTH THROUGHOUT THE MONSOON, AND

THE LOW PERCENTAGE OF ABORTIVE SORTIES DUE
TO BAD WEATHER (3.2%) SPEAKS WELL FOR THEIR
SKILL AND COURAGE.

AT 1500 HOURS ON 8TH JUNE 1945 AIRCRAFT 'X'
KK 167 SET OUT FOR A ROUTINE SORTIE AT
TOUNGO WITH A LOAD OF 6,500 LBS OF TINNED
FOOD SUPPLIES TO BE LANDED AT TOUNGOO. THE
AIRCRAFT FAILED TO RETURN TO BASE.

DURING THE MONTH, SEATING ARRANGEMENTS TO
THE CINEMA WERE IMPROVED AND A REFRESHMENT
BAR WAS ADDED WHICH SERVED COLD DRINKS. 500
MEN COULD BE COMFORTABLY SEATED AND THE
SCREEN WAS ENLARGED TO PROVIDE BETTER
VISION FOR THOSE AT THE BACK OF THE HALL.
SOUND DEFECTS, CAUSED THROUGH VIBRATION AND
ECHO FROM THE CORRUGATED STRUCTURE OF THE
BUILDING, WERE OVER-COME BY THE ARRANGING
OF U/S SUPPLY DROPPING PARACHUTES AROUND
THE ROOF AND WALLS. THE SQUADRON LIBRARY
WAS USED EXTENSIVELY THROUGHOUT THE MONTH
AND A GOOD SELECTION OF BOOKS WERE ALWAYS
AVAILABLE. AS IN THE PREVIOUS MONTH,
SWIMMING PROVED TO BE THE MAIN ATTRACTION –
AS WELL AS BEING AN ALLEGED CURE FOR
PRICKLY HEAT. THREE TRUCKS A DAY WERE RUN
TO THE BEACH AND THEY WERE ALWAYS WELL
FILLED. FOOTBALL AND RUGBY WERE BOTH KEENLY
PLAYED AND FOLLOWED. A SQUADRON LEAGUE,
CONSISTING OF ELEVEN SIDES FROM DIFFERENT
SECTIONS WAS FORMED AND A CHAMPIONSHIP
COMPETITION WAS COMMENCED. (Operations Records
AIR 27/354 3-4 JUNE)

Chaps in Jeep, with Lancaster in background on Ramree Island. (The Lancaster was a rarity in the Far East Theatre.)

Sun 10 June
Wrote letter to Pegs: tent alterations, monsoon, showers, tent leaks – only consolation barrels fill up. Very hot – digging trench 130 degrees in sun.

Received letter from Mother dated 6th June 1945:

My dear Peter

I am not surprised you are in Burma, I thought as much. You expect you will be in England before March (when you may be demobbed) I should think as you will have been in India 4 years at that rate! You would enjoy the operational trips, I hope you cannot manage to get too many as I think they are dangerous, but then I should. Mrs. Wall told me on the phone yesterday that Alec Lickorish had met with an accident: he was travelling in a jeep and was thrown on his head and taken to Aldershot Hospital, but is making good progress. Alec was one of the officers who found Lord Haw Haw. Am pleased you are on the coast, it should be more refreshing and nice to get sea bathing; you certainly have had some roughing to do.

Much love Mother

L to R Bill Slowcombe, myself & Ron McKenzie outside our tent.

Sat 16 June
Wrote letter to Mrs Samuel:

Dear Mrs Samuel

Thank you very much for your letter of April 29ᵗʰ. I am glad to hear you have been keeping reasonably well and am hoping you are feeling much fitter now that the European war is over and flying bombs, rockets etc are a thing of the past. It must have been very worrying living through all that.

Well, it's up to us out here to get this war finished and then we can really set our minds on the problems of peace. Fortunately things are going very well at present and I don't think it will be so very long before the Japs are completely beaten. We have had a move since I last wrote and we are now stationed in Burma – fortunately very close to the sea. In fact my tent is within 20 minutes walk of the beach. It is most pleasant and refreshing having a swim after a hot day's work. However, we don't get down there quite so often now as the monsoons have broken and consequently we are liable to get caught in a heavy shower as these storms break so suddenly – often without any warning at all.

I think you would be amused if you could see my tent. I share it with 5 other chaps and we have made many gadgets and contraptions for making life a little more comfortable and easier – Heath Robinson has got nothing on us!! For instance, at the side of the tent we have erected a contraption for catching rain water – it also acts as a shelter above the 'showers' and wash basins which we have made out of small petrol tins. The other night we collected 22 gallons with this contraption which of course saved us quite a few walks to the pump which is some way from our tent. We were fortunate in getting hold of an old supply parachute which we have put up in front of the tent like a huge sunshade. Beneath it we have built a couple of long chairs out of scraps of metal and lengths of thick webbing which we have woven together to make the back and sides. I think the biggest 'bind' of all out here is doing one's own dhobi (washing). We spent all morning boiling our clothes today. We have no difficulty in finding wood for our fire as there is thick jungle around our tent – I expect we spend a day thrashing a clearing large enough for our needs. However, when the washing was half dry a heavy shower suddenly came upon us before we had time to take it down! It will probably be days before it is thoroughly dry.

Now that the censorship has been relaxed somewhat I am able to tell you that I am in a supply squadron. In fact this squadron *and others like it have been responsible for entirely supplying the troops in Burma with food and all kinds of war material during their victorious advance. We've transported everything from tins of milk to Jeeps and light guns. My small part in this squadron is concerned with the maintenance and repair of the aero-engines.*

Best wishes from Peter

Sat 23 June

Wrote to Parents: flew to Calcutta for shopping trip, a 3 hour interesting flight over the Ganges Delta; writing under difficulty as much noise, rain and mosseys; 200" of rain, dhobi difficult but water collectors help; have had 3 visits to the beach recently. Good food, cornflakes and condensed milk.

DURING JULY, THE SQUADRON WAS STILL BASED AT KYAUKPYU, RAMREE ISLAND. THERE WERE SEVERAL DETACHMENTS, EACH OF THREE AIRCRAFT, STATIONED AT TOUNGOO, AND SUPPLYING GUERRILLA FIGHTERS OF FORCE 136 ALONG THE MAWCHI ROAD AND THROUGHOUT THE LENGTH OF THE SHAN HILLS.

THE MAIN TASK OF THE SQUADRON WAS THE FLYING IN OF SUPPLIES TO THE IRRAWADDY PLAIN, AT SUCH STRIPS AS MYINGYAN, MEIKTEILA, MAGWE, TOUNGOO AND MINGALADON. AT THE SAME TIME, AIRCRAFT OF THE SQUADRON DROPPED REGULARLY ON SMALL UNITS ENGAGED IN GARRISONING DUTIES, KINDAUNGGYI, SANDOWAY AND TAUNGUP. THESE OPERATIONS WERE CARRIED OUT THROUGH SOLID MONSOON WEATHER, AT ONE TIME THE RAIN WAS ALMOST CONTINUOUS FOR THREE WEEKS WITH NEVER A BREAK OF MORE THAN ONE HOUR. THE RUNWAY WAS IN A SHOCKING CONDITION. AS THE RAIN WASHED AWAY THE SAND FROM BENEATH THE

RUNWAY IT BECAME CORRUGATED, AND FREQUENTLY AIRCRAFT WERE HAVING TO LAND AND TAKE OFF IN THE CENTRAL PORTION OF THE STRIP WHICH WAS ABOUT 1,200 YARDS LONG.

THE GROUND CREWS OFTEN WORKED STRIPPED TO THE WAIST AND SOAKED THROUGH FOR HOURS ON END IN ORDER TO KEEP THE AIRCRAFT SERVICEABLE. STRANGE AS IT MAY SEEM, AFTER HAVING BEEN SOAKED ALL DAY, ALMOST EVERYONE WENT TO THE BEACH AT THE NORTH END OF THE STRIP AND SWAM BEFORE DINNER.

THE BATTLE OF THE SITTANG BEND PROVIDED SOME VARIATION TO THE REGULAR ROUTINE FLIGHTS. ON ONE OCCASION OUR AIRCRAFT WERE BRIEFED TO RENDEZVOUS WITH B.25 AIRCRAFT OVER THE RESERVOIR NEAR PAYAGYI, TO GO IN WITH THE BOMBER STREAM AND DROP SUPPLIES AS THEY DROPPED THEIR BOMBS. AS USUAL WHEN AN OPERATION PROMISED TO BE SPECTACULAR, NOTHING OF INTEREST OCCURRED; B.25'S WERE SEEN FLYING IN A DIFFERENT DIRECTION, BUT NO BOMBS WERE DROPPED, AND SO THE DAKOTAS DROPPED ON THE D.Z. IN THEIR OWN TIME.

THE DETACHMENT AT TOUNGOO WAS SENT THERE BECAUSE SO MANY TIMES AIRCRAFT HAD LEFT THEIR BASES AT RAMREE OR AKYAB TO DROP ONLY TO FIND THAT THE D.Z.'S WERE UN-LOCATABLE, OR IF THEY COULD BE PINPOINTED, THERE WAS TOO MUCH CLOUD ON THE CIRCUIT FOR A DROP TO BE CARRIED OUT, THAT MUCH FLYING TIME WAS WASTED. IT WAS THEREFORE DECIDED THAT A DETACHMENT OF OUR AIRCRAFT SHOULD BE USED AT TOUNGOO WHERE THE CAPTAINS COULD WATCH THE WEATHER AND TAKE OFF WHEN THEY THOUGHT THAT IT WAS CLEAR ENOUGH TO GIVE A

REASONABLE CHANCE OF SUCCESS.

THE D.Z.'S IN THE SHAN HILLS WERE VERY REMINISCENT OF THOSE IN THE CHIN HILLS JUST AFTER THE ADVANCE FROM IMPHAL. THEY WERE SMALL AND EITHER ON TOP OF THE HILLS WHERE AIR CURRENTS MADE THE DROPPING OF 'CHUTES ON THE D.Z. VERY DIFFICULT, OR ELSE IN THE SMALL VALLEYS BETWEEN THE HILLS WHERE FLYING WAS MOST UNPLEASANT DUE TO BUMPS AND SCATTERED CLOUD. DETAILS OF THE LOAD ARE UNAVAILABLE BECAUSE THE ARMY INSISTED SO MUCH ON SECRECY THAT THE CREWS NEVER KNEW WHAT THEY CARRIED.

THE COMPOSITION OF THE DETACHMENT VARIED AS AIRCRAFT AND CREWS WERE RECALLED TO BASE, THE FORMER FOR INSPECTIONS AND THE LATTER FOR REST. MAIL AND BEER WERE FLOWN REGULARLY TO TOUNGOO. THE SITUATION OF TOUNGOO DETERIORATED SUDDENLY WHEN JAPANESE FORCES IN THE PEGU YOMAS BEGAN THEIR ATTEMPT TO CROSS THE ROAD NEAR TOUNGOO OR JOIN THEIR MAIN BODY EAST OF THE SITTANG. TO COUNTERACT THIS THREAT, THE DEFENCES OF TOUNGOO WERE STRENGTHENED, THE SQUADRON FLYING IN LOADS OF BARBED WIRE FOR THIS PURPOSE.

AS IN JUNE MUCH PLAYING OF FOOTBALL, RUGBY AND SWIMMING TOOK PLACE. UNFORTUNATELY IN THE MIDDLE OF THE MONTH, A BULLDOZER REMOVED A QUARTER OF THE RUGBY PITCH TO OBTAIN SAND FOR REPAIRS TO THE RUNWAY. THE CANADIANS ON THE SQUADRON PLAYED SEVERAL GAMES OF SOFTBALL. THE SQUADRON CANTEEN OPENED TWICE DAILY AND THE CINEMA SHOWED FILMS NIGHTLY. TWO AIRCRAFT WERE RUN TO CALCUTTA, ONE ON MONDAYS AND ONE ON

THURSDAYS FOR PEOPLE GOING ON LEAVE AND ALSO TO BUY CANTEEN STORES. (Operations Records AIR 27/354 5-6 JULY)

Sun 1 July
Letter to Parents: Hope you spend a happy holiday. Car prices doubled – am willing to sell OY and run Hillman. Leave postponed; dhobi is a bind.

Fri 13 July
Wrote to Pegs: apologise for yesterday's letter, am rather lonely; home mail means everything – enjoy receiving mail from you. Volunteered for electrical work.

Received letter from Grannie, Battlefield Road, St Albans dated July 20th, 1945

My dear Peter

Thank you for your cheery letter. It is wonderful how you dear boys pull things along as you do. The wonderful ideas to make chairs and tables out of almost nothing or I should say anything you can find around you where you are. I should think it is like living in a great wilderness with many sorts of nasty creeping things about – I think you are all so brave and try and look on the bright side. It is a great help. I was sorry to hear your leave was put off when you were going to see the dear Padre you were with sometime, but perhaps you are there now, I hope so. It would be such a cheer up. We are looking forward to your return home soon. I do not think it will be long now. You will love the garden here; if you want to be quiet you can and if not the City is full of life and plenty going on.

My love dear boy,

Grannie

Tue 24 July

Wrote letter to Barbara: busy because of rain; not much swimming; volunteered for electrical work; cinema for squadron; trip to Calcutta; food good; will hold you to your promise, you treat me to lunch at Dickys and I'll take you to Theatre.

WITH THE END OF JULY 1945 CAME THE END OF OPERATIONS AT RAMREE FOR THE SQUADRON. TWO DETACHMENTS EACH OF THREE AIRCRAFT WENT TO TOUNGOO BUT THE MAIN TASK WAS TO MOVE THE SQUADRON TO TILDA IN THE CENTRAL PROVINCES OF INDIA, THERE TO TRAIN AND PREPARE FOR PARATROOPER AND GLIDER OPERATIONS WHICH WERE TO OPEN THE WAY TO THE RECAPTURE OF SINGAPORE. AN ADVANCE PARTY, UNDER THE COMMAND OF F/LT. N. CURRELL AT THE BEGINNING OF THE MONTH AND HE, WITH THE AID OF THE HOLDING UNIT AT TILDA, AND W/CDR MACNAMARA WHO WAS C.O. OF 238 GROUP DETACHMENT AT BILASPUR ORGANISED THE STATION BOTH DOMESTICALLY AND TECHNICALLY FOR THE INGRESS OF THE SQUADRON.

THE FLYING PROGRAMMES WERE SCHEDULED SO THAT AN AIRCRAFT LEFT KYAUKPYU AFTER LUNCH, NIGHT-STOPPED AT DUM DUM, CALCUTTA, THEN FLEW TO TILDA, UNLOADED THERE AND GOT BACK TO KYAUKPYU VIA DUM DUM THE NEXT DAY. THIS LEFT THE FOLLOWING MORNING FOR SERVICING THE AIRCRAFT AND LOADING IT. AS MORE EQUIPMENT AND PERSONNEL WERE CONVEYED TO TILDA, THE PROGRAMME BECAME MORE DEPENDENT UPON THE CAPTAINS OF THE AIRCRAFT WHO FLEW TO AND FROM TILDA OR RAMREE AS QUICKLY AS THEY COULD. MONSOON WEATHER EAST OF CALCUTTA OFTEN CAUSED ENFORCED NIGHT STOPS AT DUM DUM SINCE FLYING CONTROL THERE WOULD ADVISE AIRCREWS TO WAIT UNTIL NEXT DAY

BEFORE ATTEMPTING THE TRIP TO KYAUKPYU.

TOWARDS THE 12TH OF THE MONTH, MOST OF THE LOADS HAD BEEN CONVEYED TO TILDA, WHEN A RUMOUR WAS HEARD THAT JAPAN HAD ASKED FOR PEACE TERMS, AND SOON THIS BECAME OFFICIAL. THIS OF COURSE MEANT THAT TRAINING PROGRAMMES WERE CANCELLED AND FOR A SHORT WHILE NO-ONE KNEW WHETHER THE SQUADRON WAS TO REMAIN AT TILDA OR RAMREE. FINALLY A SIGNAL CAME ORDERING THE SQUADRON TO MOVE TO MINGALADON AIRFIELD, RANGOON. THE SQUADRON WAS SPLIT UP AT FIVE DIFFERENT LOCATIONS: TILDA, AKYAB, RAMREE, TOUNGOO AND MINGALADON.

THE SERVICING SECTION HAD MEN AT ALL THE LOCATIONS WHERE OUR DETACHMENTS WERE, SO THAT, SHOULD AN AIRCRAFT BECOME U/S AT ANY POINT OUR OWN PERSONNEL COULD SERVICE IT.

DUE TO THAT STATE OF CHAOS REIGNING DURING THE LATTER HALF OF AUGUST, WITH SIGNALS ARRIVING THAT CANCELLED OR CONTRADICTED SIGNALS RECEIVED ONLY A SHORT TIME PREVIOUSLY AND WITH THE SQUADRON SPLIT UP SO MUCH, THE AMOUNT OF USEFUL WORK THAT COULD BE DONE BY THE SQUADRON WAS SEVERELY REDUCED AND ADMINISTRATION WAS ALMOST IMPOSSIBLE.

AT RAMREE, THE USUAL FOOTBALL MATCHES, SOFTBALL GAMES AND SWIMMING WERE ENTHUSIASTICALLY CARRIED OUT. AT TILDA, THERE WAS NO SWIMMING BUT THE GROUND THERE WAS VERY FLAT AND FREE FROM SHRUBBERY COMPARED WITH RECENT LOCATIONS OF THE SQUADRON, AND SO BOTH FOOTBALL AND CRICKET PITCHES WERE EASY TO CONSTRUCT AND INTER-

SECTION GAMES WERE PLAYED. AT AKYAB ONLY
FOOTBALL GAMES WERE ENGAGED IN, DUE TO THE
LACK OF PITCHES FOR CRICKET OR RUGBY.
SWIMMING WAS PROHIBITED DUE TO THE STRONG
UNDERCURRENTS WHICH HAD CAUSED THE DEATH OF
SEVERAL SERVICE PERSONNEL.

A CANTEEN FOR AIRMEN AND ANOTHER FOR SNCO'S
WAS OPENED AT TILDA UNDER A CONTRACTOR. THE
BEER SUPPLY THERE WAS MAGNIFICENT AND
APPROXIMATELY 25,000 BOTTLES OF AMERICAN
BEER WERE CONSUMED BY THE SQUADRON AND
MEMBERS OF THE HOLDING UNIT OF 668 SQUADRON
WHO WERE USING THE SAME MESS. (Operations
Records AIR 27/354 5-6 AUG)

Mon 6 Aug
Letter to Parents: 1 Ration of cigs 100 per week, choc. Keeping
extremely fit.

Wed 8 Aug
Promoted Act Cpl. Left Ramree Island 13.45 hrs and flew in 'D' for
Donald for Calcutta, arriving there 16.35 hours. Trip uneventful,
visibility excellent. Had tea and toast at the Dum-Dum restaurant and
afterwards took Liberty Wagon to Calcutta. Visited Hogg market and
bought pyjamas, mothballs, batteries, bootlaces and batteries.

Visited Firbo's for Dinner, had chicken, two eggs and chips, mince pies
and custard. Later visited YMCA and played table tennis with Bill, Dave
Williams & George Fermin. Returned to Dum Dum by midnight and slept
under main plane of kite.

Thu 9 Aug
Got up at 0445 and had breakfast at Restaurant. Later inspected York &
Ensign transports. Left Dum Dum 0645 and arrived Tilda 1030. Visibility
good but considerable cloud. Lost way when nearly there and flew to
wrong aerodrome. After circling round it we flew back along the main
line until we came to Tilda. Living in billets near old station.

Tue 14 Aug

Jap peace rumours. Flew with CO and Adj to Bilaspur to get 'gen' on station move. Asked CO for permission to fly a Tiger Moth but not granted. However, he allowed me to fly the Dak back part of the way from Bilaspur to Tilda.

Wed 15 Aug

Played for servicing football team – lost 4 nil.

Letter received from Mother, dated 16th August 1945:

Dearest Peter

What do you think of the wonderful news of Peace to the World! It all came so suddenly and may there be no more wars anyhow not for 100 years! Strangely Robert went off yesterday for Malta and then the Far East; one good thing he will have no dreadful War conditions and the young ones must go to relieve the older men who have gone through it all. We wonder if you may be home by Christmas, there is a good chance I should think. You would send us a cable when you start your journey home no doubt. Strangely we heard the War was over at 7.30am/The Feast of the Assumption so Father did not pop up to Town. Wednesday evening we held a Thanksgiving Service at 8pm and after went to the Catons for coffee and after hearing the Kings Speech (I expect you, Eustace, John & Robert also heard it) went up to the City of St Albans and saw the lights, bonfires and dancing in the Market Square in front of the Town Hall, everyone was most quiet and orderly. So glad the Telegraph is arriving so you will know all the news. Don't forget your migraine tablets, they are most important; someone we met at The Hotel was a Dr, they said if you should get malaria there was no recurrence with those tablets, they do turn one's skin yellow at first but it goes off, is that right! That is why at first the men did not like taking them.

If on your journey back, I wonder if you could get some material to line four new windows as quality is all very poor here, and you are bound to feel the cold at first. We have 1 ton of coal, 1 ton of coke and logs so far, our allowance until May is another 14 cwt coal and 1 ton of coke but with care we shall be OK. Last winter they cut the electric off at times but not gas but they have not done so this year.

Yes, you can take over the Hillman, I shall hope to get some runs! We can't book up for going away until I know when you are starting your journey home can I! Uncle Eustace and Di are going to Bournemouth Oct 6th for a week and I am going with them if we can fix up somewhere. I feel so much better since my last holiday, am writing in the garden in the sun. St Peter's bells have been peeling all the morning.

Father is quite excited at the thought of you both coming home and at 97 [W R Walker Ltd] father has worked hard the last six years and I'm so glad you will both be able to take responsibility, it should progress well as it has stood up well in six War years. As you know there are great possibilities. Hope you are fit, we all are.

Much love Mother

Thu 16 Aug

Took train to Raipur – an Indian city some 20 odd miles from Tilda and spent day there. We walked into the town and bought a few small articles. The quality of the cotton material was very poor indeed (no linen or silk etc). Returned by tonga to station and had lunch in the restaurant. Caught the 5pm train back and on arriving at the camp were told to prepare to leave by kite the following morning at 5.30am, we being the advance party going to Rangoon. Rumour that I have at last received my tapes!

Fri 17 Aug

Left Tilda in Q-queenie at 8am, arrived Dum Dum 10.30am. Strong tail wind with poor visibility. Cloud ceiling over Calcutta was 300ft – almost flew between tall factory chimneys! Flying conditions extremely bad so decided to stay night. Took bus to Calcutta and after finding Bank closed had a snack at the Normandie Restaurant. Bought the following articles from the gift centre:-

Embroidered Kashmir table cloth Rs 30-0
   "   "   "   table centre & set 8-0
1 small Kashmir rug 9-0
1 half moon shaped rug 12-0

Saw 'Henry V' at the Lighthouse Cinema – an excellent film. Dinner at Firbo's with drinks on private verandah and returned to Dum Dum at 1am.

Sat 18 Aug

Slept on verandah of passengers' waiting room until 5am when we were woken up by the arrival of a number of Bombay bound passengers. Had tea and toast at restaurant and left for Rangoon at 0900 hrs. Low cloud & poor visibility for first hour but flying was smooth. However we soon ran into some thick weather and got tossed about badly so turned North and made for the coast; this we followed as far as Chittagong where we flew further inland as we hoped to find better weather. Instead visibility deteriorated and we got tossed around a lot; we climbed high but were unable to get out of it. Altered course again intending to make the Irrawaddy Valley but were unable to cross mountain range owing to low clouds. Returned to coast and followed same towards Rangoon but conditions grew worse so made for Ramree where we landed at 2.50pm. A 5hr 50min flight from Calcutta.

Sun 19 Aug

Stayed on Ramree all day and attended evensong at St John's Church. Padre Keeble took service and Padre Heap gave the address.

Letter to Parents: back in tent, flying 6 hours yesterday, over 2000 miles in last fortnight, in Calcutta on Victory night, little celebration. Bought presents and rugs (being sent on).

Mon 20 Aug

Departed Ramree 8.20am and arrived Mingaladon (Rangoon) at 10.10. Pleasant trip with little cloud – flew down Irrawaddy Valley. Unloaded kit and waited 1½ hours for transport. Taken to 195 Squadron site but found no available accommodation there. Had 'picnic' with Squadron and were kept waiting 2½ hours before being allotted a site for the Squadron in the midst of a rubber plantation. Heavy shower before tents were completely erected; rushed around in 'birthday suit' to carry kit into tent.

Fri 24 Aug

Hitchhiked into Rangoon. Walked up Pagoda Street and visited the Shwe Dagon (the largest pagoda in the world). Took a few snaps there and bought a miniature Buddha carved in wood (Rs 1). Also bought a set of Japanese treasury notes. Had meal at the International Restaurant which cost us Rs 2-4 each (omelette, slice of cucumber and tea). Town badly damaged previously by our bombers.

Japanese Surrender at Rangoon, 26th August 1945. Lt General Numata Takazo and Rear-Admiral Chudo before entering reception tent.

Sat 25 Aug

Busy erecting tents and moved into another tent, ½ mile walk to stream. 3 tent moves. Busy erecting tents for Advance Party. Dave and I fix up water collection. Bitten at least 20 times, literally thousands of mosquitoes.

Sun 26 Aug

Two Jap planes arrive 10am escorted by Squadron of Spits. Took snap as first kite lands. Mad rush to dispersal area in jeep. Took snaps of Jap Commanders before entering reception tent. Newsreel cameramen there – probably in picture. Took close up of Jap commander in car.

Japanese Commanders marching down Main Street, Rangoon.

Thu 30 Aug

Snake enters tent and slithers over Bill's foot whilst he is writing! It eventually hides under my tin box. I pulled the box away smartly and struck its back with a spade. Was only a small non-poisonous snake (about 2ft long). Expect to move shortly to rejoin Squadron.

Japanese Commander in truck.

SEPTEMBER COMMENCED WITH THE SQUADRON SPLIT UP AT FOUR LOCATIONS, AKYAB, TILDA, RAMREE AND MINGALADON. MANY RUMOURS CONCERNING THE FUTURE MOVES OF THE SQUADRON WERE HEARD, BUT IT WAS KNOWN THAT ITS TASK WOULD BE TO ASSIST IN SPEEDING UP THE RESCUE AND REPATRIATION OF ALLIED PRISONERS OF WAR AND INTERNEES. DURING THE FIRST WEEK, THE FLYING PROGRAMME CONCENTRATED ON GETTING THE DETACHMENTS AT TILDA AND RAMREE MOVED TO AKYAB. AS THE PROBABILITY OF THE SQUADRON BEING MOVED TO EITHER RANGOON, BANGKOK OR SINGAPORE WAS CONSIDERABLE, IT WAS DECIDED TO CONTINUE WITH THE MINGALADON DETACHMENT SO THAT IT COULD FUNCTION AS A TRANSIT CAMP FOR SQUADRON PERSONNEL NIGHT-STOPPING THERE.

ON ABOUT THE 7TH OF THE MONTH, W/CDR R.

ALTMAN, DSO, DFC, WHO HAD BEEN THE OFFICER COMMANDING THE SQUADRON SINCE FEBRUARY, LEFT FOR WORLI, BOMBAY TO BE MEDICALLY REPATRIATED TO ENGLAND DUE TO EAR TROUBLE. ON THE 16TH SEPTEMBER, THE NEW C.O., W/CDR B R MACNAMARA JOINED THE SQUADRON AT AKYAB. VERY SOON AFTERWARDS A SIGNAL CAME INTO SQUADRON HQ GIVING ORDERS FOR THE SQUADRON TO MOVE TO KALLANG AIRFIELD AT SINGAPORE. THE SIGNAL ARRIVED ONE EVENING, NEXT DAY WAS SPENT ORGANISING THE MOVE, AND ON THE FOLLOWING ALL AVAILABLE AIRCRAFT COMMENCED THEIR JOURNEY. THIS WAS SCHEDULED FOR AIRCRAFT TO REACH MINGALADON AND NIGHT-STOP THERE, THEN FLY TO PENANG (AFTER CROSSING THE MALAY PENSINSULA AND FLYING DOWN THE EAST SIDE OF IT TO AVOID THE MONSOON ON THE WEST SIDE). FROM PENANG, THE AIRCRAFT WERE TO PROCEED TO SINGAPORE, UNLOAD, THEN RETURN TO PENANG AND NIGHT-STOP THERE. NEXT DAY THEY WERE TO FLY BACK TO AKYAB, OVERFLYING MINGALADON IF THEIR FUEL WAS ADEQUATE. MUCH BAD WEATHER WAS ENCOUNTERED CROSSING THE MALAY PENINSULA FROM RANGOON TO JUST SOUTH OF BANGKOK. SOME CAPTAINS OF THE AIRCRAFT FOUND THAT IT WAS EASIER TO KEEP TO THE WEST OF THE PENINSULA UNTIL THE BAD WEATHER RAN OUT ABOUT HALF WAY TO PENANG.

AT FIRST, ONLY ONE AIRCRAFT WAS STATIONED AT KALLANG WHILE THE REMAINDER CARRIED SQUADRON PERSONNEL AND STORES. WITH VERY LITTLE DELAY, THE SINGLE AIRCRAFT, JOINED AFTER A DAY OR TWO BY OTHERS, BEGAN TO OPERATE IN SUMATRA AND JAVA, TAKING IN SUPPLIES AND BRINGING OUT R.A.W.P.I.

THE ORGANISATION OF THESE OPERATIONS WAS VERY DIFFICULT OWING TO THE LACK OF ANY ARMY ORGANISATIONS TO TAKE OVER THE RESPONSIBILITY FOR MANIFESTING LOADS AND PASSENGERS. THE SQUADRON HAD TO EVOLVE ITS OWN MANIFESTS AND GENERALLY COMBINE THE DUTIES OF A SQUADRON, A R.A.M.O., AND A WELFARE AND INFORMATION BUREAU. HOWEVER, RIGHT FROM THE BEGINNING OF THIS NEW PHASE, THE SQUADRON SUCCEEDED IN OPERATING WITH A HIGH STANDARD OF EFFICIENCY.

MEANWHILE THE DETACHMENTS WERE BEING CALLED IN. ALL PERSONNEL AND STORES AT TILDA WERE FLOWN TO AKYAB, THERE TO BE MANIFESTED AND LOADED FOR PASSAGE TO SINGAPORE. THE DETACHMENT AT MINGALADON CONTINUED TO FUNCTION AS A STAGING POST FOR SQUADRON PERSONNEL. AS IN AUGUST THE LACK OF INTELLIGENCE OFFICERS AND DE-BRIEFING FACILITIES COMBINED WITH THE SPEED OF TURN-AROUND OF OUR AIRCRAFT MEANT THAT THERE WAS NO DE-BRIEFING AND SO THERE ARE NO RECORDS TO COMPILE STATISTICS FROM.

THE ORDERLY ROOM AND SQUADRON HQ REMAINED AT AKYAB DURING THE MONTH BECAUSE ITS FUTURE ACCOMMODATION AT KALLANG HAD NOT BEEN DECIDED UPON. ALL REDUNDANT AIRCREW, SUCH AS AIR BOMBERS, FLIGHT ENGINEERS AND STRAIGHT AIR GUNNERS, WERE POSTED OFF THE SQUADRON TO REDUCE THE NUMBER OF PERSONNEL AND THEIR KIT THAT HAD TO BE TRANSPORTED TO SINGAPORE.

AT THE COMMENCEMENT OF THE MONTH, THE MAJORITY OF SERVICING WAS BEING CARRIED OUT AT TILDA. IT HAD BEEN FOUND NECESSARY,

HOWEVER, TO HAVE A SMALL SERVICING PARTY AT RAMREE CAPABLE OF DOING A RESTRICTED NUMBER OF MINOR INSPECTIONS, AND ANOTHER AT MINGALADON TO ARRANGE FOR TECHNICAL ACCOMMODATION IN THE EVENT OF THE ANTICIPATED MOVE THERE MATERIALISING. WHEN FINALLY A DECISION WAS GIVEN TO MOVE THE SQUADRON TO SINGAPORE, SERVICING WAS WITHDRAWN TO RAMREE LEAVING A REAR PARTY AT TILDA TO TAKE CARE OF AIRCRAFT WHICH WERE THERE AWAITING SPARES.

ON THE 18TH OF THE MONTH, AN ADVANCE PARTY (CONSISTING OF 1 SNCO, 2 CPLS AND 11 AIRMEN) WAS SENT TO SINGAPORE, TO PREPARE FOR THE SQUADRON'S ARRIVAL. THE PARTY SUCCEEDED IN COMPLETING SEVENTEEN MINOR INSPECTIONS BEFORE THE END OF THE MONTH WHEN THE MAIN SERVICING PARTY ARRIVED. (Operations Records AIR 27/354 5/6)

Mon 3 Sep
Left Mingaladon 8.30am and arrived Ramree 10.10am. Pleasant flight although very bumpy for about 10 minutes, fairly cloudy.

Tue 4 Sep
Letter to Pegs, congrats on engagement; re acting corporal. Jap surrender, me on news reel, snaps of Shwe Dagon.

Wed 5 Sep
Letter to Siddie Prince. Moved several times, expect to go home soon. Shall try for leave again and hitchhike by air, may see you at Bangalore.

Thu 6 Sep
Applied for compassionate leave; told to fly to Akyab and get Adjutant's permission. Left Ramree 8.45am and arrived Akyab 9.20. Told that Adjutant was still at Tilda. Continued to Dum Dum in transport plane, intending to fly to Tilda following day (Akyab to Calcutta 2½ hours).

However, the trip was cancelled and we were directed back to Ramree instead.

Spent afternoon and evening in Calcutta; withdrew remainder of my bank account after much persuasion as bank was then closed. Ordered rugs for Bill and shopped at the Hogg Market (bought material and swim suits). Dinner at Firpo's and then listened to a pianoforte recital in YMCA. Returned to Dum Dum 12pm to find all my kit had disappeared! Reported same and eventually found it in the luggage despatch dept! Slept in kite and woke about 6am.

Fri 7 Sep
Left Dum Dum 8am and arrived Ramree 11am. Left Ramree 2.30pm and arrived Akyab 2.55. Spent night at Akyab.

Sat 8 Sep
In the morning found that our Squadron Orderly Room had only just arrived; therefore got pass stamped and railway warrant made at wrong orderly room. Enquired at Staging Post re lift to Calcutta on mail kite but turned down. Explained position to CO and was promised a lift in his kite the following morning. (CO flying to Bombay on repat). Slept in kite, heavy showers during night.

Sun 9 Sep
Left Akyab 7.30am approx. Visibility very poor – rough trip flying about 50ft above sea. Arrive Dum Dum 9.35am. Attended evensong at Cathedral. Booked berth in Madras Mail.

Letter to Parents re leave, flew over 800 miles to get my pass stamped. Catch Madras Mail tomorrow, change twice. Hope to see Siddie in Ooty if lucky.

Mon 10 Sep
Left Calcutta by Madras Mail at 4.20pm.

Wed 12 Sept
Arrived Madras 11am. Had light refreshments in Canteen. Caught the special troop train for Bangalore at 13.10, arrived Bouringhat at 8.30pm. Slept in 1st class waiting room.

Thu 13 Sep

Caught the 9.30 train for Oorgaum and arrived there at 10.10. Was met by Church Caretaker and taken to Parsonage. Introduced to the Patriarch, Mr Griffins Jones on golf course; also called on Mr Rowe to enquire re tennis etc.

The Parsonage at Oorgaum, Kolar Gold Fields. Padre Rowland is standing on steps.

Fri 14 Sep

Went swimming in afternoon. Enjoying leave, will probably stay here for 10 days and hope to meet Siddie in Ooty.

Sat 15 Sep

Visited power house and air cooling plant of Oorgaum gold mine. Cage winches driven by GEC motors and generators. Capacity of air cooling plant:- 160,000 cubic ft per min @ 37 degrees F. Ammonia is compressed and cooled alternately. This cooling action draws off heat from a series of spiral pipes containing brine which are placed in the ammonia system. The cold brine is then passed into the air cooling chamber where it passes through 40 miles of coiled piping which in turn cools the air which passes through it.

Sun 16 Sep

Attended morning prayer and sung Eucharist. Read lesson at Children's Service.

View of the Kolar Gold Fields taken from the top of the Church tower. Bullins Shaft can be seen on left.

Tue 18 Sep

Went down Bullins Shaft in company with 13 others. This shaft is the 3rd deepest in the world being over 9000ft deep. We didn't go below 6,200ft. The cage was jerked violently from side to side as we got low down. At 5,000ft we left the cage and traversed some of the passages. Noted where some of the concrete walls were bulging in through the tremendous pressure. Went down another 1,200ft in an inclined shaft which was much smoother running. Were taken to bottom of air duct where it was reasonably cool. The temperature at the bottom of the mine is approx. 120 degrees F.

Wed 19 Sep

Visited the gold extracting and processing plant. Mighty, power driven hammers pulp the quartz. Water washes the pulped quartz over blankets which collect the small pieces.

Thu 20 Sep
Played tennis in afternoon. Lazy time with 5 servants to wait on me. Hope to meet Siddie in Ooty.

Sat 22 Sep
Letter to Parents writing on verandah: very pleasant leave, spent most of day reading, swimming, tennis. Visit to gold mines. Had tea with confirmation candidates, attended children's services and read lesson. Squadron was moving to Akyab when I left, probably there again! Or may possibly have moved to Rangoon. Stayed at Mission House, advantage being able to invite Siddie there in evenings. Met Siddie in evenings and one afternoon on lake.

Tue 2 Oct
Left Kolar Gold Fields in evening and caught 4.50 train for Bouringhat. Changed here for Madras and had no difficulty in finding a compartment in the 7pm Madras train.

Madras, Hindu Temple.

Wed 3 Oct

Arrived Madras 5.30am. Had light refreshment in WVS Canteen at 7.30 and then went for walk round the city. Spent some time in the WVS rest room drinking iced lime under a fan (very hot day) and later walked to beach. Saw some fishermen pull into shore in their dug out boats – was amazed how they prevented them from turning over. Had Tiffin at the Stewart Canteen and then ambled back to the Station where I spent the rest of the afternoon in the rest room. Boarded Calcutta Mail at 5pm but was later turned off by R.T.O. to make room for ex-prisoners. Luckily met Indian friend with whom I travelled down with; he very kindly invited me to share his compartment with himself and his family. Left 6.20pm Wed.

Sun 7 Oct

Letter to Parents, at Calcutta trying to get air lift – if unsuccessful may have to go by ship – week's delay. Left Parsonage day late, Padre taken suddenly ill – had job getting doc, he assured me he would pull through. Made rapid recovery. Service at Cathedral, staying at transit camp.

Father Douglass of Oxford Mission, Behala, Calcutta.

Mon 8 Oct

Visited Father Douglass of the Oxford Mission at Behala. Found him reading in his 'den'. He lives a very ascetic life, having nothing but a hard wooden bed, chair and table in his 'room'. This room in which he lives is nothing more than a raised concrete platform about 12ft square with a thatched roof above. It has no sides except for some wire netting. Was shown the Church – most impressive and well kept. Promised to call on Rev. Pearson of Audley Chapel when I return.

TRANSPORT COMMAND, ROYAL AIR FORCE

AIR PASSAGE AUTHORITY **N⁰ 688845**

BOOKING REFERENCE...... /......

AUTHORITY has been granted by the Air Priority Authority at the place of issue for the following air passage :—

Rank, Initials, Name.	Service or Department.	Passport or Identity No.	Baggage Allowed.	Flight No.
Cpl. Walker	RAF/4		65#	LS 77
From	Via		To.	
CAL.			Akyab	

When any part of above flight is performed on a Civil Air Line, the cost will be :—

* (A)—chargeable to British Government Funds, viz., to..................................Dept. (unless R.O.A.C. waiver applied to that Dept.)
* (B)—not chargeable to British Government Funds, but recoverable from.................

Delete which is not applicable.

Signature of Issuing Officer.

William s/o

Date Stamp. 8/10/45

(8.8390A) 19,600 Bks. Hw. 8/44

P.T.O.

Cpl Walker's Air Passage Authority from Calcutta to Akyab.

Tues 9 Oct

Left Dum-Dum at 6.30am on mail kite and arrived Comilla at 7.40am. Smooth trip – some cloud. Had char in canteen. Left Comilla at 7.50am and arrived Chittagong at 8.30am. Left Chittagong at 8.45am and arrived Akyab at 9.30am. Spent night at Akyab.

Wed 10 Oct

Left Akyab at 10am and arrived Ramree at 10.20am. Back in 'old tent'.

Aerial View of RAF Kyaukpyu, Ramree Island. (Courtesy of Ian Hall)

AT THE BEGINNING OF OCTOBER THE SQUADRON WAS ENGAGED IN ITS MOVE FROM AKYAB (BURMA) TO SINGAPORE. HOWEVER, MANY SORTIES WERE ALREADY BEING FLOWN, CARRYING ESSENTIAL SUPPLIES INTO AND EVACUATING EX-POW'S EVACUATED FROM THE MANY CAMPS BOTH IN MALAYA AND THE DUTCH EAST INDIES. 17 SORTIES WERE FLOWN TO AND OVER 350 AUSTRALIAN EX POW'S EVACUATED FROM BANGKOK TO BASE.

BESIDES THE ROUTINE WORK FIVE OTHER EXTREMELY INTERESTING TRIPS WERE FLOWN DURING THE MONTH.

1) ON 2ND OCT, A SQUADRON A/C PILOTED BY F/O GRIMMETT CARRIED GEN. SEGHALT AND HIS TWO ADC'S, CAPTS SHAH NAVAG & DHILLON, WHO LED THE I.N.A. FROM MEDAN TO SINGAPORE UNDER ESCORT.

2) W/CDR. REYNOLDS, DABMRAF WAS TWICE FLOWN TO KUCHING IN BORNEO. ON THE FIRST OCCASION (9.10.45) THE PILOT F/L CURRELL HAD THE DISTINCTION OF BEING THE FIRST PILOT TO LAND AN RAF PLANE IN BORNEO SINCE THE JAP OCCUPATION. THIS TRIP RECEIVED A WRITE UP IN ONE OF THE DAILY PAPERS AND MUCH AMUSEMENT WAS DERIVED FROM THE FACT THAT THE REPORTER WHO WROTE THE STORY HAD AWARDED F/L CURRELL WITH THE FICTITIOUS TITLE OF 'INVADER'.

3) IN JAVA F/O BATESON FLEW GEN. SOERKARNO FROM BATAVIA TO SOERABAYA, IN ORDER THAT HE MIGHT BROADCAST AN APPEAL TO THE EXTREMIST ELEMENTS THERE, TO LAY DOWN THEIR ARMS AND CO-OPERATE WITH THE AUTHORITIES UNTIL AN AGREEABLE SETTLEMENT WAS REACHED. THE AIRCRAFT WAS SHOT AT AND HIT BY S/A FIRE BOTH ON LANDING AND TAKE-OFF FROM SOERABAYA AND ONE IR CASUALTY WHO WAS BEING EVACUATED WAS HIT IN THE HIP BY THE FIRE.

4) WHAT MUST BE THE MOST UNIQUE CONSIGNMENT EVER ASSIGNED TO AN RAF CREW SINCE THE FORMATION OF THE ROYAL AIR FORCE WAS CARRIED OUT THIS MONTH. 'CHINESE COMFORT GIRLS' WHO WERE FOUND IN A 'BROTHEL' (WE DON'T KNOW WHO FOUND THEM) AT MEDAN WHERE THEY HAD BEEN FORCIBLY EMPLOYED BY THE JAPANESE AS 'WELFARE FACILITIES' AND HAD BEEN BROUGHT FROM PENANG TO MEDAN BY THE

ENEMY DURING THEIR OCCUPATION, WERE RETURNED TO PENANG FOR 'REHABILITATION' BY OUR AIRCRAFT.

5) F/O GARNETT FLEW A ROUND TRIP OF 7,220 NAUTICAL MILES IN 14 DAYS TO RABAUL, NEW BRITAIN, PAPUA NEW GUINEA.

AT THE BEGINNING OF THE MONTH THE SQUADRON WAS IN THE MIDDLE OF A MOVE FROM AKYAB TO KALLANG. THE ADVANCE PARTY HAD ARRIVED AT THE END OF THE PREVIOUS WEEK HEADED BY W/CDR MACNAMARA. SQUADRON HEADQUARTERS MOVED IN AT THE END OF THE FIRST WEEK AND CAME UNDER THE CONTROL OF 903 WING WHICH LATER IN THE MONTH CHANGED ITS NAME TO RAF STATION KALLANG. THE DISCIPLINE OF THE SQUADRON WAS VERY GOOD, THERE WERE NO CASES OF PERSONNEL OF THIS UNIT BEING APPREHENDED IN BROTHELS. SQUADRON HEADQUARTERS WERE SITUATED IN A PARTIALLY COMPLETED HANGAR ON THE AIRSTRIP AND THE DOMESTIC SITE WAS 2-3 MILES AWAY IN CIVILIAN HOUSES, THE BEST ACCOMMODATION THE UNIT HAD KNOWN FOR MANY MONTHS.

CONSEQUENT UPON THE END OF HOSTILITIES WITH JAPAN, ALL DOMINION PERSONNEL WERE WITHDRAWN FROM THE UNIT THIS MONTH. FOR ALMOST A YEAR, ABOUT ONE THIRD OF THE AIRCREW ON THIS SQUADRON HAD BEEN CANADIAN AND THERE WAS ALSO A GOOD PERCENTAGE OF AUSTRALIAN AND NEW-ZEALAND PERSONNEL.

SINCE THE SQUADRON HAS BEEN SCATTERED AT SEVERAL DIFFERENT STATIONS DURING THIS AND THE PREVIOUS MONTH, IT HAS BEEN IMPOSSIBLE EITHER TO BRING INOCULATIONS AND VACCINATIONS UP TO DATE, OR TO GIVE ANY

LECTURE ON HYGIENE. GOOD PROGRESS IS HOWEVER NOW BEING MADE WITH INNOCULATIONS, AND A CIRCULAR LETTER IN LIEU OF A LECTURE HAS BEEN PREPARED.

AT FFL INSPECTIONS, NO INFECTION WAS FOUND IN THOSE PERSONS AVAILABLE, SHOWING THAT V.D. IS BEING REPORTED AS SOON AS CONTRACTED, AT THE SAME TIME THERE HAS BEEN A REGRETTABLE INCREASE IN THE INCIDENCE OF V.D. ON THIS SQUADRON, SO THAT IT HAS BEEN NECESSARY TO PUT ALL BROTHELS OUT OF BOUNDS, INSTEAD OF ONLY CERTAIN AREAS.

EAR TROUBLE AND DENGUE FEVER HAVE BEEN LESS SINCE ARRIVAL IN SINGAPORE. THERE HAS HOWEVER BEEN AN INCREASE IN FATIGUE AMONG AIRCREW, OWING TO INADEQUATE FOOD AND SLEEP, NECESSITATING SEVERAL OF THEM HAVING TO BE GROUNDED FOR A FEW DAYS TO RECOVER. AT BATAVIA, AIRCREW HAVE ON SEVERAL OCCASIONS HAD TO FLY SIX AND A HALF HOUR SORTIES WITH NO BREAKFAST, POOR RATIONS FOR LUNCH AND AN INSUFFICIENT MEAL ON RETURN TO BASE, A CONSIDERABLE TIME AFTER TOUCHING DOWN. THEY ALSO HAVE BEEN SLEEPING ON STONE FLOORS, WITH NO MEANS OF HANGING UP THEIR MOSQUITO NETS.

ABSENCE OF TELEPHONE OR TRANSPORT, AND DEPLETED MEDICAL STAFF, WITH A HEAVY BURDEN OF STATION DUTIES, HAVE CONSIDERABLY IMPEDED THE PROPER CARE OF THE SQUADRON, AND MANY COMPLAINTS RE SANITATION AND OTHER MATTERS HAVE REMAINED UN-INVESTIGATED FOR UNREASONABLE LENGTHS OF TIME. THE MEDICAL OFFICER REGRETS THIS AND HOPES FOR MORE ASSISTANCE IN THE FUTURE.

THE FACT THAT THE UNIT DOMESTIC SITE WAS
SITUATED NEAR TOWN, LED TO THEIR BEING LITTLE
ORGANISED WELFARE OR SPORTS FACILITIES.
SEVERAL FOOTBALL MATCHES WERE PLAYED HOWEVER
AGAINST SINGAPORE F.C. AND AGAINST SERVICE
TEAMS. ALL THESE MATCHES WERE WON BY THE
UNIT. ABOUT THE MIDDLE OF THE MONTH, THE
'TONG SWIMMING POOL' RE-OPENED AFTER THE
DAMAGE SUSTAINED DURING THE JAPANESE
OCCUPATION HAD BEEN REPAIRED AND FULL USE WAS
MADE OF THE POOL BY UNIT PERSONNEL.

TWO LIBERTY RUNS, ONE FOR SNCO'S AND THE
OTHER FOR AIRMEN WERE MADE NIGHTLY TO 'THE
GREAT WORLD AMUSEMENT PARK' SITUATED IN THE
TOWN. HERE THE RECREATIONAL FACILITIES
INCLUDED DANCING, BOXING, WRESTLING AND
CINEMA SHOWS AS WELL AS THERE BEING AN
ABUNDANCE OF RESTAURANTS AND SHOPS ETC.
(Operations Records AIR 27/354 5/6)

*Taken on the beach at Ramree Island. L to R myself, Bill
Bulcher, Paddy Stanbridge, Jock Johnstone.*

Thu 11 Oct
Trip to Volcano – cannot go, am put in charge of duty crew.

Sat 20 Oct
Letter to Parents: Squadron split up, only 8 of us left, well organised, in hut. Plenty of swimming. Closing down unit. Expect to stay here another week then proceed 1000 miles south by boat as going ahead with Advance Party to Singapore. Expect to be home by Christmas. Expect no mail until I rejoin Squadron.

THIS MONTH (NOV) THE SQUADRON WAS WELL SETTLED IN AT KALLANG (SINGAPORE) WITH A DETACHMENT AT BATAVIA. THIS DETACHMENT CONSISTED OF THE C.O. BOTH FLIGHT COMMANDERS AND THE MAJORITY OF THE PERSONNEL FROM EACH FLIGHT.

THE SQUADRON HEADQUARTERS AND THE SERVICING FLIGHT WAS LEFT AT KALLANG UNDER THE COMMAND OF F/L B.M. CLARKE. THERE WAS STILL A DETACHMENT AT AKYAB, CONSISTING OF ABOUT 80 MEN WITH F/L P. BAKER AS C.O. THE ADMINISTRATIVE SECTION OF THE SQUADRON WAS AT LAST SETTLING DOWN AFTER THREE AND A HALF MONTHS OF CONTINUAL CHANGES OF LOCATION. THE RATE OF RELEASE UNDER A&S GROUPS HAS BEEN INCREASING EVERY MONTH, BOTH OF AIRCREW AND GROUND PERSONNEL; REPLACEMENTS FOR AIRCREW WERE PROMPT AND SUFFICIENT BUT MANY TRADES IN GROUND PERSONNEL WERE SADLY DEPLETED.

APART FROM A FEW MINOR OFFENCES THE DISCIPLINE OF THE SQUADRON WAS VERY GOOD, THE MAIN TROUBLE BEING DRESS REGULATIONS, BUT AS THE SQUADRON HAD ONLY JUST ARRIVED FROM BURMA, THIS WAS UNAVOIDABLE AS THE AIRMEN WERE DEFICIENT OF CLOTHING.

OWING TO THE DISPERSAL OF THE SQUADRON, V.D. LECTURES HAVE BEEN IMPRACTICABLE. ACCORDINGLY A BRIEF PAMPHLET HAS BEEN CIRCULATED THROUGHOUT THE SQUADRON (SEE APPENDIX 2). IT MUST BE EXPLAINED THAT THE "GREAT WORLD" IS AN AMUSEMENT PARK IN SINGAPORE. HOWEVER, THE TERM "GOING TO THE GREAT WORLD" HAS NOW BECOME ALMOST SYNONYMOUS ON THE SQUADRON FOR ANY TYPE OF EVENING SPENT IN TOWN.

APPENDIX 2: BRIEFING FOR SORTIES TO THE "GREAT WORLD"

ARE YOU GOING TO THE BIG CITY TONIGHT, IF SO, REMEMBER THAT WINE AND WOMEN DO NOT GO WELL TOGETHER SINCE, AFTER THE INTAKE OF ALCOHOL, INDISCRETIONS SO OFTEN TAKE PLACE WHICH ARE AFTERWARDS REGRETTED. BEAR IN MIND THAT 99% OF THE WOMEN YOU MAY HAVE CONTACT WITH WILL BE INFECTED WITH ONE OR OTHER OF THE CONTAGIOUS DISEASES, NOT TO MENTION LICE OR SCABIES. IF THE CALL OF NATURE CANNOT BE DENIED, THEN STILL MODERATE THE ALCOHOL SO THAT YOU WILL REMEMBER TO TAKE PROPER PRECAUTIONS.

THE FRENCH LETTER (CALLED ENGLISH LETTER IN PARIS) IS NOT 100% SAFE, EVEN IF IT IS GOOD QUALITY AND DOES NOT BURST, SO USE E.T. AS WELL, BUT IN ANY CASE URINATE, AND USE SOAP AND WATER AS SOON AS POSSIBLE AFTER CONTACT. ABOVE MATERIALS ARE AVAILABLE BOTH AT

THE M.I. ROOM AT THE MAIN GUARD HOUSE, AND AT THE SURGERY.

IT IS COMMON SENSE AS WELL AS AIR FORCE LAW, THAT IT IS IMPERATIVE, IN THE INTERESTS OF BOTH YOURSELF AND OF THE COMMUNITY, TO REPORT ANY SUSPICIOUS SYMPTOMS OR ANXIETY AT ONCE, REPEAT AT ONCE. THE LONGER IT IS DELAYED, THE LESS QUICK, AND THE LESS COMPLETE IS THE CURE; AND THERE IS NO PROTECTION FROM ONE ATTACK, EACH SUBSEQUENT INFECTION WILL TAKE ITS TOLL. YOU SHOULD REPORT A SORE OF ANY KIND, ESPECIALLY ON LIPS, TONGUE OR GENITALS, EVEN IF PAINLESS, OR QUICKLY HEALING. A RASH ALSO MAY OCCUR, AND TAKES MANY DIFFERENT FORMS.

THERE HAS BEEN A REGRETTABLE INCREASE IN THE NUMBERS OF MEN IN THIS SQUADRON WHO HAVE FALLEN VICTIM TO THIS SCOURGE, SO THAT IT HAS NOW BEEN NECESSARY TO PUT ALL BROTHELS OUT OF BOUNDS.

ON 1ST OF NOVEMBER 1945, THE ORIGINAL ADVANCE PARTY FOR THE DETACHMENT AT BATAVIA WAS ENLARGED BY THE ADDITION OF A SKELETON HEADQUARTERS STAFF TO PREPARE FOR LARGE-SCALE OPERATIONS. THIS DETACHMENT WAS NECESSARY BECAUSE THERE WERE INDICATIONS THAT THE INDONESIAN EXTREMISTS WERE PREPARING TO "DECLARE WAR" ON THE BRITISH FORCES IN JAVA.

ON 3RD NOVEMBER ONLY 2 A/C OPERATED, ON THE

4TH, 5TH AND THE 6TH, ONLY ONE. IT WAS ON THE 5TH THAT F/L CURRELL STARTED HIS FLIGHT TO DELHI AND BACK WITH MR DENNING, POLITICAL ADVISOR TO SUPREME COMMAND SEAC. ALTOGETHER F/L CURRELL AND HIS CREW FLEW 41 HOURS IN 4½ DAYS INCLUDING ½ A DAY IN DELHI. (Operations Records AIR 27/354 7/8)

Sat 3 Nov
Letter to Barbara: On Ramree Island, shortly leaving for Akyab. No repat gen until I rejoin Squadron there. Hope to be home in December, easy time. Personal effects parcel sent off. Peggy officially engaged – has been for some time, lovely ring.

Sun 4 Nov
Left Ramree at 5pm and flew to Akyab, arrived there 5.30pm. Raining hard on arrival and got very wet carrying kit to Canteen where we slept that night.

Old canteen in which we lived at Akyab.

Sun 11 Nov

Letter to Parents: At Akyab, leaving for Singapore tomorrow. Must visit orderly room to learn repat gen. Toss up whether I return before Christmas. Repats are posted individually. Hope to see Robert in Singapore. Is Eustace back and when does he return to Business?

Aerial View of Akyab Airfield. (Photo courtesy of Ian Hall)

Dakota DC3 being repaired on PSP (pierced steel plank).

DC3 having a propeller fitted.

Dakota DC3 having been repaired.

Mon 12 Nov
Left Akyab 3am. Very tired, slept on stack of bed rolls which were piled up in front of fuselage. Smooth trip. Arrived Penang 10.30am, had lunch there. Left 11.30 and arrived Selita aerodrome Singapore at 2.30pm. Total flying hours 10. Billeted in private houses near Kallang Airport – quite comfortable. Saw wrestling match at Great World Stadium that evening. Seats cost 2 Dollars.

Wed 14 Nov
Letter to Pegs. Glad to receive your letter. Am glad you spent a happy birthday – when is Dick due out? Flew from Akyab and slept on bed rolls. Doubt whether I shall arrive back before Christmas. Toss up between repat and demob. Trying to contact Robert Caton.

Fri 16 Nov
Bought snake skin handbag dollars 24 (16 pkts cigs), also jade bird D26 (10 pkts). Saw 'Blithe Spirit'.

Sat 17 Nov

Letter to Francis. Hope to be out by end of January. Toss of whether I return by repat or demob. We 'foreigners' are among the few remaining Bachelors of the old gang – however still plenty of girls. Hope to repair Hillman and OY, live at St Albans with Mother & Father. Singapore clean city but cost of living very expensive, fags worth 3/6 a packet. Food scarce, 10s for eggs on toast and tea.

Sun 18 Nov

Took snap of Jap plane dump and of Mosquitoes.

Mosquito FB VI.

Sun 25 Nov

Letter to Parents: re censorship. 31 Squadron mentioned in Telegraph. Re car at Clarks, insure it 3rd party and tax it. Will send cable giving date to tax from, another cable when I am on way. May fly. Robert's ship not in. Out between Jan 1st and Feb 28th. Sent off another personal effects parcel.

Mon 26 Nov

Flew as second pilot and took snaps of docks, town, Cathay building etc. in Singapore.

Mosquitoes. (Note the markings are South East Asia Command having a light blue instead of red centre to the roundel to avoid confusion with the Japanese 'Meatball').

Wed 28 Nov

Attended Forces Fellowship Meeting at Toc H at 8pm. Subject 'The Christian and Social Problems'. Speaker, a Colonel in the Salvation Army.

ALTHOUGH THE SQUADRON WAS STILL OFFICIALLY AT KALLANG DURING DECEMBER, IN POINT OF FACT ONLY A REAR PARTY COMMANDED BY F/LT B.M. CLARKE, AND CONSISTING OF SERVICING FLIGHT AND THE HEADQUARTERS ORGANISATION WERE STATIONED THERE. THE REMAINDER OF THE SQUADRON WAS AT KEMAJORAN AIRFIELD, BATAVIA, JAVA.

SERVICING REMAINED AT KALLANG BECAUSE THE FACILITIES FOR INSPECTIONS, ENGINE CHANGES AND STORAGE OF SPARES WERE IMMENSELY SUPERIOR TO ANYTHING THAT WAS POSSIBLE AT

KEMAJORAN AIRFIELD.

AS AGE AND SERVICE GROUP RELEASE NUMBERS CREEP SLOWLY UPWARDS, MANY MEMBERS ARE BEING WITHDRAWN FOR REPATRIATION.

REPLACEMENTS FOR THE AIRCREW ARE COMING QUICKLY ENOUGH FROM OTHER SQUADRONS THAT HAVE BEEN DISBANDED, BUT UNFORTUNATELY EXPERIENCED GROUND PERSONNEL ARE RARER AND IT REFLECTS GREAT CREDIT ON THE GROUND CREWS THAT THEY GET ALL THEIR WORK DONE ALTHOUGH OVERWORKED.

THERE WAS LITTLE SPORT PLAYED AT SINGAPORE DUE TO THE CLOSE PROXIMITY OF A CITY OF 3,000,000 INHABITANTS. THERE IS A GREAT LACK OF PLAYING FIELDS AND EQUIPMENT BUT BETTER PROSPECTS ARE HOPED FOR AS THE SITUATION QUIETENS DOWN. (Operations Records AIR 27/354 7/8)

Sat 1 Dec
Letter to Pegs: on my way, standing by for repat. Thought boat was worst part of tour. Last flights – took snaps. Hope to meet you and your fiancé soon.

Sun 2 Dec
Letter to Parents. Service at Cathedral. Sent off cable. Due at Calcutta 20th, if very lucky might arrive before and reach home by Christmas. Flying: 5-7 days. Expect me 10 days after last cable. Another cable when I arrive. No luck with meeting Robert.

Mon 3 Dec
Went to Garrison Theatre with Bill, Henry & Dave and saw a three act comedy 'Without a Prince'. Bought a wallet $7 (17 in cigs), bought a table set $10 (8 pkts cigs).

Tin Box weighs 54.5 lbs (this includes kit bag, shoes 1 pair). Less: 2 pairs shorts, 1 pair socks, writing pad, cigarettes, shaving kit, water bottle, shoe brush, webbing, monsoon cape. Bedroll weighs 24.5 lbs, 1 blanket 5.5 lbs, 1 pillow 2¾ lb. Total: 70 ¾ lbs.

Problems of Packing – some of the Kit I had to take with me.

Chapter 7 – Chronology of War:

26th July: Churchill was forced to resign as the Conservative Government ended and Clement Atlee took over as Prime Minister. The Russians were quite bewildered by Churchill's defeat, and Churchill found himself unsuited to address the challenges of peace. Although he had not commanded the respect and trust of the British people all of the time, his rhetoric had explained the struggle as no-one else could and in terms that the Allies could comprehend and relate to. Many American historians were to be more generous in their use of Winston Churchill's quotations than from their own president, Franklin Roosevelt! Of paramount importance was Churchill's personal influence in securing the commitment of American power to the Mediterranean and Europe following Pearl Harbour.

July: The Japanese were subjected to intense shelling and gunfire by guerrillas and the Burmese Defence Army: well over 12,000 Japanese were killed in the massacre in the Pegu Yomas area – a huge range of hills north of Rangoon. Special duty Lysanders were fitted with 150 gallon long-range tanks under the fuselage, increasing their range from 600 to 1250 miles; runways of bamboo matting were constructed in jungle clearings.

2nd August: British forces succeeded in liberating Burma from Japanese control. As the Americans got closer to the Japanese mainland, the Japanese became even more fanatical in their resistance, and many allied planes and ships were lost to the Kamikaze pilots. On 4th August, Mountbatten was able to announce that the Japanese resistance had ended, drawing to a close the bitter campaign in the mountains and jungles of Burma.

6th August: The first atomic bomb was dropped on the city of Hiroshima and 3 days later Nagasaki suffered the same fate.

14th August: The Japanese surrendered unconditionally: 3 years and 8 months after the beginning of the Burma Campaign, the Japanese signed the preliminary surrender arrangements at Rangoon, thus ending the longest campaign fought by the Commonwealth Army on any front.

27th August: Lieutenant-General Numata Takazo, Chief of Staff to Field-Marshal Terauchi at Southern Army Headquarters, went to Rangoon to negotiate the surrender. He took with him Rear-Admiral Chudo of the Imperial Japanese Navy plus two Japanese officers, including a medical lieutenant, and two civilians, Katsumori and Fuji, from the Hakuyo Trading Company, as interpreters.

Naturally enough, accounts of the negotiations differ. The British were intent on showing who was master; the Japanese on showing that they still had muscle. "The senior representative was Lieutenant-General Numata, Chief of Staff to the Supreme Commander, Count Terauchi" wrote Mountbatten, who was represented by Lieutenant-General F.A.M. Browning, his Chief of Staff. "His attitude, and that of his officers, was entirely correct; but there can be no doubt that they had come to Rangoon feeling that they were in a position to bargain over, or at least comment on, the terms which I had laid down for the execution of the surrender." (Mountbatten Report, p.184 para 643, Report to the Combined Chiefs of Staff by the Supreme Allied Command South-East Asia 1943-1945 HMSO 1951.)

As Mountbatten recalls it, Chudo made difficulties by asking for separate naval arrangements, although the Tenth Area Fleet under Vice-Admiral Fukudome, was in fact under Terauchi's direct operational control.

The document laid full responsibility on Terauchi for ordering all his forces to cease fire and ensuring the order was complied with, to remove minefields, to forbid signals between units and to be responsible for maintaining law and order, with Allied forces arriving to take over the various countries of SE Asia.

The Japanese delegation's morale was far more desperate than they allowed it to appear. Tomura, his staff officer, turned to Numata and said, "General, we can only die once. If we take our lives now, even the British will take note of that. There are probably those among them who know we cannot do what is unreasonable. We have potassium cyanide with us. Should we not take our own lives now?"

26-30th Aug: Medical teams and supplies were dropped to POW locations in Burma and Siam (Operation Birdcage and Operation Mastiff).

2nd September 1945: The Japanese officially surrendered on board the USS Missouri.

10th September: The re-occupation of Singapore took place.

12th September: A surrender ceremony took place at Singapore. A wary American medical officer, fearful they might imitate Goering's successful suicide at Nuremberg, had the Japanese delegates' mouths probed before they entered the surrender ceremony. It was even more repellent, Numata recalls, because the officer did not disinfect his hands after each probe with an instrument like a shoe-horn.

Mountbatten did not compel Field Marshall Terauchi to go to Singapore for the surrender ceremony on 12th September. Why should Mountbatten have been so concerned over the fate of Field Marshall Terauchi? It has been suggested that like Terauchi, Mountbatten was a peer of the realm and the heir to a family with a service tradition. Family and personal connections with Great Britain were not lacking in Terauchi's past.

21st September: The last shots were fired in Bolo-Auk, Salween District, well after the Japanese surrender.

31st October: Tiger Force was disbanded.

6th November: The surrender of all Japanese troops in Burma was completed, nearly 72,000 of them. The rest had moved across the hills into Siam and surrendered there.

CHAPTER 8

HITCHING HOME BY PLANE
DEC 1945 – JAN 1946

Editor's Note:

After 15 days in Singapore, where he did quite a bit of shopping (I fortunately have inherited the snake skin handbag and other items), Peter left on 4th December bound for Dum Dum (Calcutta) via Penang and Akyab – a total of 1715 miles which took nearly three days. The British forces were obviously not that welcome in India by then as in the Calcutta area there were mounted police and Peter was told to quit India many times.

Christmas was spent in Dalbhumgarh, and Peter again helped with the Christmas activities, this time their slogan was 'Roll on the Boat'. Together with a colleague, Peter helped to treat a native baby over several days – one of the 'Untouchables'. Whilst at RAF Dalbhumgarh, he travelled by train to Jamshedpur to visit Tata, the largest steel works in the Empire at that time (now the owners of Jaguar/LandRover).

There was a problem with the Air Trooping Scheme causing considerable delays in getting personnel back home, explained to the troops by Air Marshall Goddard, but Peter appears to be one of the lucky ones chosen to fly to RAF Mauripur at Karachi.

31 Squadron had historical connections with Karachi as it was based in the north-west frontier of India from its formation in 1915 until it moved to the Far East in 1942. At the end of the war, after being stationed in Java, the squadron then moved back to be based in Mauripur during the independence and partition period when their job was ferrying refugees: Muslims from south to north and Hindus in the opposite direction.

From Karachi, Peter would fly for many days across the Middle East and Europe, before finally reaching RAF St Mawgan, Cornwall on 26th January

1946. His term of service officially ended in July 1946 but he wasn't finally discharged from the RAF until June 1959.

But, after a massive correspondence of 178 letters, Peter would not be going home to his girlfriend, Peggy Caswell, as in September 1945 she had become engaged to an RAF Officer. On the 1ˢᵗ December Peter writes to her that he hopes to meet her and her fiancée soon.

Tue 4 Dec
Left Kallang Airport, Singapore at 3pm. Arrived Butterworth (Penang) at 6pm. Smooth passage all the way. Had dinner in combined officers/airmens mess. Service very poor – had to wait half an hour before being served. Small helpings and cold when served!

Dinner consisted of:

Pea soup
Filleted fish
Chicken, sweet potatoes, veg
Fruit salad
420 miles, total flying hours 3.

Wed 5 Dec
Breakfast at 7.30am. Another long wait! Consisted of:- 2 eggs and one small slice of sweet potato, 1 cup of tea.

Left Butterworth at 10.00am, arrived Akyab at 5pm. Long and tiring trip – slept part of way. Very bumpy for five minutes when passing through some dense clouds over a mountaineous region. Followed coast most of way. Scenery rather monotonous. Flew over miles and miles of jungle so thickly covered with trees that only the tops could be seen.

980 miles, total flying hours 7.

Letter to Barbara: on way, probably get held up in Calcutta a few weeks. Not due at trooping centre till 20th, lucky so far. Missed Robert in Singapore. Looking forward to seeing you early next year.

Thu 6 Dec

Left Akyab 9.15am and arrived Dum Dum 11.30. Taken to 35 PTC Ballygung. Billeted in Nissan Huts.

315 miles, total flying hours 2.15.

Singapore to Calcutta total of 1715 miles.

Fri 7 Dec

New identity card. Ordered 12 months supply of tea from Brooke Bonds. Sent off two rugs.

Sat 8 Dec

Saw 'Arsenic & Old Lace' at Tiger Cinema. Big Congress meeting on Madan Street, trams and buses packed. Was told to Quit India many times that day!

Sun 9 Dec

My birthday! Received Holy Communion at 8.30. Sung Eucharist service at Cathedral. Lunch at Firpo's. Visited Fr Douglass at Oxford Mission in afternoon, and attended Children's Service. Took snaps and stayed to tea with Sisters. Attended Evensong at Cathedral and afterwards went to Forces Social in Calcutta Club, where we had community singing.

Mon 10 Dec

Paraded at 9am with kit. Loaded same on gharri and drove to station. Had to re-arrange load on way. Many wogs gathered in Dalhousie Square. Mounted police out. Left by troop train at 3pm and arrived Dalbhumgarh about 8pm, serious delay. Some chaps been here for days. Entertainment – pictures only. Comfortable billets here, food poor.

Thu 13 Dec

Informed on parade of temporary breakdown of Air Trooping Scheme.

Interviewed CO with intention of transferring from repat to demob. Signal being sent off to BAFSEA. Reply probably in 5 days.

Sat 15 Dec
Officially posted to HQ Karachi but still at Dalbhumgarh.

Letter to Parents: Christmas greetings, little hope of returning by then. At ATC awaiting kite to fly us to Karachi. Only 2 kites left since I arrived, over 600 in front. Interview with CO, trying to transfer to demob quicker and save £20. Little chance awaiting signal. Present system unfair. Some chaps home after 3.5 years, others 4 and still here.

Sun 16 Dec
Attended Morning Service at No. 1 Site. Went to Chakulia in evening to attend Evensong. Bought sweets, glucose D, cheese, razor set etc from Canteen.

Wed 19 Dec
Hitchhiked by rail into Jamshedpur. Travelled most of way in Engine. Rather slow. Arrived at Tata Institute in time for Tiffin. Shopped in afternoon and bought: 2 photo albums, 8 pkts corners, 3 towels, rug, padlock, hooka, 2 prs canvas shoes, case. Stayed night at Institute very comfortable. Food excellent. Tennis, badminton, swimming, billiards, table tennis etc.

Thu 20 Dec
Visited Tata Steel Works in morning – most interesting. These are the largest single steel works in the British Empire. Saw engine wheels being made. Left by the 9.45 train and arrived back at Dalbhumgarh about 1am. Still no gen from HQ re transfer; almost certain to be demobbed when I return. Probably here for another 3 or 4 weeks.

Sun 23 Dec
Attended morning service at 10.30. Went to Chakulia in evening for Carol Service.

Mon 24 Dec
When returning from Orderly Room across paddy fields, John and I came across a little baby who was covered with scabies sores. Cow dung was plastered all over them – apparently to prevent the disease from spreading. John suggested treating it so we returned to camp for soap

and ointment and arranged for warm water to be fetched from the village. Took over half an hour washing cow dung from sores – baby was howling all the time! Covered sores with Milton ointment and bandaged legs and hands. John gave his pants to baby which covered it up to its chin! Promised to come again in two days time.

John holding the baby, with other 'Untouchables'.

Tue 25 Dec

Holy Communion at 9am. After the Christmas dinner, John and I fed about 40 'untouchables' down near the local village. Gave them curried meat, rice and spices which were all cooked together by the dhassi contractor. Looks like another 3 weeks here.

Fri 28 Dec

Treated Baby again on outskirts of village. Gave it a thorough washing with soap and water and covered sores with Eusole. Bandaged up legs, arms and buttocks. Many of the village males watch on! Others come for treatment. Padre's hour in evening followed by gramophone recital.

'Roll on the Boat', Christmas at Dalbhumgarh 1945.

Sat 29 Dec

Afternoon walk with John and friend to river where we had a pleasant swim.

Sun 30 Dec

Morning service taken by lay reader – good address. Dressed child in afternoon. Attended evening service.

Mon 31 Dec

Air Marshall Goddard visits us to give reasons for breakdown of Air Trooping:

(1) 1500 Dakotas and 500 Skymasters promised for RAF were not handed over.

(2) Lack of Dak spares.

(3) Halifax & Sterlings taken off Air Trooping. Halifax need too much maintaining and catch fire easily and electric motors on Sterling give trouble in tropical weather.

(4) Lack of suitably trained aircrew.

(5) Bad weather.

(6) Liberators now carrying only 18 passengers instead of 28.

Sat 5 Jan
John, George, Joe and I go for day's trek into Jungle. Left 9.30am. Entered forest after leaving villages behind and continued up valley. Saw elephant dung and spore marks of a tiger or leopard on the bank of a watering spot. Had tiffin in pleasant valley. George chatted with some villagers on way home – were shown some bows and arrows. Slipped whilst climbing over rocks and sprained ankle rather badly (very painful that night).

Sun 6 Jan
Attended morning service at 10.30am. My name was called out on day's airlift, so reserve was sent in my place! Went to Chakulia in evening to attend evening services.

Mon 7 Jan
Paid No. 205!! Apparently got an extra month's pay. Treated child who is getting better and took snaps. Packed food parcel.

Tue 8 Jan
No air lift.

Wed 9 Jan
96 on air lift – I am included in first 12! Left Dalbhumgarh at 1.15pm and arrived at Chakulia 2pm. Weighed in (50 lbs & 30 lbs). Beds already made – very comfortable. First class bar here – best I've seen in India.

Thu 10 Jan
Waiting for air lift to Karachi. 2 kites leave but none of our crowd go. 4 kites scheduled to leave tomorrow – am on first (KJ 934)[a Dakota IV].

Fri 11 Jan
Depart Chakulia at 8.30am, arrived Palam at 1.30pm. Had quick lunch

and returned to kite immediately. Took off 2.15pm and arrived Mauripur (Karachi) at 5.30. Saw snow covered Himalayan mountains as we approached Palam; flew into bird. Passed over Alahabad & Jodphur. Billeted in large air conditioned huts with three tiered beds. Chakulia to Mauripur 1238 miles.

Sat 12 Jan
Visited Karachi, meal at YMCA. Shopping – bought 3.5 yards of silk and 4 yards of cotton and a watch. Here in Karachi for 5-7 days.

Sun 13 Jan
Attended gospel service. Visited Ron Ayres in evening and went with him to evening service.

Mon 14 Jan
Sprained ankle is swollen and painful – reported sick.

Tues 15 Jan
Had left ankle x-rayed at Karachi hospital, found to be OK.

Wed 16 Jan
Am posted on air lift tomorrow in Liberator (128) carrying 24 passengers. Driven 5 miles to army transit camp. Passed many orange groves, gharries keep to right. Exchange some currency, £1 = 1000mils.

Thu 17 Jan
Take off 0610, arrived Shaibah (Iraq) 1335. Turning points Jiwini (India), Jask, Sharjah, Bahrein (Arabia) (7 hrs 30 mins).

Take off 1500, arrived Lydda 1930 (5.30pm standard time). Turning points Habsyah (near Baghdad) (4hrs 30mins).

Very cramped in Bomb Bay, no windows. Smooth trip to Shaibah. Took snap of desolate, hilly country near River Jordan. Saw Dead Sea in distance. Billeted in tents. Averaged 180mph.

Fri 18 Jan
Departed Lydda 1305 and arrived El Aden 1705 (near Tobruk,

Cyrenaica). Flew over sea practically all the way with coastline just visible. Port engine out momentarily – probably due to empty tank. Last 20min of flight took us over the old battle ground – saw the remains of some artillery equipment, etc. Endless view of sand. Had excellent meal on arrival – served by German waiters. Very comfortably billeted, four in room – beds already made – hot showers. Cold during night.

Sat 19 Jan
All aircraft grounded owing to bad weather over Sardinia.

Letter to Parents: At El Aden, held up owing to bad weather. Hope to be home before this reaches you. Unable to send cable. Transit camps excellent.

Sun 20 Jan
Board aircraft at 8am for early take off but were recalled after run up at end of runway owing to bad weather en route. Spent morning in control building. Another attempt was made at 3pm but this time a mag drop on the port engine prevented us taking off. Taken down to the accommodation site again. Attended evening service in Nissan hut chapel – very nicely constructed.

Mon 21 Jan
Took off 9.10am from El Aden and arrived Catania (Sicily) 12.10. Smooth trip – flew along North African coast a considerable way. Sea along coast covered with black crude oil. Poor billets – no sheets issued – two tiered beds. Visited town, very dirty and damaged considerably by bombing. Bought some oranges and lemons. Exchanged currency 400 lire = £1. (600 miles, 4 hrs.)

Tue 22 Jan
No take off owing to bad weather over Europe.

Wed 23 Jan
Ditto

Thu 24 Jan
Ditto

Fri 25 Jan

Took off 7.30am and arrived Marseilles 1.15pm. Bumpy in places, flew over Sardinia. Very cold here, billeted in old hospital quarters. Went to pictures in local town in evening.

Sat 26 Jan

Left Marseilles 2pm, took snap of aerodrome from air. Plenty of cloud and slightly bumpy. Light fall of snow over a large area of France – mostly south – lakes frozen. Temp -4 degrees. Speed 170 ground MPH. 40 mins ahead of schedule, expect to arrive St Mawgan, Cornwall 17.30 GMT.

DC2/3 at aerodrome on way home.

Chapter 8 – Chronology of War:

Jan 1946: Mutinies occurred, shaking the British government out of its lethargy. India was a vitally important military resource for Britain and its Empire, having an inexhaustible supply of manpower together with a fully functional army, air force and naval bases. Back in August 1942 when Congress passed its 'Quit India' resolution and wanted the immediate dismantling of the Raj, hundreds of Congress leaders were arrested and violent protests broke out causing the Viceroy, Lord Linlithgow, to describe the disorder as "the worst since the Mutiny". Order was restored by the Indian Police and the still loyal Indian Army.

Paul Scott's *Raj Quartet* was a mirror of the long British-Indian affair in which he felt the resentment of Indians at the ruthless suppression of Gandhi's Quit India Movement, "... a country whose history had been that of our own for more than three hundred years and which contributed more than any other to our wealth or well-being". David Holloway writing in *The Telegraph* of 1975 said that "In 100 years' time when men are wondering what India in the 1940s was like, they should read Mr Scott's 'Raj Quartet' for a portrait of the real India in a way no formal history could".

Apparently in the middle of January, a mutiny took place amongst British RAF servicemen infuriated by delays over demobilisation and repatriation, presumably due to the breakdown of the Air Trooping Scheme.

August 1946: Calcutta rioted for several days and some 5,000 were killed and 15,000 injured. The Viceroy at the time, Wavell, warned that the Raj would progressively be unable to remain in control and that it was time to escape from the burdens of Empire. Wavell was one of the few to consider the complex problems of Anglo-Indian relations. Lady Manners in Paul Scott's *The Jewel in the Crown* observed that "...the creation of Pakistan is our crowning failure... and they should never have got rid of Wavell".

Wavell succeeded Lord Linlithgow in 1943 as India's last but one

Viceroy, probably the most difficult tenure that any Viceroy had had to face. Wavell was good as the Viceroy and gained a reputation as a humane man as he did something about the Bengal Famine whereas Lord Linlithgow did not manage to achieve much. He vigorously promoted co-operation between Indian Muslims and the Raj. However, Sabhas Chandra Bose managed to recruit about 50,000 Indian prisoners-of-war from Japanese prison camps and for a time the Indian National Army was quite detrimental to Britain's war effort: a non-Gandhian way of opposing the Raj.

Wavell was rather summarily dismissed from his position and replaced by Lord Louis Mountbatten in 1947, who then proceeded to wind up the Raj with the agreement of all parties concerned. He had less than five months to accomplish a transfer of power of intense complexity and significance. The problem was that many Britons at home were totally indifferent and ignorant of Indian affairs and this may well have led to the dividing up of India in 1947. Although Lord Mountbatten, India's final Viceroy, cared about Indian unity, he failed to carry this out.

However, the legacy that the Raj left for India was an amazing infrastructure of roads, railways, telegraph, High Court, colleges for education to university standard, state legislature for democratic government as well as the English language.

APPENDIX A

DIARY DETAILS OF FLIGHTS, JULY 1943 – NOV 1945

(1) RAF BAIRAGARH, BHOPAL, July – October 1943

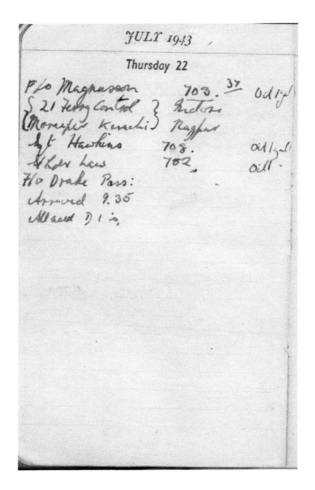

Thu 22 July   F/O Magnusson 703 oil 1 gall; S 21 Ferry Control, Indore,
Mauripur Karachi, Nagpur Sgt Hawkins 708 oil 1 gall
S/Ldr Law 702 oil 1 gall
F/O Drake, Pass; Arrived 9.35
all need DI's.

| Sat 24 July | AN 783 100 Oct; |
| | AN 127 3 galls oil |

AN 660 100 Oct, 3 galls oil

Douglas DC3 100 Oct, oil 4 galls port, 3½ galls starboard, 342 galls.

Wed 4 Aug   AN750, 94, 100 Oct

AN 650, 104, 100 Oct

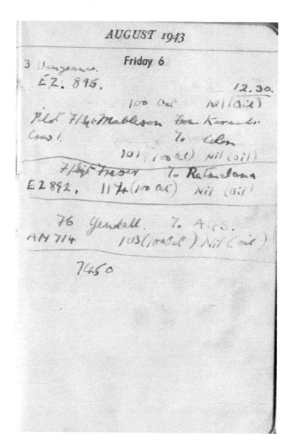

Fri 6 Aug   3 Vengeance:

EZ 895, 101 (100 Oct), nil (Oil)

Pilot F/Sgt Mableson from Karachi to Cahors, Crew 1

EZ 892, 114 (100 Oct), nil (Oil)

Pilot F/Sgt Fraser to Ratmalana

AN 714 103 (100 Oct), nil (Oil)

76 Yendall to AGS

Sat 7 Aug	FH 264,
	Pilot P/o Forman, Crew 3, Pass 3
	Tanjore, 210 (96) 35

Tue 10 Aug   FE 677

Pilot F/Sgt Sadler from Karachi to Ratmalana, 1 Pass

49 (90 Oct) ½ gall

FE 547

Pilot W/o Menzies 51, ½ gall

FE 683

Pilot Sgt Morgan 48, ½ gall

Wed 11 Aug   FK 441

F/Sgt Hall from Allahabad, 22 FC

Fri 13 Aug   FK 130

Hudson

Pilot, Crew, Pass

Sat 14 Aug   FK 730

4 galls oil, 170 (90 Oct), 14 (100 Oct)

Flew in Hudson on D.F. test. Up for 3 hrs 10 min.

Very cloudy and visibility poor at times.

Had difficulty flying through to station owing to low cloud –
success on 6th attempt.

Flew over rivers and mountains.

Thu 14 Oct   Flt/Sgt Thompson, Ahmedabad to Allahabad, 23 F.C.

APRIL 1945

TUESDAY 24

Flew to Taungtha on supply trip. Kite B. (DC IV) Pilot W.O. Curtis. Cargo Petrol. F. Time 3 hrs 20 min (½ hr night)

Left Hathazari 14.45
Arrived Taungtha 17.15
Left " 17.30
Arrived Myingyan 17.40
Left " 17.45
Arrived Taungtha 18.05 Crossed
Left " 18.10 Chins &
Arrived H.— 19.50 Arakan hills.

Flew through smoke of Jungle fire: crossed Irrawaddi just below the joining of the Chindwin river. passed Mount Popa (5000 ft) (the home of the King Cobra which was recaptured from the Japs a few days ago) Flew through clouds & rain — bumpy at times. Brought back 20 10 Rs Mobile canteen at Taungtha

---

Tue 24 Apr   Flew to Taungtha (near Mandalay) on supply trip. Kite B (Dakota DC IV),
Pilot W.O. Curtis, cargo petrol. Flight time 3 hrs 20 mins (½ hr night)

Left Hathazari	1445
Arrived Taungtha	1715
Left Taungtha	1730
Arrived Myingyan	1740
Left Myingyan	1745

Arrived Taungtha hills	1805	Crossed Chino and Arakan
Left Taungtha	1810	
Arrived Hathazari	1950	

Flew through smoke of jungle fire: crossed Irrawaddy just below the joining of the Chinwin River. Passed Mount Popa (5,000ft), the home of the giant King Cobra snake which was recaptured from the Japs a few days ago. Flew through clouds and rain – bumpy at times. Brought back 20 IOR's [Indian Other Ranks]. Mobile canteen at Taungtha.

Sun 29 Apr — Engine change on U. Flew on air test with C.O. (throttles vibrated back during take off!).

Tue 1 May — Flew on afternoon sortie to Myitcha (on west bank of Irrawaddy).
Left Hathazari 1540, climbed to 1,000 feet but were unable to get above thick bank of cloud.
Severe bumps experienced for about 10 minutes.
Rate of climb indicator registered 2,000ft per minute.
Climb one minute and a few seconds later would drop to 2,000ft per minute descent!
Cargo 7,000 lbs tinned milk.
Arrived Myitcha 1720. Left 1745.
Flew further north to miss densest part of cloud and climbed to 15,000ft at which height we just managed to pass over the thick banks of clouds.
Arrived 1945.
Kite (H), Mark IV, Pilot W.O. Curtis.

(3) RAF KYAUKPYU, RAMREE ISLAND, JUNE 1945

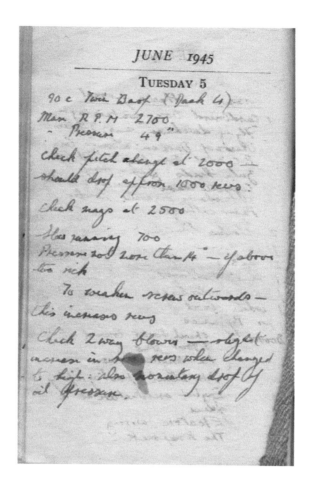

Tue 5 June

90c Twin Wasp (Dack 4)
Max RPM 2700
Max pressure 49"
Check pitch change at 2000 – should drop approx. 1000 revs.
Check mags at 2500, Slow running 700.
Pressure not more than 14" – if above too rich.
To weaken screw outwards – this increases revving.
Check 2 way blower – slight increase in revs when changed to high, also momentary drop of oil pressure.

(4) RAF AKYAB, NOV 1945

Fri 9 Nov   60** (60 hour servicing) inspection on kite which is to fly us to Singapore.

(5) SELITA AERODROME, SINGAPORE, NOV 1945

Sun 18 Nov   60** inspection at Selita aerodrome, Singapore.

Sun 25 Nov   60** inspection on 'Y'. Repair broken cable controlling oil shutter.

Mon 26 Nov   Inspection completed. Air tested at 4.30pm. Flew as second pilot and took snaps of docks, town, Cathay building etc. in Singapore.

APPENDIX B

DIARY DRAWINGS OF DESIGNS FOR PLANE PARTS/SERVICE TOOLS – MAY 1945

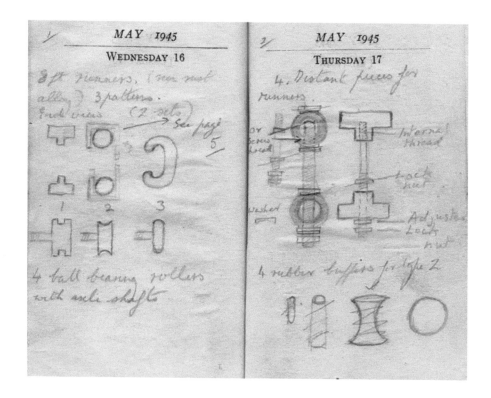

6 strengthening pieces

2 end pieces

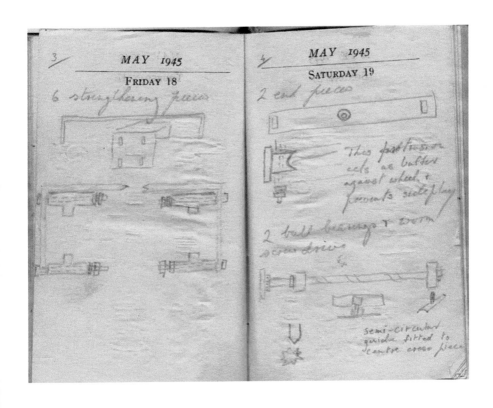

This flat portion acts as buffer against wheel & prevents side play

2 ball bearings + worm screwdrive

semi-circular guide fitted to centre cross piece

SUNDAY 20

6 cross pieces
12 ˮ ˮ

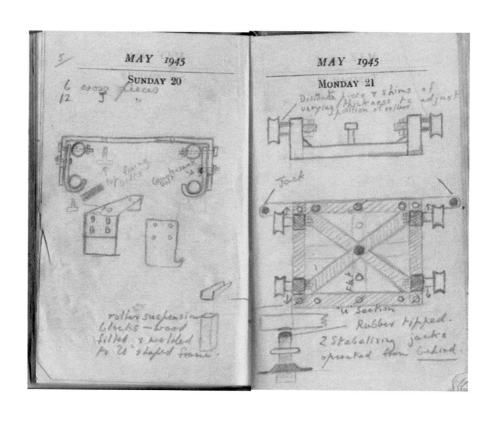

roller suspension
blocks — wood
fitted & moulded
to "U" shaped frame.

MONDAY 21

Distance piece + shims of
varying thickness to adjust
position of rollers.

Jack

Flat

"U" Section
Rubber tipped.
2 Stabalising jacks
operated from behind.

APPENDIX C:

DIARY AND OPERATIONS RECORDS DESCRIPTIONS OF PLANES: 1942 – 1945

ANSON

AVRO 3-seat monoplane general reconnaissance and fighter aircraft, in use by the RAF for many years before the war. Its famous predecessor was the Avro 504 biplane. Two Armstrong Siddeley Cheetah engines each of 350hp of unlimited endurance which stand up to hardest usage without developing defects. Max speed 188mph, range 790 miles. One forward gun and one gun in turret, bomb-load of 360 lb.

ARGUS

FAIRCHILD light communications aircraft supplied to Britain under Lend-Lease arrangements from 1941 onwards. Single 145hp Super Scarab engine, max speed 112mph, range 720 miles.

AUSTER

BRITISH TAYLORCRAFT 3-seat Air Observation Post light cabin monoplane. One 145hp de Havilland Gipsy Major VII engine. Max speed 124mph.

AUDAX

HAWKER 2-seat Army Co-operation biplane, adapted from the Hart. Total production for RAF of 624 when construction ended in 1937. One 530hp Rolls Royce Kestrel in-line piston engine. Max speed 170mph. One forward-facing machine gun and one Lewis gun on flexible mount in rear cockpit plus 4 x 20lb bombs or 2 x 112lb supply containers on underwing racks.

BEAUFIGHTER

BRISTOL 2-seat night fighter or anti-shipping Whispering Death.strike-fighter combining long range and horsepower with hitting power. Twin engines of Bristol Hercules (radial engines with sleeve valves). Top speed over 330mph, range of 1,500 miles. Four cannon mounted in central fuselage and 6 machine guns in wings. Known as *Whispering Death* by Japanese troops because of the unique quietness of the sleeve valve engines.

BEAUFORT

BRISTOL 4-seat torpedo-carrying bomber also used for mine-laying, photography and reconnaissance duties. An anti-shipping plane equipped with radar from quite early on in the war. It was very rare in India. Two Bristol Taurus engines, sleeve-valve units, top speed 270mph. Air-borne torpedo attack.

BLENHEIM

BRISTOL 3-seat mid-wing monoplane, the first multi-seat bomber to come into action in WWII. Two 840hp Bristol Mercury engines, top speed 260mph, range 1,125 miles. Both forward-firing and rear-firing guns and can carry small bombs. Used for daylight raids combining speed with load-carrying capacity. The backbone of Britain's day bombing fleet.

CORNELL

FAIRCHILD Single-engined monoplane, it was the Canadian-built version of the USAAF's PT-19 and PT-26 primary trainers. One 175 or 200hp Ranger engine, max speed 124mph, range 420 miles.

DAKOTA

DOUGLAS Military transport with a crew of 3 and 28 troops, manufactured in Santa Monica, California. This great workhorse aircraft served in every battle zone of the war and was the mainstay of both RAF and USAAF transport squadrons. Dakotas were active on all fronts as glider-tugs, para-troop carriers, personnel transports, freighters and ambulances. They also played an important part in the Berlin Airlift of 1948-49. Two Pratt & Whitney Twin Wasp engines, max speed 230mph, range 1,500 miles.

Developed as a military transport from the 21-seater DC-3 commercial airliner, which first flew in December 1935, the aircraft first entered service with the USAAF as the C-53 Skytrooper in October 1941, followed by the C-47 Skytrain in January 1942. The RAF operated over 1,200 of these aircraft and called it the Dakota, the name allegedly deriving from 'Douglas Aircraft KOmpany Transport Airplane'. The aircraft became an icon and President Eisenhower reckoned it was one of the primary elements in winning the war (the others being the Jeep, the bazooka and the atom bomb).

In June 1942, Dakotas joined 31 Squadron on the Burma front, replacing Douglas DC-2s and elderly Valentias. In Burma, Dakotas of Nos. 31 and 194 Squadrons played a large part in supplying the Chindits.

DEFIANT

BOULTON PAUL 2-seat turret fighter. A single Rolls Royce Merlin engine of 1,030hp. Max speed 303mph. Four Brownings machine guns in power-operated turret.

EXPEDITER

BEECH 6/8-seat communications and light transport aircraft. Built in USA as military variant of Beech 18 civil transport and first flown in 1941. Total of 411 supplied to Britain under

Lend-Lease and used largely in SEAC. Two 450hp Pratt & Whitney Wasp Junior engines, max speed 230mph, range 900 miles.

HART   HAWKER 2-seat biplane light day-bomber that first entered RAF service in 1930 and was withdrawn from front line service in UK in 1938 but at outbreak of war continued to be operational in Middle East. One 525hp Rolls Royce Kestrel in-line piston engine. Max speed 184mph, range 470 miles. 1 forward-firing machine gun and 1 Lewis gun in aft cockpit and up to 520lbs of bombs.

HARVARD   NORTH AMERICAN 2-seat advanced trainer. One Pratt & Whitney Wasp engine of 550hp. Top speed 206mph, range 730 miles. Characteristic rasping note caused by its direct-drive propeller with high tip speeds when in flight.

HUDSON   LOCKHEED 5-seat maritime general reconnaissance and transport aircraft. One of the outstandingly successful aircraft of the war, it was the first US designed and built machine to go into action with the RAF. Good performance, handling and robust. Chased submarines and fought off every aircraft which tried to raid the British convoys across the Atlantic. Many of the Hudson VIs were converted for transport work, with the turrets removed, serving in the Far East. Two Wright Cyclone engines of 1,100hp. Top speed over 260mph, range 2,000 miles. Twin forward guns, twin guns in dorsal turret, one gun in ventral position and bomb-load of 1,000lb.

HURRICANE	HAWKER single-seat fighter-bomber first manufactured in 1937 which formed the mainstay of RAF defences in the war for escorting and sweeps over occupied territory. The most heavily-armed single seater fighter in the world during WWII. One 1,280hp Rolls Royce in-line piston engine, 2 speed supercharger for aiding performance at height. Max speed 335mph.
KITTYHAWK	CURTISS single-seat fighter-bomber developed from the Tomahawk, it first entered service with the USAAF in May 1941 under the designation P-40D. One 1,600hp Allison engine, max speed 362mph, range 1,000 miles. Armament: 6 guns in wings and provision for 1,000lb of bombs.
LEOPARD MOTH	DE HAVILLAND 3-seat high-wing cabin monoplane.
LIBERATOR	CONSOLIDATED 8-seat (up to 9) American B-24 heavy bomber with a wing span of 110 feet, making it one of largest bombers built in the USA. Four Pratt & Whitney Twin Wasps engines of 1,200hp. 320mph top speed and range of 3,000 miles.
LIGHTNING	LOCKHEED single-seat twin-engined fighter, it was famous as the P-38 of the USAAF. It was a very effective low-level attack aircraft. Two Allison liquid-cooled engines of 1,150hp, top speed of 400mph, range 1000 miles. Good fire power and performance.
LODESTAR	LOCKHEED used for general transport duties, it was the RAF version of the USAAF's C-56, C-59 and C-60. Two 1,000hp Wright Cyclone or two 750hp Pratt & Whitney Hornet engines. Max speed 272mph, range of 1,890 miles.

LYSANDER	WESTLAND 2-seat monoplane Army Co-operation aircraft used for message-dropping and picking up/dropping of supplies by parachute and artillery observation; it had been in service since before the war. Bristol Perseus XII engine, top speed 230mph, range of 600 miles. Armament: 2 machine guns in wheel spats, 2 guns on housing in rear cockpit plus light bombs on wings.
MARTINET	MILES 2-seat, first seen in April 1944, it was the RAF's first target-tug. One 870hp Bristol Mercury radial piston engine, max speed 240mph, range 694 miles. No armament.
MITCHELL	NORTH AMERICAN AVIATION 5-seat light bomber. Two 1,350hp Wright Double-Row Cyclone GR-2600 engines. Max speed 292 mph, range 1,635 miles. It was good at attacking ground targets in support of ground troops.
MOHAWK	CURTISS single-seat tactical reconnaissance and ground attack American fighter, being the earlier version of the Tomahawk. A single Allison engine of 1,040hp. Max speed of 345mph and range of 730 miles. Although obsolete by 1941, it was retained by the RAF for use in India and Burma.
MOSQUITO	DE HAVILLAND 2-seat fighter-bomber/high level reconnaissance aircraft. Two Rolls-Royce Merlin 1,230hp engines, max speed 380mph, range 1,205 miles. Although not quite as fast as a Spitfire, it was considerably faster than most other Allied or enemy aircraft. However, the wooden construction of the plane was to prove a serviceability problem in Burma because of the extreme climate of the summer monsoons and

the numerous termites. Armament: 8 guns forward and 2 x 500lb bombs in fuselage plus 2 x 500lb bombs under wings.

OXFORD · AIRSPEED 3-seat advanced trainer with 2 x 370hp Armstrong Siddeley Cheetah X engines. Max speed 188mph. In November 1937 it became the RAF's first twin-engined monoplane advanced trainer. To aircrews it was known as the *Ox-box.*

PUSS MOTH · DE HAVILLAND 3-seat high-wing cabin monoplane.

PROCTOR · PERCIVAL 3 to 4-seat radio trainer and communications aircraft. One 210hp de Havilland Gipsy Queen II inline piston engine. Max speed 160mph, range 500 miles. No armament.

RELIANT · STINSON 5-seat high-wing cabin monoplane.

SPITFIRE · SUPERMARINE single-seat fighter of Battle of Britain fame which was to prove superior to the Japanese Zero and Oscar fighters. Spitfire Vs began operations in Burma in October 1943. One 1,440hp Merlin engine, max speed 374mph, range 1,000 miles. Armament: 4 guns plus one 500lb bomb.

TIGER MOTH · DE HAVILLAND 2-seat biplane of 1930's design of steel tubing construction with fabric covering. One de Havilland Gipsy Major engine of 130hp, max speed 109 mph. Robust, simple aircraft suited to elementary training.

TOMAHAWK · CURTISS single-seat tactical reconnaissance and ground attack fighter which developed from the earlier Mohawk. One 1,040hp Allison engine, max speed 345mph, range 730 miles. In RAF service the Tomahawk corresponded to the USAAF's P-40. Armament: 2 guns in fuselage and 4 guns in wings.

VENGEANCE | VULTEE 2-seat dive-bomber, ordered from America in 1940, of classic layout and having exceptional powers in matters of bomb-load and range. Decided it could best be used to advantage against difficult jungle targets in Burma, where it was first reported in action in July 1943. They supplanted Blenheims and proved very effective weapons on the Arakan front. One 1,700hp Wright Double Row Cyclone engine, max speed 279mph, range 1,200 miles. Armament: 4 guns in wings and 2 guns in rear cockpit plus bomb-load of 2,000lb.

WAPITI | WESTLAND 2-seat general purpose biplane, first flown in 1927 and used extensively on the North-West Frontier of India and over the deserts of Iraq. Total Wapiti production of 517 ceased in August 1932 but about 80 were still with the RAF in India in 1939. One 550hp Bristol Jupiter VIII radial piston engine. Max speed 135mph, range 360 miles. Armament: 1 fixed Vickers gun forward and one Lewis gun in rear cockpit plus up to 580lb of bombs.

WELLINGTON | VICKERS-ARMSTRONG 6-seat long-range night-bomber speed of 265mph known as the *Wimpey*, it was one of most successful twin-engined bombers of the war. Wellingtons were the first RAF long-range bombers in the Far East from the beginning of 1942. Two 1,000hp Bristol Pegasus engines, max speed 235mph, range 2,200 miles.

Armament: 2 guns in each of nose and tail turrets and 4,500lb of bombs.

YORK   AVRO Long-range transport with a crew of 5 and 24 passengers, manufactured by AV Roe of Manchester and Yeadon. Four 1,280hp Rolls-Royce Merlin XX engines. Maximum speed 298mph, range 2,700 miles. Before 1945 the thin trickle of Yorks consisted mainly of VIP aircraft. The most famous York named *Ascalon* was furnished as a flying conference room and took Sir Winston Churchill and Allied commanders to Algiers via Gibraltar on 25th May 1943 and a few days later flew H.M. King George VI on his tour of troops in North Africa and the Mediterranean area. 257 Yorks were built, one remaining with the RAF in the Far East until 1957. They played an important part in the Berlin Airlift of 1948-49.

EPILOGUE

After the War, my father returned to St Albans to live with his parents in their lovely Edwardian house in Battlefield Road, where our family continued to live for over thirty years. In August 1947 he met my mother, Dulcie Roberts, at the Townsend Tennis Club in St Albans, they became engaged in November and were married in May 1948. I was born in 1950, with my brother (Michael) and sister (Ruth) following at three yearly intervals.

L to R: Michael, Peter, Elizabeth, Ruth, Dulcie, Grandfather Robert Walker, December 1957.

Peter continued working for the family business of W.R. Walker Ltd in Mayfair where he became the Managing Director until his retirement in the 1970s. The Hillman car was lovingly maintained for many years by my father (usually wearing his RAF overalls!) and we used it for many family holidays all over England.

My father had been profoundly moved by his experiences in India and Burma; he was a very spiritual man and a committed Christian. At our local church in St Albans, St Saviours, he was Church Warden for many years and organised the Christian Aid collections. He was very tolerant of other cultures: whilst a teenager, I thought it quite normal to have a recently arrived West Indian family to share Christmas Day with us!

My sister and I inherited colour blindness from our father, as well as neuro-endocrine tumours from which Dad died in 1983, giving his body for research into this rare genetic condition (Multiple Endocrine Neoplasia Type 1). Having unknowingly passed this onto my three children, in 2002 together with my elder daughter Emily, I decided to set up the patient support group known as AMEND. 10% of any profits from the sale of this book will be donated to AMEND (www.amend.org.uk) and 10% to the NET Patient Foundation (www.netpatientfoundation.org).

BIBLIOGRAPHY

Primary Sources

Owen, Lt Colonel Frank, *The Campaign in Burma*, HMSO, 1946.

Sunny Natal with View of Natal, The Knox Printing & Publishing Company, Durban, 6d, 1940s.

The Flying Dutchman, composed and published on H.M.T. Westernland, June 18th, 1942.

Secondary Sources

Allen, Louise, *Burma – The Longest War 1941-1945*, Ebury Press, 2009.

Annett, Roger, *Drop Zone Burma*, Pen & Sword Aviation, 2008.

Arthur, Max, *Forgotten Voices of the Second World War*, Ebury Press, 2004.

Bowyer, Chez, No. *31 Squadron, The History 1915-1960*, RAF, 1960.

Chant, Chris, *The World's Great Bombers from 1914 to the Present Day*, Amber Books Ltd., 2000.

Conyers Nesbit, Roy, *RAF in Action 1939-1945*, PRO, 2000.

Delve, Ken, *The Source Book of the RAF, Far East 1941-1945*, Airlife Publishing Limited, 1994.

Farringdon, Karen, *Witness to World War II*, Abbeydale Press, 2007.

Fowler, William, *We Gave Our Today, Burma 1941-1945*, Weidenfeld & Nicholson, 2009.

Franks, Norman L.R., *First in the Indian Skies, 31 Squadron*, RAF Association, 1981.

Hall, Ian, *A Goldstar Century, 31 Squadron RAF 1915-2015*, Pen & Sword Aviation, 2015.

Hastings, Max, *Finest Years, Churchill as Warlord 1940-45*, Harper Press, 2009.

Hawkins, Doreen, *Drury Lane to Dimapur*, The Dovecote Press Ltd, 2009.

Ioan-ap-Llywelyn, *Padgate to Warton via India*, published by the author, 1990.

Jackson, Robert, *The World's Great Fighters from 1914 to the Present Day*, Amber Books Ltd, 2001.

Jefford, Wing Commander C.G., *RAF Squadrons*, Airlife Publishing Ltd, 1988.

Judd, Denis, *The Lion and the Tiger – The Rise and Fall of the British Raj 1600-1947*, Oxford University Press, 2004.

Martland, Peter, *Lord Haw Haw, The English Voice of Nazi Germany*, The National Archives, 2003.

Mehra, Parshotam, *A Dictionary of Modern Indian History 1707-1947*, Oxford University Press, 1985.

Mondey, David, *The Hamlyn Concise Guide to British Aircraft of World War II*, Chancellor Press, 1994.

Moore Williams, Robin, *Paul Scott's Raj*, Heinemann Ltd., 1990.

Rawson, Andrew, *Victory in the Pacific & Far East*, Pen & Sword Military, 2005.

Shales, Melissa, *Travellers Delhi, Agra & Rajasthan*, Thomas Cook Publishing, 2007.

Somerville, Christopher, *Our War – How the British Commonwealth Fought the Second World War*, Weidenfeld & Nicholson, 1998.

Stewart, Adrian, *They Flew Hurricanes*, Pen & Sword Aviation, 2005.

Stewart, Major Oliver, *The Royal Air Force in Pictures*, Country Life Limited, 1942.

Sturtivant, Ray, *Flying, Training & Supporting Units since 1912*, Air-Britain (Histories) Ltd, 2007.

Thetford, Owen, *Aircraft of the Royal Air Force since 1918*, Putnam & Company, 1968.

Thompson, Julian, *Forgotten Voices of Burma*, Ebury Press, 2009.

Watson, Francis, *India – A Concise History*, Thames & Hudson, 1974.

Wood, Michael, *The Story of India*, BBC Books, 2007.

A big **Thank You** to all those who made pledges to the crowd-funding site, Kickstarter. Without your generosity this project would probably never have reached fruition.

John Adams

Yvonne Aird

Peter Anthony

Ema Brunton

Jay Bunyan

Mark Chapman

Fred Cooper & Barb Ferrell

Anne Craig

Colin Deady

Nicholas Dent

Rebecca Dent

Robert Dent

Bob Dickerson

Lorenzo Dutto

Oliver Dwyer

Ed

Emily & Andy Fazal

Tony Foster

Edward Gale

Carolyn & Stuart Heseltine

Marie-Anne & Earl Hintze

Neville Isles

Ivan Jalaluddin

Nikie Jervis

Muriel Liddle

Terry & Bunty Marsh

Mike and Bonnie Lawson

Nick & Julia Opperman

Mary Payne

Pat Pelton

Jagan Pillarisetti

Martin Reithmayr

Susan Salt

Geraldine & Paul Sauvage

Kirsty Shepherd

Vic Sole

Lavinia Sonnenberg

Mike Walker

Duanne Warnecke

Aaron Young

Mick Young

Zetetics

LIST OF PHOTOS AND IMAGES

INDEX

PEOPLE

PLACES

PRINTED AND BOUND BY:

Copytech (UK) Limited trading as Printondemand-worldwide,
9 Culley Court, Bakewell Road, Orton Southgate.
Peterborough, PE2 6XD, United Kingdom.